PLANET GOLF USA

PLANET GOLF USA

The Definitive Reference to Great Golf Courses in America

DARIUS OLIVER

PRINCIPAL PHOTOGRAPHERS: JOHN & JEANNINE HENEBRY

ABRAMS, NEW YORK

Contents

Foreword by Ben Crenshaw viii

Introduction xii

West Coast & Hawaii   1

Cypress Point 4

Pacific Dunes 8

Pebble Beach 12

Bandon Trails 16

Pasatiempo 20

Los Angeles CC 24

Riviera 26

Bandon Dunes 28

The Quarry at La Quinta 32

The Valley Club of Montecito 36

Kapalua 38

Shadow Creek 40

Chambers Bay 44

Forest Highlands 46

Monterey Peninsula CC 48

Nanea 50

Spyglass Hill 52

The Olympic Club 54

Mayacama 56

Desert Forest 58

San Francisco GC 60

The Preserve 60

Bel-Air CC 62

Estancia 62

Eugene CC 64

Sahalee 64

Rustic Canyon 66

Princeville 66

Torrey Pines 68

The Midwest & Rocky Mountains   70

Sand Hills 74

Crystal Downs 78

Ballyneal 82

Prairie Dunes 86

Chicago GC 90

Whistling Straits 92

White Bear Yacht Club 96

Colorado GC 98

The Golf Club 102

Oakland Hills 104

Victoria National 108

Kingsley 112

Muirfield Village 114

Interlachen 116

Lost Dunes 118

Erin Hills 120

Inverness 122

Sutton Bay 124

Camargo 128

Wolf Run 130

Olympia Fields 132

Double Eagle 134

Butler National 136

Medinah 138

Blackwolf Run 140

Crooked Stick 142

Cherry Hills 144

Hazeltine National 146

Castle Pines 148

Shoreacres 150

Scioto 150

Bellerive 152

Arcadia Bluffs 152

Canterbury 154

Sand Ridge 154

Milwaukee CC 156

Flint Hills National 156

Sycamore Hills 158

Tullymore 158

Rich Harvest Links 160

Sanctuary 160

The South   162

Augusta National 166

Seminole 170

Pinehurst 172

Pete Dye GC 176

TPC at Sawgrass 180

Wade Hampton 184

Kiawah Island – Ocean 186

Yeamans Hall 190

Kinloch...............................192
Long Cove...........................194
Black Diamond Ranch...............196
The Honors..........................200
Harbour Town........................202
Peachtree...........................204
World Woods.........................206
Dallas National.....................208
Southern Hills......................210
Jupiter Hills.......................212
Valhalla............................214
The Bear's Club.....................216
Calusa Pines........................216
Holston Hills.......................218
Colonial CC.........................218
The Homestead.......................220
Ocean Forest........................220
East Lake...........................222
Grandfather.........................224
Sea Island..........................224
Sage Valley.........................226
Hawks Ridge.........................226
Kiawah Island – Cassique............228
Briar's Creek.......................228
Shoal Creek.........................230
Trump International.................230

The Northeast 232

Pine Valley.........................236
Shinnecock Hills....................240
National Golf Links of America......244
Merion..............................248
Oakmont.............................252
Old Sandwich........................256
Fishers Island......................260
Sebonack............................262
Winged Foot.........................266
Eastward Ho!........................270
Friar's Head........................274
Essex County Club...................278
Somerset Hills......................280
The Country Club....................282
Boston GC...........................284
Myopia Hunt Club....................286
Bethpage Black......................288
Garden City.........................292
Plainfield..........................294
Galloway National...................296
Quaker Ridge........................300
Maidstone...........................302
Oak Hill............................304
Baltusrol...........................306
Kittansett..........................308
Baltimore CC........................310
Yale University.....................312

Hudson National.....................314
Ridgewood...........................318
Piping Rock.........................320
The Creek...........................320
Lehigh..............................322
Laurel Valley.......................322
Bayonne.............................324
Salem...............................326
Congressional.......................326
Newport CC..........................328
Trump National......................328

Ratings & Rankings 330

Best Par Threes.....................334
Best Par Fours......................336
Best Par Fives......................338
Miscellaneous.......................339

Planet Golf World 100...............342

Acknowledgments.....................344
Photo credits.......................344
Index...............................345

Foreword

"Planet Golf USA should further one's appreciation for the building of courses, and serve as an educational tool as well."

BEN CRENSHAW

My love of golf history and golf architecture started when I was a 16-year-old playing in the 1968 United States Junior Amateur at The Country Club in Brookline, Massachusetts. My father and I enjoyed Boston that week, but, for me, the appeal was in attempting to learn how to play a course that was far different from those in my native Texas. The Country Club is one of our oldest and most historic clubs, and the golf course is very natural, rustic and distinctively New England. There are a few blind shots, slick, undulating greens, craggy bunkers cut into slopes, and many stately trees.

Experiencing The Country Club and playing where Francis Ouimet won the 1913 US Open, in a play-off with the great Harry Vardon and Ted Ray, really piqued my curiosity, and I have been reading books about the game of golf ever since. Of this much we can be certain: American golf owes its existence to our cousins in Britain. Scottish and English immigrant professionals took a great leap of faith when they came to our country to help spread this timeless and honorable export. These men were hired to perform many duties, including teaching the game and club making. They were also largely responsible for the layout of new golf courses.

The first courses that appeared in the United States were rudimentary at best, but there were knowledgeable minds that desired more and, importantly, these men had studied the famous links of the British Isles. Among the first courses to gain international respect were Garden City Golf Club, Myopia Hunt Club and then, triumphantly, the watershed National Golf Links of America. Charles Blair Macdonald was after something completely different at the National, and expressly desired to build a "classical golf course in America, one which would eventually compare favorably with the championship links abroad, and serve as an incentive to the elevation of the game in America." It remains one of my favorites to this day. As a matter of fact, I rate the National and Cypress Point as the two most fun golf courses in America on which to play.

The trio of Pine Valley, Merion and Oakmont came into being around this time as well. Pine Valley, built by George Crump, is nothing short of a work of art. Its end result is the collaboration of many minds, but the grand scheme and the formation of the course was Crump's. The evolution of this layout is a great story in itself but, simply put, there is no other course quite like Pine Valley—you have to be lucky enough to see it to believe it.

Merion is as graceful as a Main Line debutante. The course is distinctive and memorable, and gives one the impression that every inch of its oddly shaped property was properly utilized. There is a distinct quality to all of the holes at Merion, a tribute to Hugh Wilson, who, along with his brother Alan and a young construction foreman named William S. Flynn, would complete Pine Valley after George Crump's death. Flynn later remodeled Shinnecock Hills and The Country Club. Oakmont, like the Fownes family that built it, is as tough as steel, its challenge unbending but enduring and its greens able to strike fear in all players, including myself. Putting on the 1st, 2nd, 9th, 10th, 12th and 15th greens is so daunting, if you miss the hole your ball might just continue on down the Pennsylvania Turnpike!

There are many names associated with the clubs listed above who would contribute to the great courses and the Golden Age of the 1920s. George C. Thomas, who watched as Pine Valley was being built, gave us Los Angeles Country Club, Riviera and Bel-Air. In the case of Riviera, I think that it may be one of the finest man-made courses ever built, Thomas having nothing but the desert floor of a canyon to work with. But he did have a barranca, which facilitated drainage and ensured high interest from the golfer's standpoint.

A.W. Tillinghast also witnessed the formation of Pine Valley, and claims credit for convincing Crump to add to the character of the diabolical 7th, the par five with a vast waste area to be carried on the second shot. The adaptation of this hole would appear on many of Tillinghast's designs, including at the delightful Somerset Hills, Baltusrol, Baltimore Country Club (Five Farms) and Ridgewood. We designed our par five 9th hole at Austin Golf Club to be a distant cousin to this hole, and named it "Tillie." Tillinghast's work elsewhere was equally full of character. The collective quality of his holes, be they long ones, short ones or doglegged ones, is remarkable

OPPOSITE The 8th hole on Merion's elegant East Course, one of the treasured Golden Age layouts that continues to influence Ben Crenshaw in his course design work

Looking across the 8th green at Tillinghast's underrated Somerset Hills Country Club in New Jersey

The recently restored 3rd hole at Dr. MacKenzie's beloved Pasatiempo

OPPOSITE The par five 14th hole at Friar's Head. Coore and Crenshaw are blessed to have been able to "chase classical ghosts" on such magnificent golfing terrain

and lasting, even today. His greens are especially interesting, and designed to keep a golfer honest throughout the round. As a set, his greens at Somerset Hills are among the most fascinating that I have seen.

Donald Ross, after arriving in America at Oakley Country Club near Boston, found that of his many duties golf course design interested him the most. I am sure the possibilities of this profession grew when he traveled to Pinehurst in North Carolina and started building courses for the Tufts family. There is no one associated with golf design who has had his breadth of work associated with quality more than Donald Ross. He had a profound influence on the game in America, and at the same time his work was a significant business, and employed many men as construction foremen and supervisors. A list of his creations would be too long to mention here, but this I can say—whenever I visit a course where Donald Ross worked I get unusually excited, for I know that there are interesting ways of solving problems on the ground.

Dr. Alister MacKenzie was perhaps the most vibrant architect of all time. His training as a camouflage artist, employed by the British Army, perfectly coincided with his early interest in golf design. The features he built on most of his courses reflect this training, and his enduring lesson to all of us in golf design is to work with the land. His bunkers, mounds, undulations, and the graceful lines that they produce are truly beautiful. And his greens were built to remind us that while it may take two strokes to "get there" on a par four, you can still have your work cut out to secure a par. Augusta National, Cypress Point, Crystal Downs and Pasatiempo are all majestic.

I must mention Perry Maxwell, who was one of my favorites, and who for three years was a partner or associate with MacKenzie. Both were ardent admirers of nature, and perhaps Maxwell put it best when he said: "It is my theory that nature must precede the architect, in the layout of links. It is futile to attempt the transformation of wholly inadequate acres into an adequate course." No one will ever forget Perry Maxwell's greens; they are works of art unto themselves.

Another important "Golden Ager" was Seth Raynor, initially hired as an engineer by Charles Blair Macdonald during the building of the National Golf Links of America. That he went on to build so many courses of distinction, and so successfully adapted the principles and themes of replica holes like Alps, Biarritz, Short, Eden, Punchbowl and Cape, is truly amazing. I have never played a Seth Raynor course that I didn't admire a lot, and they are always fun to play.

While the likes of Pete Dye, Jack Nicklaus, Tom Fazio, Tom Weiskopf, Tom Doak, Greg Norman and Gil Hanse are responsible for some excellent modern courses, it's the older creations that these fine golf designers built during the Golden Age that stand out most in my studies and throughout my playing career. As for my own design work, Bill Coore and I have had so much fun "chasing classical ghosts of the past." We enjoy the appeal of what possibilities a certain property might bring, and working together with a loyal and talented crew. We hope people continue to enjoy our courses for many years to come.

Planet Golf USA will be fun for you to delve into. Darius Oliver's second installment, which contains much work and study, should further one's appreciation for the building of courses, and serve as an educational tool as well. It is my honor to contribute this foreword to his beautiful book.

Ben Crenshaw

Ben Crenshaw

Introduction

The seeds for *Planet Golf USA* were planted prior to the completion of the first *Planet Golf* book, which took the best part of three years to compile and involved travel to more than 600 golf courses in 41 countries. The ambitious aim of that publication was to provide readers with a definitive reference to the finest golf available outside the United States. With half the world's 32,000 courses here in America, its logical companion seemed a follow-up directory to the greatest golf country on earth.

My principal goal with this US edition was to make it as comprehensive and credible as *Planet Golf*, which meant ensuring that every worthwhile course in the nation was included. Rather than research all 16,000 candidates myself, I allowed the expansive ranking panels of *Golf Digest* and *GOLF Magazine* to do the preliminary research, narrowing my focus to those layouts featured on their Top 100 ranking lists. I then set out, rather ambitiously, to review every one of America's Top 100 courses, as well as more than a dozen gems somehow overlooked by these august publications.

Like the first book, the compilation process was exhaustive but highly rewarding. Driving the length and breadth of this endlessly fascinating land, I put more than 22,000 miles on the odometer and passed through 41 states in order to visit around 230 leading golf clubs. While I was truly blessed to have been able to see so many fabulous courses, the one major reservation I have about enthusiastically endorsing golf here is exclusivity. In *Planet Golf*, more than 80 percent of the courses reviewed were readily accessible to visiting golfers, while in this volume the number that are open for outside play is less than 20 percent.

OPPOSITE **The heavily undulating par four 9th at the Eastward Ho! Country Club, a remarkable old layout in Massachusetts that the major magazine ranking panels continue to ignore**

The mid-length 6th at Pine Valley in New Jersey, long regarded as the planet's premier golf course

Florida's Seminole Golf Club is considered by many to be the best layout in Donald Ross's extraordinary design portfolio; pictured is the 10th hole

OPPOSITE The par three 3rd at Hawks Ridge near Atlanta, one of countless modern courses in the US inspired more by the look of Augusta National than the design

The origins of elite golfing institutions are inextricably tied to the origins of the sport here. Unlike the United Kingdom, where many early links were formed on public land for the enjoyment of all, in America the game was driven largely by wealthy businessmen building private clubs and retreats for themselves and their well-connected associates. Although there is evidence of the sport being played in South Carolina during the 1780s, it wasn't until the 1880s that formal fields of play were established and lasting golf clubs formed. Most of the early activity was in the Northeast, but golf's popularity quickly spread, and the game was being played across the Midwest, in the South and along the West Coast by the end of the 19th century.

Not surprisingly, the earliest examples of quality golf were found at private clubs like Myopia Hunt Club, Garden City, The Country Club and Ekwanok in Vermont. Aside from the likes of Pebble Beach and Pinehurst, this trend continued through the Golden Age of golf, which loosely began with the 1909 opening of Charles Blair Macdonald's momentous National Golf Links and lasted through to the end of the 1930s. Arguably the most noteworthy courses built during this era were perennial world No. 1 Pine Valley and Dr. Alistair MacKenzie's spectacular Cypress Point, which so impressed Bobby Jones that he selected MacKenzie as the man to build his field of dreams at Augusta National.

Of course, Augusta's influence has been the most wide-reaching, particularly in terms of how golf courses the world over are now groomed and presented. What is often overlooked, however, is just how strategic the original plans were. Jones and MacKenzie were both passionate disciples of The Old Course, and built an intelligent layout full of fascinating subtleties. The putting contours were wild and severe, but targets were mostly open in the front, the idea being to keep the turf keen and firm like St. Andrews to encourage a bounced-on approach. The thought that their masterpiece had inspired thousands of lush, overwatered courses would likely horrify both men.

Other influential early architects included Donald Ross, William Flynn, Hugh Wilson, Seth Raynor and A.W. Tillinghast, all of whom believed, like MacKenzie and Macdonald, that the essence of interesting golf was designing holes that were devoid of unnaturalness and offered strategic routes to the green. Ross was a particularly interesting figure, having been responsible, in some shape or form, for a staggering 400 golf courses across the United States.

Another legendary Golden Ager was George Thomas, who expressed similar views about the importance of strategy to the golf architect and also famously wrote that he expected his design work, and that of his peers, to be surpassed by future generations of course creators. Strangely, this wasn't the case, and following the Great Depression golf somehow became homogenized in America, variety and tactical interest replaced with formulaic arrangements, dull use of terrain and the profusion of penal hazards. The game went from one played along the ground and between the ears, to an aerial activity where the shots to hit were dictated by the nature of design.

The demanding inland holes at Spyglass Hill, such as the 6th, typify how courses were arranged during the "Trent Jones Decades"

The 2nd at Sebonack Golf Club, where the modernism of Jack Nicklaus merged with the traditional ideals of Tom Doak

OPPOSITE Pure golf land is back in fashion, thanks to the likes of Pacific Dunes; pictured is the 13th hole

OVERLEAF Approaching the final green at the venerable National Golf Links of America

The decades from the 1950s to the 1980s almost entirely belonged to the Robert Trent Jones school of design, with its focus on conditioning and easy bogey, hard par golf. By contrast, earlier architects felt unrestricted by hole length, slope ratings, balance or difficulty. Most rounds were played as part of a match, so par was irrelevant and holes could be fun. The introduction of the 7,000-yard course and the rise of professional golf changed this mindset completely, as clubs started to recognize the value of hosting prestigious events and sought to ensure their layouts fit the requirements of championship play. This usually involved making holes longer, narrower and more penal under the misguided assumption that such changes would make their courses more outstanding. There is a big difference, however, between difficult holes that punish the slightest mistake and offer few chances to make birdies, and challenging ones, which use multiple routes of attack and the lure of a likely birdie to entice players into bogey-making mistakes. The latter type are much more enjoyable and interesting to play.

Thanks, in part, to the likes of Sand Hills and the hugely successful Bandon Dunes Resort, American golfers have been reintroduced to classical design and the joys of playing on quality golfing ground. There also seems to have been a reawakening to the importance of the country's Golden Age layouts, with countless traditional clubs now looking to restore the integrity of their altered courses. Whether it's the removal of intruding trees, the widening of fairways or the return of lost bunkers and green shapes, sensible restoration programs have helped many of the nation's finest classics recover spectacularly from what, in some cases, had been decades of mismanagement and neglect.

Despite continuing issues with the cost of golf, the time taken to play, exclusivity and the nature of modern design, there is no doubt that the ancient Scottish game has been most successfully exported to America, and this book was written to pay tribute to her most astonishing venues. Like the earlier edition of *Planet Golf*, the reviews focus on the quality of the actual golf course rather than unnecessary peripheral elements like the makeup of a club's membership or the number of tournaments it has hosted. For completeness, all of those courses listed among the most recent *Golf Digest* and *GOLF Magazine* Top 100 lists are featured, regardless of whether the ranking seemed warranted or not. The reviews are arranged according to the four official census regions of the United States, with the only deviations being to include Maryland with the Northeast and to bunch the Rocky Mountain courses with those in the Midwest, due to more apparent golfing similarities.

What made *Planet Golf USA* so fascinating to research and compile was the diversity of an industry that relentlessly leads the world forward yet continually has an eye on its past. There are so many differing styles of golf on display across this great nation, and though I fully expected to be blown away by the likes of Pine Valley, Cypress Point and Shinnecock Hills, in many ways it was discovering the pleasures of Ballyneal, Bandon Trails, Eastward Ho!, Essex, Fishers Island, Old Sandwich and White Bear Yacht Club that made this journey so unforgettable. My sincere hope is that you enjoy reading up on these hidden gems as much as the more celebrated championship venues that you may instinctively skim through first.

West Coast & Hawaii

West Coast & Hawaii

Cypress Point

Pacific Dunes

Pebble Beach

Bandon Trails

Pasatiempo

Los Angeles CC

Riviera

Bandon Dunes

Quarry at La Quinta

Valley Club of Montecito

Kapalua

Shadow Creek

Chambers Bay

Forest Highlands

Monterey Peninsula CC

Nanea

Spyglass Hill

The Olympic Club

Mayacama

Desert Forest

San Francisco GC

The Preserve

Bel-Air CC

Estancia

Eugene CC

Sahalee

Rustic Canyon

Princeville

Torrey Pines

OPPOSITE The growth of golf throughout
California has included desolate regions like
Palm Springs and the Coachella Valley; pictured
is the opening hole at Tom Fazio's immaculately
groomed Quarry at La Quinta course

While golfing roots in this country are generally traced to the Northeast, the American West has a long and proud tradition in the sport, the game first played on this side of the nation around 1888, when a few rudimentary holes were established on the northern Oregon coast at Gearhart. Between this event and the opening of southern Oregon's Bandon Dunes Resort, more than a century later, golf along the West Coast and throughout this vast region grew dramatically.

With its fertile terrain and ideal climate, California is an American golfing powerhouse, and now home to around 900 courses, up from less than 300 in the 1970s. Not surprisingly, its best courses tend to date from the heady pre-Depression decades of the 1910s and '20s, when leading Golden Age architects like George Thomas and Dr. Alister MacKenzie were prolific and environmental regulations less restrictive. Milestone layouts include the classic Thomas and A.W. Tillinghast courses of Los Angeles and San Francisco and the spectacular Monterey Peninsula double act of Pebble Beach and Cypress Point. Comparisons between these two giants are always interesting, but with wonderful coastal dunes, a superior set of greens and more design variety, including outstanding short par fours and fives, Cypress Point is the area's clear standout. Pebble Beach is a much more difficult test, thanks to its modern length, thicker roughs, narrower fairways and smaller greens, but difficulty has never really been an accurate measure of greatness. MacKenzie's beloved Pasatiempo is another important layout here, partly because it is one of the few he designed in America that is still open for public play.

Elsewhere, the ability of resourceful modern architects to overcome obstacles of topography and soil has allowed the game to spread rapidly across the islands of Hawaii and through the arid, rocky deserts of California, Nevada and Arizona. The opening of the Desert Forest Golf Club during the 1960s was particularly significant, as it helped popularize this form of golf and encouraged further development within these inhospitable reaches. Beyond the layouts featured in the following chapter, other interesting desert layouts include Tom Doak's Stone Eagle course near Palm Springs and both Troon Golf & Country Club and the Saguaro Course at We Ko Pa in Scottsdale.

Cypress Point Club

COURSE OPENED 1928

DESIGNER Dr. Alister MacKenzie

GOLF DIGEST 4

GOLF MAGAZINE 2

"For years I have been contending that in our generation no other golf course could possibly compete with the strategic problems, the thrills, the excitement, variety and lasting and increasing interest of the Old Course, but the completion of Cypress Point has made me change my mind."

DR. ALISTER MACKENZIE

OPPOSITE Those who seek more than pristine turf and a high slope rating are likely to find Cypress Point the ultimate golf experience; pictured is its celebrated par four 17th hole

A near-perfect collaboration between the greatest golf architect of all time and the finest piece of golfing ground yet discovered, the Cypress Point Club is situated on the westernmost tip of California's Monterey Peninsula and first opened for play in 1928. The course was the vision of champion golfer Marion Hollins, who convinced Del Monte developer Samuel Morse of the need to establish a private club within his subdivision as an alternative to the more accessible golf available on the Peninsula. Hollins had identified an ideal stretch of coastline for the club and hired Seth Raynor as its course designer. When Raynor passed away prior to construction commencing, she appointed Dr. Alister MacKenzie as his replacement. It was an inspired decision.

With its dramatic seaside cliffs, large coastal dunes and almost mythical pines and cypress trees, MacKenzie fell instantly for the property and spent a great deal of time ensuring his routing fully exploited the natural bounties available. Ignoring all perceived golfing conventions, the layout is neither arranged in a large out and back loop nor with its nines returning to the clubhouse. Instead, it starts on open ground and finishes with an extraordinary sequence of holes along the Pacific, in between moving effortlessly between the dense woodlands and spacious dunes. The sequence of holes is also unusual, with consecutive par fives on the outward nine and consecutive threes toward the close. Aside from this bold routing, what makes MacKenzie's work here so incredible is the strategic arrangement of his holes, the sublime green settings, creative putting contours and the naturalistic style of bunkering, the sprawling traps artistically shaped to appear part of the virgin landscape.

To the surprise of those who think Cypress Point's appeal is solely due to the ocean holes, the quality of the earlier golf is quite extraordinary. The 8th and 9th, for instance, are among the finest back-to-back par fours in America, both rewarding accurate driving but each with ideal landing areas that are increasingly difficult to hit the more club you take from the tee. The 8th is played across the shoulder of a large sandhill to a fairway leaning away from the green; those able to hug its dangerous right side are given the best line into a remarkable multitiered target with four or five distinct pinable shelves. The 9th is then a brilliant driveable par four, its fairway dropping along a narrowing ridge toward a terrifying green that is benched into a sizeable dune, angled across the approaching golfer and squeezed between some of the most formidable traps on the course. Other special holes include the strategically bunkered par fives, the cross-valley par three 7th and the perfectly proportioned dogleg 12th. Also unforgettable is the mid-length 13th, its putting surface cut into a dune and surrounded by some of the most magnificent bunker shapes ever constructed by man.

As memorable as these holes may be, they are but a mere prelude to the closing section and the sheer exhilaration one feels when stepping onto the 15th tee for the very first time. After crossing Seventeen-Mile Drive, the golfer emerges from a cypress grove to be presented with a coastal golfing scene of almost inconceivable beauty. The hole itself requires little more than a short-iron, but the exquisitely bunkered green is positioned atop a rocky bluff and beyond a violent ocean cove. The visual splendor of this gem would be unsurpassed in golf were it not for the very next hole, the 16th—regarded almost universally as the most spectacular par three on the planet. Again the golfer heads directly across the Pacific, this time needing to carry at least 220 yards in order to reach a target perched on a distant promontory.

This unforgettable hole was actually suggested by Marion Hollins, but what makes it so impressive is the fairway area to the left that MacKenzie insisted on including to allow nervous players to approach it as a strategic short par four.

Completing a three-hole stretch unrivaled anywhere on earth is a Cape-style par four that heads across and then along the craggy shoreline. Set obliquely to the tee, the fairway here is dominated by a central clump of cypress trees, which forces you to flirt with the water in order to set up an optimum view of the green. Steering players away from the sea, the 18th is a much-maligned finisher that zigzags up a narrow fairway and back to the elevated clubhouse. Though the hole is overcrowded by trees, those able to safely find the short grass with their drive are left with a lovely approach shot into a putting target pitched steeply from back to front.

Like many clubs of this vintage, Cypress Point has undergone periods of neglect, but a recent restoration program successfully returned the greens and bunkers to near their original proportions. The club has also consciously tried to expose more of the native sand and return holes to the rugged appearance that the designer so desired.

Understandably, MacKenzie took enormous delight in the success of Cypress Point and the pleasure it brought people from across the golfing spectrum. About the only disappointment he might have with how the club has evolved is that it has become so exclusive that few visitors ever get to experience his masterpiece. Regardless, this is a layout that truly has it all—great architecture, a great setting, incredible sand dunes and the finest stretch of holes anywhere on the planet. Although there have been numerous coastal sites uncovered since the course was built, the sad truth for global golfers is that there is still only one Cypress Point.

OPPOSITE **Whether played as an all-carry par three or a strategic short par four, the 16th at Cypress Point is surely the most magnificent hole in golf**

Bandon Dunes Golf Resort – Pacific Dunes

COURSE OPENED 2001
DESIGNER Tom Doak

GOLF DIGEST 14
GOLF MAGAZINE 9

"Every architect dreams of building among the sand dunes, in the same terrain where golf was conceived in the British Isles. For me and my associates, Pacific Dunes is that dream come true."

TOM DOAK

OPPOSITE **Despite having built a number of great courses since Pacific Dunes, this remains Doak's signature creation and it's a layout that, hole for hole, is the equal of any in America. Pictured is the fabulous par three 11th**

The opening of Pacific Dunes in 2001 not only launched the international career of outspoken architect Tom Doak, but also firmly established the remote Bandon Dunes Resort as a genuine must-play destination for all serious golfers. Doak had actually first toured the property that would become Bandon Dunes in 1994, and immediately began lobbying owner Mike Keiser to let him design its first course. He lost out to David McLay Kidd, but Keiser later gave him the contract to design the second course, Pacific Dunes, on an adjacent and even more spectacular piece of land.

With the same coastal cliffs as Bandon, as well as huge dunes and natural sandy blowouts, this was one of the finest parcels of virgin golf land anywhere in the United States, and the ideal platform for this self-proclaimed Renaissance man to showcase his prodigious design talents. Shunning a conventional out and back routing, Doak instead chose an irregular plan that resembles Ballybunion for the manner in which it loops toward the sea, teasing players by quickly turning inland and then returning for an ocean encore to start the back nine. This arrangement enabled the course to incorporate the best features on the property, though, unusually, it left the inward half with three par fives and four par threes, including consecutive short holes at the turn. For Doak, it was never the makeup of par here that mattered, but rather how many world-class holes he could squeeze out of the magnificent terrain.

Despite significant variances in topography, to the designer's great credit the entire layout feels as if it was "discovered" rather than designed, and there isn't a single out-of-place hole anywhere on the course. Although some clearly designed themselves, such as the 13th, which is sandwiched between cliffs and a mighty 60-foot sand dune, the rest were carefully crafted to retain as much of the lumpy ground movement and natural wind-blown bunkers as possible. The green sites complement the surrounding landforms and, where appropriate, feature wild contours and imaginative chipping areas.

The two opening holes are ideal starting points. Neither is within sight of the ocean, but their rugged bunkers, cool fairway and green undulations and fascinating recovery shot options introduce players immediately to the charms of links golf. The next is a par five which, like the adjacent 12th and 15th holes, eats up some of the flatter land and connects the duneland to the sea. Doak is on record as admiring Tom Simpson's use of par fives over dull ground at Ballybunion, and here he similarly built long holes to swallow up such land, the difference being his superior green complexes. The 3rd, in particular, has a wonderful target that sits on a sharp ledge and is only reached after some strategic bunker dodging.

The first to touch the coastline, the 4th is a pin-up par four that hops along sheer cliffs plummeting 100 feet down into the Pacific Ocean. The next turns away from the sea and heads through a sandy valley toward a tiered green that is angled sharply right and full of humps and bumps. It is the first in a terrific set of one-shotters that includes the long 10th, played into a shallow bowl beside the ocean, the 14th with its target perched atop a shaved dune and the mighty downhill Redan at the 17th, which is framed by an

immense gorse-covered ridge. The short hole highlight, however, is the all-world 11th, played directly along the cliffs and across native grasses and stunning blow-out bunkers expertly crafted by Doak's shapers.

Other thrills include an ingeniously contoured green complex at the 7th, the half crowned, half basin-shaped putting surface on the 8th and the wonderfully sporty two-target, high road/low road 9th hole. There are also two brilliant short par fours. The 6th is driveable under certain conditions, but its green is tucked beyond a large bunkered ridge on a small plateau and is very difficult to hit and hold from the left side of its wide fairway. One of Doak's favorites, the 16th is a fun hole that bends along a narrowing spine toward a skinny shelf green built at the base of a dune and falling cruelly into a deep hollow.

With an enviable mix of sand, surf and strategic design, Pacific Dunes is a course that caters to all tastes and golfing preferences. The bounces may not always be straight, the stances are rarely level and the color and texture of the firm fescue fairways and bouncy greens may be off-putting to some, but this is golf in its purest form, and is the sort of raw experience that all golfers should embrace.

ABOVE **The quirky short par four 16th**

OPPOSITE **Squeezed between the West Coast and a massive Bandon sand ridge, the 13th is one of several world-class holes at Pacific Dunes**

Pebble Beach Golf Links

COURSE OPENED 1919
DESIGNERS Jack Neville,
Douglas Grant,
H. Chandler Egan

GOLF DIGEST 6
GOLF MAGAZINE 4

Pebble's notorious 106-yard 7th
hole, surrounded on three sides by
Monterey Bay

OPPOSITE The one-shot 5th,
designed by Jack Nicklaus on land
that for decades had been part of
a private estate

Situated at the southern end of California's
Monterey Peninsula, Pebble Beach was
developed by business entrepreneur Samuel F.B.
Morse, who first saw the property while acting as
liquidator for a company wanting to offload its
failed investment in the region. Morse felt that a
golf course along the sea would help residential
sales and managed to convince the company to
invest in the building of the Pebble Beach Golf
Links. When it was completed, he purchased the
course as part of a greater 18,000-acre Peninsula
property that incorporated the vast Del Monte
forest as well as further coastal land later used to
build additional courses, including Cypress Point.

Pebble Beach occupies a site of unparalleled
scenic beauty, its holes stretching along a rocky
coastline and boasting wondrous views across
Carmel Bay and Stillwater Cove. This was dream
land for golf, yet the responsibility for designing
the layout was given to local amateur players
Jack Neville and Douglas Grant, who, with little
experience, cleverly arranged the holes so that
half could follow the continually curving bay.

Despite being well received, the course was
constantly refined in the decade following its
1919 opening, most substantially by another
amateur, H. Chandler Egan, who reshaped
almost all the greens and bunkers prior to the
1929 US Amateur. Egan also moved the 1st
and 10th tees, pushed the 16th green back
into a natural depression and extended the
fairway on the 9th out to the ocean, building
a brilliant new target right beside the cliffs.

Earlier, English architect Herbert Fowler had
shifted the 18th tee onto a rocky outcrop and
moved the putting surface back and along a
seawall, transforming a tame par four into a
mighty finishing five renowned the world over.
Interestingly, during this period Dr. Alister
MacKenzie also worked on the 8th and 13th
greens, possibly to show Morse he was capable
of handling the Cypress Point assignment.

Unlike Cypress Point and the early parts of
Spyglass Hill, Pebble Beach is sheltered from
the Pacific Ocean, and as a result it lacks wild
sand dunes and natural fairway undulations.
The layout also has a more formal, manicured
appearance, although in its earliest guise things
were more rugged and the greens were actually
surrounded by vast sandy wastes. Targets have
also shrunk over the years and are now small,
circular and far from a standout feature. The
most common criticism of this course, however,
is that the inland holes are not as good as those
along the sea. Better noncoastal holes such as
the 2nd, 3rd, 14th, 15th and 16th are all very
good, though each pales by comparison to
the stunning offerings closer to the shore.

Pebble's celebrated seaside holes are
outrageously spectacular, the stretch from the
4th to the 10th without equal in this country.
With the exception of the short 5th, a Jack
Nicklaus hole built in the 1990s, this part of the
course remains essentially unaltered from the
Egan plan. The first real glamour hole is the par
five 6th, an exciting challenge with great outlooks

but played over a hill that is really too steep for most golfers to handle with their fairway wood. There are no such issues on the 7th, arguably the game's greatest dropkick par three, nor with the approach into the 8th green, which demands an awesome once-in-a-lifetime shot across a corner of the bay. Equally unforgettable are strong par fours at the 9th and 10th, each positioned alongside the sea and sloping more toward the ocean than is first apparent, their fairways and greens perfectly angled to reward those brave enough to crack a drive close to the water. The finale is also magnificent, particularly the mesmerizing par five 18th, which sweeps left along the shoreline and follows a coastal rock barrier all the way to its putting surface.

Although some criticize Pebble Beach for the disparity between its best and worst moments, the course has as many knockout holes as any in America, as well as a setting more beautiful than any other on earth. The layout itself is far from perfect and, unless playing at the right time of year, can also be frustratingly soft. These minor concerns, however, fail to take the shine off an extraordinary facility, and do little to diminish the broad global appeal of golf's most famous resort.

ABOVE The cruel away-sloping green on the par five 14th

OPPOSITE The view from the left-hand side of the 9th hole, hands down the best par four at Pebble Beach

Bandon Dunes Golf Resort – Bandon Trails

COURSE OPENED 2005
DESIGNERS Bill Coore,
Ben Crenshaw

GOLF DIGEST NR
GOLF MAGAZINE 56

"In the profession of golf architecture all one can ask for is to be given an extraordinary site and the freedom to work with it. Mike Keiser has afforded both at Bandon Trails."

BILL COORE

OPPOSITE **The 2nd hole is a long par three that takes golfers through the dunes and down toward the forested area of the property**

Following the stunning success of his first two coastal courses, Bandon Dunes owner Mike Keiser looked to add a third layout to the resort, this time within a sheltered forest away from the stiff seaside winds. His architects of choice were partners Bill Coore and Ben Crenshaw, whose greatest challenge was to deliver an inland course with enough quality to complement the existing ocean gems.

Although initial plans had the course entirely set within an elevated woodland, Bill Coore was keen to incorporate some exposed sandhills into his layout and managed to devise an ingenious routing that allowed the golf to move seamlessly through a range of contrasting landforms. Trails begins and ends within the pristine duneland and takes golfers on an absorbing journey across a sandy meadow and up into an undulating forest of spruce, pine and cedar. Located in a range of natural settings, the green sites here are superb and feature some of the pair's most creative putting contours. The bunkering is said to have been inspired by Australia's Sandbelt and is deliberately rugged, with the traps shaped to blend with the native undergrowth.

Not surprisingly, the starting and closing holes among the dunes are outstanding, but so are those carved through the forested areas. A wonderfully conceived and constructed par five on relatively flat ground, the 3rd is really the key to the routing, as it is the hole that links the sand dunes to the wooded hills. Amongst the trees, memorable features include the large fractured fairway on the 4th and the green on the gorgeous cross-gully par three 5th, which is almost 50 yards long and noted for a serious depression running across its middle. The neighboring par three 17th is an equally fabulous short hole, the tee shot heading into a beautiful plateau framed by jagged bunker shapes and protected by a cruel false front. Other back nine highlights include the bumpy par five 16th and the gently rising 15th, its green set within a magnificent sandy amphitheater. The 13th is another fine par four with an awesome target area: This time the approach is played from a slightly hanging lie into an attractive green that is benched into a forested dune and guarded on the right by one of the deepest bunkers on the layout.

There are also two cunning short par fours on the course. The first, the 8th, has a distinct Sandbelt feel as bunkers make the hole narrower the farther you hit your tee shot, yet the pitch is more straightforward the closer to the green you can drive your ball. The other is Trail's real talking point and probably the most controversial short par four of the modern era. Dropping steeply off the side of a hill, the 14th features a big, wide fairway but a diabolical target set at the end of an oblique ridge that falls sharply on all sides. Missing this tiny green can lead to big numbers, and the only way of holding the putting surface is by bouncing your ball along its skinny entrance, all but impossible from the right half of the fairway.

The severity of this green has left many unimpressed, yet a number of America's celebrated par fours feature brutal pitch shots, and this hole is not only beautiful and original but it carries a massive reward for those able to place their drive strategically down the tighter left side. Despite its obvious qualities, the 14th has already polarized opinion across the industry, and it seems to be one of those rare beasts that can not only spoil a round but can also totally shatter a golfer's perception of the entire course, which is a great shame.

Despite being built away from the coastline and the very element that has made Bandon Dunes famous, Bandon Trails is an exciting layout with a strong and distinctive identity. The course was never going to upstage its elder siblings, but the design team did a brilliant job ensuring that Trails would neither languish in their shadow nor be regarded as the resort's poorer cousin. Indeed, for many this is the best golf on the property.

ABOVE The beauty of the 325-yard 14th hole is apparent in this picture, but so is the difficulty with its tightly perched green only accepting the most precise approach shots

OPPOSITE Equally attractive but much more conventional, the 17th is the final in a delightful set of par threes

Pasatiempo Golf Club

COURSE OPENED 1929
DESIGNER Dr. Alister
MacKenzie

GOLF DIGEST NR
GOLF MAGAZINE 55

The par three finishing hole, protected
by distinctive MacKenzie bunkers
scraped into the face of the barranca

OPPOSITE Looking back across the
11th green, its fiendish contours making
par next to impossible for those leaving
their ball above the hole

The Pasatiempo Golf Club was founded by
Marion Hollins, one of the finest female athletes
of the 1920s and a woman who had driven the
development of the Cypress Point Club before
making a fortune investing in a California oil
company. With her wealth she purchased a
570-acre parcel of land in the hills above Santa
Cruz, and developed plans to create a complete
sporting and housing precinct called Pasatiempo.
Golf would be the centerpiece and its designer
Dr. Alister MacKenzie, who had impressed
Hollins with his earlier work at Cypress Point.

The site for MacKenzie's course was an elevated
ridge that overlooked Monterey Bay and included
natural sandy ravines and a large barranca. The
layout opened in 1929 with an exhibition match
featuring the great Bobby Jones, who was so
impressed with MacKenzie's thought-provoking
design that he later employed the Englishman to
help him build Augusta National. Although trees
have since grown and housing encroachments
prevent the present course from quite reaching
the heights of the original version, the intelligence
of the design and quality of the green contouring
and hazard placement remain. Here golfers are
forced to play from all levels of lie, and into greens
that vary continually in shape and slope. Even
the apparently dreary holes are elevated by their
magnificent green structures, MacKenzie using
steps, tilts, heavy breaks and irregular targets to
complicate play.

The early holes are routed along a broad, tree-
lined ridge, while the back nine is set mostly across
a series of deep natural hazards. Better parts of the
opening nine include the approach into the 2nd
green, which is angled to best hold balls played
from the right side of a left-leaning fairway, and the
bunkering on the long, uphill par three 3rd. Other
par threes at the 5th and 8th are also outstanding,
as is the small, sharply angled green on the 9th,
which rescues an otherwise straightforward, uphill
par five. Less effective are the holes hurt most by
homes and intruding tree limbs, such as the long
6th and short par four 7th, which has a terrific
target but is now cramped badly by trees that were
planted following the unfortunate death of a golfer
on an adjacent tee.

There are no such issues on a tremendous back
nine that is more spacious and houses a couple of
MacKenzie's finest pieces of design. The 10th is
a spectacular hole played across and then along
a nasty ravine, while the 11th is a brilliant uphill
par four split strategically by a diagonal barranca
and notable for an evil green that is shallow and
squeezed between sand for those driving too
safely away from trouble. Side-slope putts here
are among the scariest in the United States. Even
more impressive is MacKenzie's beloved 16th,
his favorite par four anywhere and a hole that
features a drive played blind across a slanted crest
followed by an extraordinary ravine-carry approach
into an enormous triple-tiered target cut into a
hillside. Even those familiar with MacKenzie's best
elsewhere will find this green astonishing.

Despite the success of her golf course, Marion
Hollins suffered financial hardships during the

1930s and was forced to sell the property to stave off creditors. The layout gradually started to decay soon after, as bunkers were altered or removed and putting surfaces reduced in an attempt to lessen maintenance costs. The efforts of Tom Doak in helping the club restore MacKenzie's treasure deserves special recognition, his team using hundreds of old photographs and drawings to replace lost green areas and return the bunker shapes back to near their original rugged form. The work took the best part of ten years and has been an enormous success, not only enhancing the modern Pasatiempo experience but helping to preserve the design intent of its genius creator.

Aside from great greens and world-class holes like the 11th and 16th, what makes this course so fascinating is the special place it held in the heart of Dr. MacKenzie, who spent his final years living in a home alongside the 6th fairway. Along with Cypress Point, he regarded this as his most significant achievement, and when he died his ashes were scattered across the fairways. MacKenzie remains the most celebrated International architect of all time, and given Pasatiempo is more accessible than his more famous creations, it really should be the first place interested public course golfers go to learn more about this legendary designer.

ABOVE The deceptively difficult mid-length 4th hole, noted for its wonderful bunkering

OPPOSITE Many scribes, including the designer himself, regard the 16th green at Pasatiempo as the finest MacKenzie ever designed

Los Angeles Country Club – North Course

COURSE OPENED 1927

DESIGNER George C. Thomas Jr.

GOLF DIGEST 34

GOLF MAGAZINE 27

Looking toward the clubhouse from the short 9th

OPPOSITE **Thomas's wonderful 11th hole, an almost mirror-image of the traditional Redan**

Owner of the most valuable golf real estate in America, the Los Angeles Country Club is located in the heart of Beverly Hills and significant in golfing circles for its North Course, which was redesigned by member George Thomas in 1927. An amateur architect from Philadelphia, Thomas moved to California in 1920 and helped supervise Herbert Fowler's initial renovations of the club's two courses the following year. His later work at Riviera and Bel-Air made him the hottest designer on the West Coast, and he was soon able to convince his home club to allow him to update Fowler's design, starting with the North Course.

Thomas's main issues with the existing course were the lack of strategic play and the fact that holes didn't properly utilize the land's natural golf topography. Although he kept much of Fowler's routing, Thomas designed four entirely new holes and, with shaper William Bell, added great variety and flair to the layout by rebuilding each of the greens and replacing the straight-lined bunkers with more irregular shapes. He also came up with the radical concept of building a course within a course, designing his holes with great elasticity so that a change of tee or flag location could affect the character, or even the par, of an individual hole.

With the reopening of the North Course, Thomas elevated parkland golf on the West Coast to a new level, his layout flowing beautifully across the pronounced ground contours and featuring one distinctive hole after another. Though the core of the course has survived largely intact, a number of holes were lengthened during the 1960s. Most of the work was done sensibly, but a decision to extend the 2nd hole by realigning its fairway to bend against a hillside was a major mistake—it is now the only poor hole on the course. The original, by contrast, moved the other way and approached a superb green set naturally beyond a barranca.

The other major diversion from the Thomas plan was on the harrowing short par four 6th, which is thankfully being restored by architect Gil Hanse, who is also removing hundreds of unnecessary trees and mercifully reversing the slow deterioration of Bell's incredible green and bunker shapes.

Although changes have made the front nine slightly less consistent than the back, the entire round is full of wonderful holes, with players continually confronted by interesting golf decisions and outstanding examples of strategic design. The use of ravines, ridges and a large sandy wash running across the site is exceptional. There are a couple of holes, such as the 3rd and 10th, that could use some length to bring the natural contours back into play for the longer hitters, but the layout remains relevant because its bunkers are expertly located and the putting surfaces place such a great premium on quality approach play. The par threes are particularly good: The 7th and reverse-Redan-shaped 11th are longer holes cleverly shaped to allow well-struck balls to chase toward tight flags, while both the 9th and 15th are shorter but feature exquisitely built green sites with some truly treacherous pin locations. The two-shot holes are also challenging and diverse, from the wildly undulating 3rd and crested 5th through to the stretch of strong, well-bunkered par fours that close the round.

Despite some disappointment with the current setup, today's track is still one of California's best, and its weaknesses are really only apparent after careful study of the original plans. Interestingly, George Thomas regarded this as his finest piece of work, yet he fully expected the better designs of his generation to be quickly surpassed by modern golf architects. This has still to happen, and a full restoration of the North Course would further cement its place among American golf's elite.

Riviera Country Club

COURSE OPENED 1927

DESIGNER George C. Thomas Jr.

GOLF DIGEST 61

GOLF MAGAZINE 19

Riviera's legendary par four 10th, rightly regarded as one of the world's finest holes

OPPOSITE Exquisite bunkering protects the green at the short 16th hole

Founded by members of the Los Angeles Athletic Club, the Riviera Country Club was designed by Golden Age icon George Thomas and built within a deep canyon north of Santa Monica. Thomas was initially unimpressed by the land offered him to design Riviera, and apparently only committed to the job after assurances he would be given the freedom to create whatever he pleased. He was also given a liberal budget, which he spent clearing the property and aggressively shaping the land to fit his design philosophies. When Thomas struck the inaugural drive in 1927, his course had cost more to build than any other in America.

What members at Riviera received for their money was a groundbreaking layout described by consulting architect Alister MacKenzie, as "nearly perfect". MacKenzie was particularly impressed by Thomas's creativity. Modern golfers marvel at icons like the 4th, 6th and 10th, yet when the course opened, almost all of the holes here were unique. As was the bunkering style and the use of strategic green complexes, which were continually arranged so that hitting poor drives was followed by tougher approach shots.

Starting from high atop the northern rim, the round begins with a plunging par five down into the canyon and ends with a rising two-shotter back into the base of this same hillside. In between, the golf course occupies a relatively flat basin, and the designer deserves enormous credit for being able to craft engrossing holes out of such subtle landforms. His most admired hole is the magnificently bunkered 10th, one of the world's great short par fours. There are countless ways to attack this brilliant teaser, yet even in this modern era players struggle to find a trouble-free path to a green that is only a few yards wide and angled to make driving somewhere up the tighter left side imperative. Another gem is the 4th, a super-tough Redan-esque par three famous for its away-sloping green and a mammoth sand trap that fronts the target and forces most to bounce their balls in from the side. The other major talking point is the par three 6th, which has a bunker in the middle of its green but works because the tee shot is exciting and the contouring of the putting surface has made it possible to putt around the trap.

Further highlights include the 70-foot drop from the opening tee, the wicked little par three 16th, almost entirely encircled by sand, and the mid-length 7th, a beautiful driving hole played obliquely along a ditch. Slowly rising and wonderfully bunkered, the 9th is another fine par four, as is the uphill 18th, which is initially blind over a steep ridge and then played into a bowl green set within a natural amphitheater.

Although the odd tee has been stretched to combat the effects of increased driving distances on the playing strategy of the holes, thankfully the structure of Thomas's work here has been largely preserved. The club did tidy up a once-fearsome barranca that runs through the property, and have noticeably improved the general conditioning of the course, but stepping foot on Riviera still elicits a genuine sense of nostalgia. Regardless of your preferences or golfing perspectives, Riviera is a true American treasure and the course remains one of the most interesting and challenging from this golden era.

Bandon Dunes Golf Resort – Bandon Dunes

COURSE OPENED 1999
DESIGNER David McLay Kidd

GOLF DIGEST 31
GOLF MAGAZINE 34

"From the moment I stepped out on these wild, wind-shaped sand dunes, I knew this would be the opportunity of a lifetime."

DAVID McLAY KIDD

OPPOSITE Into the prevailing winds and right along the coastline, the 5th at Bandon Dunes is a spectacularly challenging par four

One of modern golf's most extraordinary success stories, Bandon Dunes was the vision of Mike Keiser, a successful businessman from Chicago who became a genuine devotee of links golf after being profoundly affected by a trip to Ireland during the mid-1980s. He later built a terrific nine-hole course on family land near Lake Michigan, but retained a burning desire to somehow bring traditional links golf to the American mainland. His quest eventually brought him to the remote dunes of southern Oregon, near the small town of Bandon, where he discovered the perfect combination of sand, surf and spectacular coastal cliffs.

Despite being hundreds of miles from a major city, Keiser thought the 1,215-acre property was ideal and quickly negotiated its purchase for $2.4 million, about half the asking price. Although the tall sandhills were covered in dense gorse, they also had a healthy smattering of scotch broom, scrub pine, fern, cedar and spruce. The gorse was the key, however, as not only did the weed remind Keiser of Ireland, but it had grown out of control since its introduction to the region and had twice caught fire and burned down much of the town. The prospect of a developer removing most of the gorse and then controlling what remained helped him win planning approval to construct the resort.

Remarkably, Keiser employed inexperienced Scottish architect David McLay Kidd to design his first course, primarily so he could retain control and be actively involved in the decision-making process. Conscious of the potential for additional development, he kept some of the coastline for a future course but was still able to offer Kidd more than a thousand yards of prime seaside land. Kidd was also given great natural vegetation and undulation, as well as the freedom to plant fescue grasses and keep his course playing firm and fast. This allowed for the building of wide, rolling fairways, often with strategic approach-shot angles, and large greens that are contoured to present golfers with a variety of short game challenges.

While the majority of Kidd's holes are arranged within the region's wind-swept dunes, each of the nines loops beside the ocean and regularly touches the shoreline. Away from the water, better holes include the mid-length 14th, its green beautifully angled beneath a huge sandbank, and the teasing par four 10th, where golfers can select a short, blind route or play down the longer, more open left side. The cross-ridge approach into the opening green and the par three 2nd, played into a steep ledge, are also very good. The rest of the interior holes are noticeably less impressive than those along the cliffs, which is understandable given how spectacular those holes are.

First to introduce players to the Pacific is the 4th, an outstanding two-shot test that bends through dunes toward an open green site with an incredible ocean backdrop. Cleverly, the putting surface is receptive to a chasing approach, but angled toward a pair of deep bunkers. The

5th then tiptoes right along the edge of the West Coast and narrows as it approaches a target tucked beneath a gorse-covered ridge. The 6th, like the 12th and 15th, is a beautiful par three that features an exposed green and uninterrupted sea views. The final coastal hole is the mid-length 16th, the most photogenic of all and also the most unique, as its fairway is made up of staggered landing areas divided by a nasty ravine. Downwind this is a real treat, but into a headwind it can be somewhat confusing to play, as it is unclear where one needs to place the ball for a decent shot into the obscured target.

Bandon Dunes opened for play in 1999 and immediately seemed to reawaken Americans to the glories of seaside golf. The resort has since grown and, in many ways, improved, but it was Kidd's course that first put it on the golfing map and the track remains as popular with visitors as any of its neighbors. The project was an unbelievable opportunity for such a young designer, and its profile and popularity have given his career a huge kick-start. Although Kidd deserves great credit for the quality of the design work, it was the vision of Mike Keiser, and his drive to make this resort truly unforgettable, that have placed Bandon Dunes on most golfers "must-play" list.

ABOVE Options abound on the tee at 16, including hitting toward the green for the monstrously long

OPPOSITE Kidd's delightful par three 6th hole, with its stunning backdrop

The Quarry at La Quinta

COURSE OPENED 1994

DESIGNER Tom Fazio

GOLF DIGEST 47

GOLF MAGAZINE NR

The mid-length 3rd hole

OPPOSITE Approaching the final
green and clubhouse at the Quarry,
with its spectacular mountain backdrop

OVERLEAF The par five 10th hole

Situated within California's arid Coachella Valley, the Quarry at La Quinta is a luxurious private club nestled into a rocky cove at the base of the Santa Rosa Mountains. The course was opened in 1994 and designed by architect Tom Fazio, who aggressively reshaped a 370-acre gravel pit into a sumptuous golfing haven by integrating lakes, streams and waterfalls into his desert landscape.

While most of the course is built within the expansive quarry, midway through the back nine the layout briefly wanders up into an elevated valley that Fazio encouraged his client to purchase prior to completing his routing. Squeezed tightly between a couple of small mountains, these valley holes follow a winding canyon and rise as much as 200 feet above the rest of the course, which is either set down on the quarry floor or built across a central plateau.

Despite significant variances in terrain, Fazio cleverly incorporated all of the elevation changes into his routing, without holes ever feeling overly steep. He ensured visual continuity through immaculate landscaping and by continually aligning fairways and approach shots toward the magnificent mountain peaks. The design itself is playable, creative and, in places, highly strategic. Holes generally feature well-defined modes of attack and present a range of recovery situations for those off their game. Fairways and greens are generously proportioned, the putting surfaces complete with believable contours and effective false fronts and tiers.

Starting from the lower portion of the property, the round begins with a sweeping three-shotter and a strong valley par three, which are both great introductions to the fun and challenge ahead. Aside from the almost vertical dropkick 8th, the remainder of the short holes are excellent, while the par fives generally teeter on the edge of par and, although dangerous, offer aggressive players the incentive to attack. The most memorable holes, however, are the two-shotters, particularly those through the middle of the round. The first gem is the 6th. Played with a stunning backdrop, it falls toward a shallow basin green angled in from all sides and wrapped around a nasty frontal trap. The 7th is another beautiful hole, this time following a creek that runs the entire length of the fairway and with a green that is bunkered to encourage players to drive close to the water. Other strong fours include the 9th and 16th, which is also dominated by a creek down its left side, the water on this occasion cutting in front of the putting surface. Up within the higher ground, the 13th is a shorter four that bends around the canyon, its sharply contoured green favoring golfers able to bite off most of the hazard. The 14th is then a gorgeous par three played directly across this same natural ravine.

As one might expect from a club of this nature, the amenities here are outstanding and turf conditioning is of the highest standard year round. Also worthy of mention is Fazio's ingenious short course, built on land acquired by the club to protect its existing boundaries. Featuring ten greens and ten tees, this par three layout also contains a series of adjacent fairway areas, allowing the members to create their own alternate drive and pitch holes. With the quality and originality of this practice area mirroring the impressive design standards set on the full course, the Quarry at La Quinta is a real class act and one of the finest establishments in the ever-expanding Fazio portfolio.

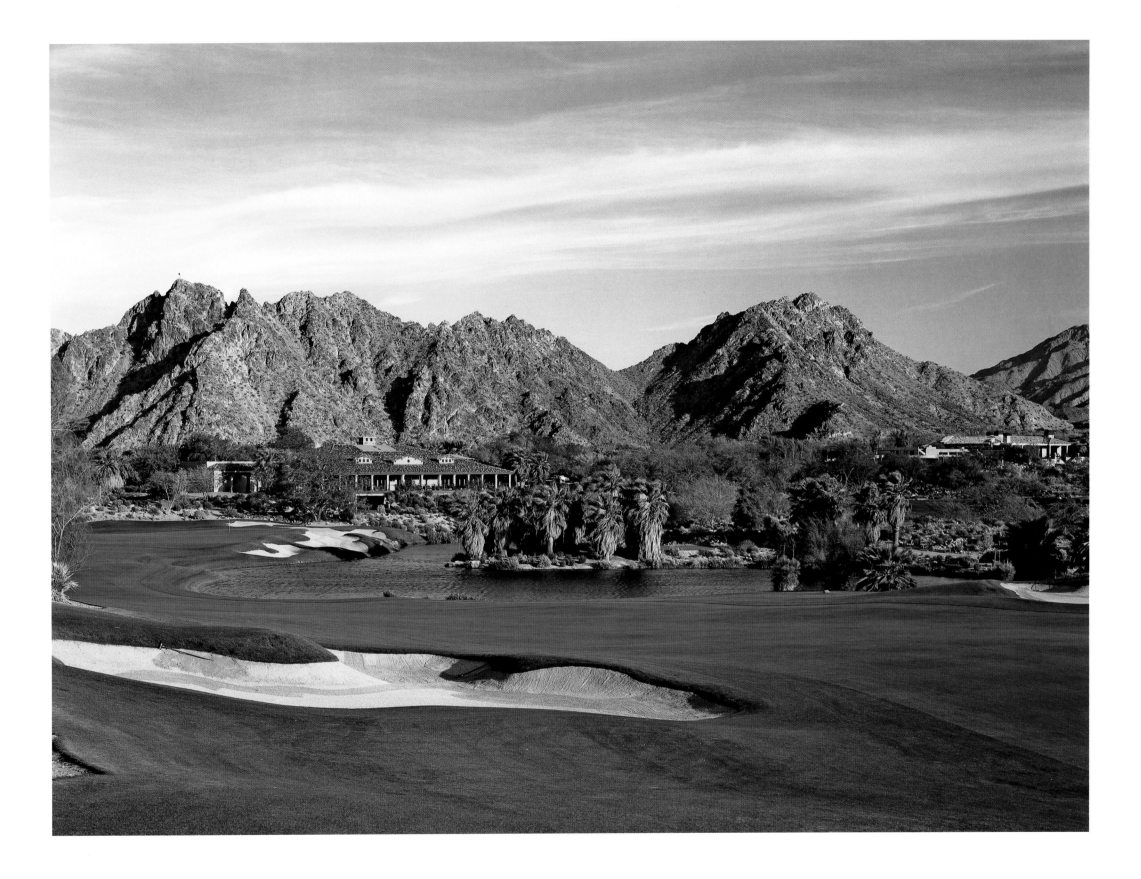

The Valley Club of Montecito

COURSE OPENED 1929
DESIGNER Dr. Alister
MacKenzie with
Robert Hunter

GOLF DIGEST 96
GOLF MAGAZINE 59

Looking toward the Valley
Club's charming clubhouse

OPPOSITE The short par five 2nd
ends at this small and dangerously
bunkered green site

Squeezed between the Pacific Ocean and the Santa Ynez Mountains, the Valley Club of Montecito was opened for play in 1929 and is located on the outskirts of the well-heeled Montecito community, east of Santa Barbara. Designed by Dr. Alister MacKenzie and built by his partner Robert Hunter, this charming course features all of the guile and ingenuity one would expect of such a design team, though on a softer, more subtle scale than some of their more noted creations.

The strength of the course is the sensible location of hazards and the ability of the designers to route interesting holes across the diverse landscape. Green and bunker shapes here are slightly less extravagant than on a course like Pasatiempo, yet the design is similarly centered on sophisticated golf holes that all players can handle but the scratch golfer can only conquer with strategic play. The artistic bunkering is outstanding, while the greens, which are generally smaller than others by MacKenzie, blend naturally into their surroundings and are full of contours and sharp angles.

The round begins with a pair of short par fives which, like the majority of holes here, can be deceptively difficult, particularly for those leaving their ball above the flag or missing approach shots on the near side. From the 3rd, the course moves across a road and into an undulating basin area that features an established forest of sycamore, oak and pine trees as well as a barranca and a small, twisting creek. This section is noted for some excellent bending par fours and a brilliant set of par threes, none of which is particularly long. The downhill 4th, for instance, is generally only a short-iron, but the narrow green is small, surrounded by sand and full of bedeviling breaks. Even more dramatic are the 8th and 11th, both beautiful one-shotters that feature tight greens which are angled across the tee and squeezed between spectacular bunkers. The approach into the 9th and a small, slippery green on the short, undulating par five 10th are also noteworthy. As are formidable traps around the 3rd, 6th and 13th greens and the cross-ravine par three 14th, which leads golfers back to an expansive closing stretch that is steeper and more difficult than it first appears.

As with many courses from this era, the Valley Club had lost some of its character and style over the decades, but pleasingly a recent program by Tom Doak has restored the integrity and quality of the initial design. Aside from returning MacKenzie's greens and irregular bunker shapes back to their original proportions, Doak and his team also reduced areas of rough grass and reinstated closely mown fringes around the putting surfaces.

Thanks to this successful restoration, the Valley Club now owns one of the best-preserved and most authentic MacKenzie designs to be found anywhere in America. Unfortunately the club is also extremely private, but for those able to make it through the gates here the experience is something quite special.

Kapalua Resort – Plantation Course

COURSE OPENED 1991
DESIGNERS Bill Coore,
Ben Crenshaw

GOLF DIGEST NR
GOLF MAGAZINE NR

The exciting all-carry approach into the right-to-left 17th green

OPPOSITE Kapalua opens with a downwind par four that plays toward a target sliding noticeably to the right

A luxury resort on the northwest shore of Maui, Kapalua is home to three golf courses—including Hawaii's most outstanding, the Plantation, which was designed by Bill Coore and Ben Crenshaw. The layout is built across a former pineapple plantation and set on the seaward side of an elevated mountain slope that leans toward the glistening waters of the Pacific Ocean.

Despite its modern resort setting, Plantation is a throwback to the good old days of golf, where the ground game ruled and holes were designed strategically to provide all standards of golfer with avenues to a good score. Fairways are wide open yet reward bold driving, while the greens are large and perfectly angled to better accept shots from preferred angles. Importantly, the holes were also arranged to accommodate the stiff trade winds that blow off the mountain toward the coast. The strength of these winds can make 660-yard par fives, like the 18th, reachable in two shots while rendering 520-yarders, such as the 9th, genuine three-shot epics.

Routing the course was the designer's greatest achievement here, as slopes are steep and the property features some sizeable canyons and dense jungle vegetation. The pair apparently started at the end, finding the colossal 18th fairway and arranging the rest of the holes around this area. The variety in terrain and the mix of uphill, downhill and sideslope holes is exceptional. As is the fact that fairways continually bend with the landforms and often follow winds that push you toward the aggressive line, making the gamble even more dangerous but the rewards even greater.

Plantation is most famous for its finishing holes, yet there is plenty of quality throughout the round. The opening hole, for instance, is a fun plunging par four, played first to a wide fairway and then across a gully to an open green leaning to the right. The falling approach into the 4th and downhill, downwind second shot into the 7th are also outstanding, as are the long cross-gully par three 8th and the three-shot 5th, which horseshoes around a huge ravine to an open green site accommodating a chasing fade. The undulating par five 15th and short 11th, played toward Molokai Island and a green angled to accept balls riding the breeze off the right, are other genuine highlights. Despite such quality, the best is undoubtedly saved for last, both the 17th and 18th noted for their massive fairways, awesome ocean outlooks and thrilling downwind approach shots. Reminiscent of the famous 13th at Pine Valley, the huge green on the 17th is perched beyond a deep ravine and sweeps noticeably from right-to-left, while the 18th is a spectacular par five that crashes steeply toward a grand target leaning away to the rear.

With numerous opportunities to ride the wind and bomb your ball long distances, the Plantation Course at Kapalua is not only tremendous fun but also one of the few courses featured in this book that will offer up regular birdie opportunities to all levels of golfer. Given how lush and demanding resort courses are now typically set up, it is refreshing to play one kept firm and fast and where you can feasibly make eagles and play without fear of losing a ball. Strangely overlooked by both *Golf Digest* and *GOLF Magazine*, the course clearly belongs among America's best 100.

Shadow Creek

COURSE OPENED 1989

DESIGNER Tom Fazio

GOLF DIGEST 27

GOLF MAGAZINE 50

"Just as Tiger Woods has raised the standard at which professional golf is played, so Shadow Creek raised the bar on the golf course design industry. It was viewed as a modern-day wonder and created higher budgets and higher standards for all new courses since it opened."

TOM FAZIO

OPPOSITE **Virtually every inch of Shadow Creek was hand sculpted, including the stream and rising fairway here at the 9th**

Carved from the flat desert plains of southern Nevada, Shadow Creek is the by-product of extraordinary vision coupled with extraordinary wealth, and its completion in 1989 was a milestone for modern golf architecture. The course was the brainchild of casino magnate Steve Wynn, who purchased a flat patch of desert in North Las Vegas and employed Tom Fazio to create a luxurious golfing oasis for his high-end resort guests. Wynn spared no expense during construction, allowing Fazio's team to plant more than 20,000 trees, move 3 million cubic yards of earth and spend around $50 million creating what is recognized today as the premier manufactured golf course in the country.

Despite inhospitable surroundings, Shadow Creek glistens like a precious stone and is able to seamlessly transport its visitors into what feels like a logical golf environment. The attention to detail here is truly astonishing. Although Fazio was blessed with a near unlimited budget, he still had to create the landforms, and he gets credit for building authentic hills, ridges and valleys and for skilfully sculpting creeks, ponds and lakes that meander so naturally they look to be part of an ancient landscape. His ability to tie the shaping and golf features together in such a believable and enjoyable manner is one of the chief reasons the layout feels so organic. Adding to the illusion, mature pines were planted around the entire perimeter of the 310-acre property to screen golfers from the outside world. They were also heavily planted within

the interior, with each of the holes enclosed by trees and isolated from the rest of the course.

The layout itself has great balance and flow, with a mix of heroic and strategic holes, interesting green complexes, appealing bunker shapes and enough general variety to keep most players fully satisfied. Despite the entire property being artificial, nothing really feels forced or manufactured here, as the contours, trees and hazards all look natural to the eye and seem to fit snugly within the design. Water features prominently throughout the round, as do the distant mountain peaks, with a number of shots aligned toward these imposing structures.

Not surprisingly, the most memorable holes at Shadow Creek tend to be those that incorporate the water, starting with the opening hole, an attractive par four that bends gently around a trickling stream. Like several others, its open target leans strategically toward the stream and favors those able to drive aggressively from the tee. The 9th and 15th are other fine par fours played along a creek, the latter with a wandering ditch that cuts in front of the green and forces tee shots closer to the hazard. Another fun hole is the dangerous par five 4th, this time bending around a large lake and heading toward a narrow green that seems able to lure most bold players into attempting a daring approach.

The standout holes, however, come at the close, with the 17th and 18th blessed with great beauty and the promise of plenty of drama. Immediately following the longest hole on the

course, the 17th is the shortest and a classic penultimate par three that features a small peninsula green framed by a sparkling waterfall cascading across rocks and feeding a lake that encircles the putting surface. The 18th is then an appropriately dramatic gambling hole: Played from an elevated ridge, it runs along a series of pools that flow down the right side of the fairway and finally cut across the front of its small green. For those playing the hole conventionally, it is a fun closer with a cool cross-pond pitch, while for courageous golfers looking at a home-hole highlight, the chance to end their day with an eagle putt is extremely tempting and exciting.

The creation of Shadow Creek reset the benchmarks for modern golf, and it seemed to encourage other developers to throw vast amounts of money at projects in the hope of emulating its success. Large budgets alone, however, can only guarantee expensive golf courses; they provide no assurance at all of quality. Without the assistance of more fertile golfing terrain, the reality is that very few courses built on such barren land will ever match what Steve Wynn and Tom Fazio achieved at Shadow Creek.

ABOVE Attractive water features and mature plantings create a "natural" setting for the 17th green

OPPOSITE Striking surroundings and vibrant colors leave a final impression on golfers as they approach the 18th green

Chambers Bay Golf Course

COURSE OPENED 2007
DESIGNERS Robert Trent
Jones Jr., Jason Blasi,
Bruce Charlton

GOLF DIGEST NR
GOLF MAGAZINE NR

*"We knew from our first day
on site that we wanted to create
a course that would be capable
of hosting a US Open."*

ROBERT TRENT JONES JR.

OPPOSITE **Approaching the 2nd green
at Chambers Bay, with its glorious
outlook over Puget Sound**

A remarkable municipal development southwest of Seattle, Chambers Bay opened in 2007 and was built within an abandoned gravel mine alongside the waters of Washington's lower Puget Sound. The course was developed by Pierce County, which employed Robert Trent Jones Jr. as its designer and invested around $20 million in the hope of creating a track to rival the best public courses in the country. Its selection as a US Open venue less than a year after its opening justified such expenditure, and also validated the design style employed by Jones and his associates.

Bordered on one side by the sparkling Puget shoreline and on the other by a steep hillside, the site appears a natural setting for golf, yet mining had stripped the virgin land of its natural ground contours and enormous amounts of earthmoving was required to make it playable. Fueled by the success of Oregon's Bandon Dunes Resort, the Jones team was determined to build a links-style course and cut away a large part of the hillside to enable themselves to create sizeable dune structures and realistic golf corridors. Most of the layout is arranged beneath this hill, with holes sloping toward the water and boasting stunning outlooks across the inlet and farther west over to the snow-capped Olympic Mountains.

The design itself is sensibly spacious, with lots of elevation change but only a handful of areas that seem overdone. Helping to make it feel an authentic links are the free-flowing teeing grounds, eroded sandy waste areas and greens that are open and widely ranging in shape and size. Pleasingly, the contouring of the putting surfaces is less extravagant than some others by this design team

and generally ties in well with the surroundings.

Despite only two holes running directly along the shore, a number of others overlook the water or are routed in close proximity. The round opens with a fairly daunting par four played toward the bay, and a narrow green flanked by an impressive dune ridge. The 2nd then runs adjacent to the shoreline and starts within the dunes before opening up and turning slightly toward the Sound and one of its secluded islands. This approach, as with the par three 3rd, is dominated by the outlook and played across a vast sandy waste toward a green sloping gently to the left. The other par threes are similarly memorable. The 15th falls sharply toward the sea and a beautifully bunkered green framed by the only tree on the property. The 17th also drops significantly, this time along a steep dune to a green engulfed by sand. Squeezed between is a par four directly along the water, which is notorious for a shallow finger of green that extends along the back right portion of the hole and is all but impossible to hit for those playing too safely away from the coast.

The rest of the course is an equally exciting mix of scenery and substance, with a number of really distinctive target areas and firm and bouncy fescue playing surfaces throughout. Although there are a couple of holes here that don't quite work, few courses are perfect and, importantly, this one is good enough to more than warrant the attention it has received. Chambers Bay was a unique development and, like other great public golf facilities, it is likely not only to attract visitors from across the country, but most importantly to inspire locals into our beautiful game for generations to come.

Forest Highlands Golf Club – Canyon Course

COURSE OPENED 1988

DESIGNERS Tom Weiskopf,
Jay Morrish

GOLF DIGEST 45

GOLF MAGAZINE NR

The par three 14th with its peninsula-shaped green

OPPOSITE One of the more impressive par fours at Forest Highlands, the 9th plunges onto a flat valley before heading over water and into a narrow target

Set high within the mountains of Northern Arizona, the Forest Highlands Golf Club was opened in 1988 and is part of a larger 1,100-acre housing development located a short drive south of the popular town of Flagstaff. The club has two golf courses; its first, the Canyon Course, was designed by Tom Weiskopf and his partner Jay Morrish, who appear to have been given first pick of the best available land for their layout.

Occupying a series of spectacular mountainside valleys and canyons, the fairways here are carved through forests of ponderosa pine and, in places, lined by copses of mature oak and aspen. The steep nature of the gradients, as well as the need to incorporate housing into the site, made routing the course quite tricky, but the designers did an excellent job ensuring the spacious layout was both user-friendly and playable. The most noticeable feature of their routing is the unusual makeup of par. Every even-numbered hole between the 4th and 14th is a par three, and there are also five par fives, including a couple that are definitely within reach in two shots. That leaves just seven par fours, but this irregular arrangement helped the designers combat the fact that golf balls travel as much as 10 percent farther at this elevation by forcing players to hit a range of different clubs into the greens.

Without question, the two holes likely to live longest in your memory are par fours at the 9th and 17th. The 9th is a magnificent looking hole that drops steeply off a hillside tee into a tight valley where trees, sand and a stream guard your drive and a pond and shallow green complicate the approach. The 17th is a classic driveable par four, but on a more daring scale. Again the tee is placed high up on a ledge, the hole falling and bending around a hill with the fairway cut by a ditch that forces you to either drive aggressively across the shoulder of the hill or to lay-up down the safer right side and try to pitch into a target now angled across you.

There are a number of other standouts as well, including cross-pond one-shotters at the 4th and 14th, the drive and pitch 16th and the long, left-bending par four 7th, which turns around large pines that interfere with the uphill second shot if too far left off the tee. The par fives are also intriguing, particularly the reachable 5th, the rising 15th and the split fairway 18th with a creek cutting the hole and creating a very narrow entry passage for the really long hitters.

Throughout the round, the variety and quality of the design work is very high, Weiskopf and Morrish using the elevation changes and a mix of hole lengths, green shapes and hazard positioning to create an interesting array of approach shot situations. The Meadow Course, which was also designed by Tom Weiskopf, opened in 1999 and is a longer, more manufactured layout that features larger bodies of water and holes arranged across a more open landscape. The course is also very good, however, and has enough quality to ensure that Forest Highlands is a 36-hole destination for most visiting golfers.

Monterey Peninsula Country Club – Shore Course

COURSE OPENED 2004

DESIGNER Mike Strantz

GOLF DIGEST 77

GOLF MAGAZINE NR

"I hope to carefully shape this new course so she will bend and sweep with the natural terrain of rocks, trees, grasses and ocean. My dream is that she will appear as if she has been dancing among the cypress on this coastline forever."

MIKE STRANTZ

OPPOSITE **The artistry with which Mike Strantz reshaped this site into a quality golf course is apparent at the par three 11th**

The Monterey Peninsula Country Club was formed during the 1920s as part of a separate residential development by Pebble Beach founder Samuel Morse. Situated on the Peninsula's western coastline and sandwiched between Cypress Point and the township of Pacific Grove, its first course was designed by Seth Raynor, while a second track, the Shore Course, was added in 1961.

Hurriedly built and long regarded as the club's poorer sibling, Shore was originally designed by Bob Baldock and Jack Neville, but by the turn of the 21st century was in such desperate need of repair that the club decided to undertake a substantial upgrade of the entire layout. A number of well-credentialed architects were considered for the job, but Mike Strantz won the contract based largely on his feel and passion for the land. Excited by the prospects, Strantz proposed a radical new routing scheme that involved reversing the existing direction of play so holes would turn toward the ocean rather than play away from the water. The designer started work on the project in early 2002, around the same time as he was diagnosed with an aggressive form of cancer that would, sadly, take his life shortly after the course reopened.

Despite his deteriorating physical condition, Strantz remained on site throughout the construction process, working side-by-side with his shapers on every feature of the design. He retained the skeleton of the opening and closing holes, but crafted 12 entirely new holes out on the expansive seaside areas, aligning a number of his greens and fairway turn points toward the Pacific or the neighboring Cypress Point Club. The broad fairways flow nicely across the terrain, while putting surfaces are generally large and sensibly contoured to thoroughly test approach play but leave a range of fun recovery options. Many are set beside attractive rock formations or protected by punishing sandy wastelands.

Although a few of the holes within the housing area remain a touch underwhelming, the heart of this course is outstanding, particularly the coastal loop from the 5th through to the 12th. There are just two par fours in this stretch, but plenty of variety and subtle elevation changes. Decorative boulders are prominent on several high-quality par threes, and also well used on the long 6th and the doglegging 15th, its approach played into a terrific skyline green framed by the distant ocean. Also excellent is the short par four 5th, bent strategically around a protruding hazard, and the outlooks beyond the 8th, 12th and 13th greens, the latter with magnificent views of the dunes at Cypress Point.

The decision to allow Mike Strantz to redesign the Shore Course was deemed risky at the time, but ultimately he proved a most astute architectural selection. Given strong local competition, this was never likely to be top dog in Monterey, but the members are now very proud of their course and its transformation has further strengthened the appeal of the area for visiting golfers. The premature death of the designer was a great loss for our sport, as there is no doubt that the success of this project would have kept him busy for many years to come.

Nanea Golf Club

COURSE OPENED 2003

DESIGNER David McLay Kidd

GOLF DIGEST NR

GOLF MAGAZINE 44

David Kidd's sprawling bunkering style on display at the par five 6th

OPPOSITE The 2nd hole is a falling four with an impressive ocean outlook

An exclusive golfing retreat on the west coast of Hawaii's Big Island, the Nanea Golf Club is situated about 15 miles north of Kailua Kona and set amongst dark lava fields on the seaward side of the volcanic Mount Hualalai. The course was designed by Scottish architect David McLay Kidd and first opened for play in 2003.

Despite the unsuitability of its soil and the fact that the property's elevation ranges from 700 to 1,300 feet, Kidd's clients wanted him to shape the land into an authentic British-style links course. They gave him the budget and freedom to cap the entire site in cinder sand and cover all the tees, greens and fairways with a drought-tolerant Paspalum grass that would permit the firm and fast conditions his shaping required. He also had his choice of 8,000 acres upon which to build his holes, the chosen parcel more than 1,000 acres in size, with much of it used as a buffer to ensure the membership enjoyed their golf totally undisturbed.

Blessed with panoramic views of the Pacific from virtually every corner of this windswept property, Kidd arranged his holes in a large figure eight with the opening nine routed across the lower portion of the site and the back nine heading into the higher ground. Full of deep hollows and crimped ridges, the linksy playing areas are relatively generous and attractively framed by shimmering meadow grasses and black volcanic rock. The large, undulating green complexes are particularly good, while the sprawling grass-faced bunkers are generally well positioned and nicely cut into the rolling ground.

The course opens with three downhill holes that

bend to the left, each offering long hitters a big advantage not only in terms of getting into wider landing areas but also in being able to access preferred approach angles. Tracking back up the slope, the bumpy and bunkerless mid-length 5th is the first real standout, its green set on a ledge and protected by a deep frontal depression and a significant left-to-right gradient. The other cool mid-length hole is the 16th, which rises impressively into a shelf green falling severely at the front and divided by a vertical tier. The par fives are also very good, the last half of the 6th climbing dramatically beyond a bunkered ridge and the 13th with its green also set beyond a ridge but angled across the fairway and benched between deep bunkers. The plunging 18th is another exciting three-shot challenge, with a wildly shaped putting surface and plenty of gambling options. Other quality features include the tiered plateau target at the 7th, the built-up back ledge on the 10th green and the nasty dogleg 12th, which turns and tumbles along a lumpy fairway. The approach into the 15th is also really good, the shot pointing toward the ocean and heading down through a valley and into a unique half plateau, half punchbowl target.

Nanea is an impressive layout on a difficult site and a pleasant break from much of the other golf available across the Hawaiian Islands. Kidd clearly had his issues here, yet he did well to fashion a convincing golf course out of this steep and inhospitable terrain. It isn't really a genuine links course, but the holes are fun to play, the views are outstanding and the superior turf conditions make it a pretty memorable experience for most visiting golfers.

Spyglass Hill Golf Course

COURSE OPENED 1966

DESIGNER Robert Trent Jones

GOLF DIGEST 52

GOLF MAGAZINE 48

The green at the par three 3rd hole, with its Pacific Ocean backdrop

OPPOSITE With options from the tee and an uncomfortably tight green surrounded by coastal vegetation, the mid-length 4th is one of the standout holes at Spyglass

Designed by Robert Trent Jones at the height of his prolific career, Spyglass Hill was the vision of Pebble Beach founder Samuel Morse, who had long planned for a series of golf courses along his spectacular Monterey coastline. Sandwiched strategically between Cypress Point and the Monterey Peninsula Country Club, the land he made available to Jones for Spyglass Hill was a combination of untouched coastal dunes and forested high ground two miles northeast of Pebble Beach.

Deriving its name from a hill in Robert Louis Stevenson's landmark novel *Treasure Island*, the course opened in 1966 and was designed from the outset to be a long, demanding test of golf's premier players. Rather than ducking in and out of the coastal dunes, Jones preferred to introduce golfers immediately to the sea and then finish with an extended stretch of holes through the Del Monte forest. These forested holes tend to play much longer than the opening loop, as the ground always seems damper and many of the approach shots are played uphill or into large plateau greens.

The course opens dramatically by diving into the pristine sandhills, starting with a fearsome par five that turns through a chute of pines before tumbling down and toward the Pacific. The next few holes are cut among the sand and ice plant. Par threes at the 3rd and 5th boast fun tee shots and superb ocean outlooks, while the 4th is a legendary mid-length par four that bends around a vast sandy scrub toward an anorexic green squeezed obliquely between small dunes. This was apparently one of Jones's favorite holes, and he gives golfers the option of either laying back and leaving a full wedge over the frontal mound or trying to hit the ball aggressively farther up the fairway and then pitching through the saddle.

From the 6th tee play turns inland, away from the surf and onto a continuous stretch of holes through the pines that are strong and difficult but a lot less memorable than the stunners preceding them. This total change of character is the most obvious sore point with Spyglass Hill, along with the fact that the green complexes and driving challenges of these wooded holes at times becomes a little monotonous. Many of the targets are pushed up, with most having sharp contours and bold flanking bunkers. Approach shots from the fairway are manageable, but stray off the tee and bogey quickly becomes a decent score. The steeply uphill 8th and long 16th, which bends around a central pine, are particularly harsh on inaccurate play.

One of the hardest courses in California, Spyglass Hill is rightly renowned for Jones's early holes, although those within the trees are still full of quality and are probably better than many first realize. It may struggle when compared directly with neighbors like Cypress Point and Pebble Beach, but this layout is one of the best from its iconic architect and is well worth including in any Monterey Peninsula golf itinerary.

The Olympic Club – Lake Course

COURSE OPENED 1927

DESIGNER Sam Whiting

GOLF DIGEST 23

GOLF MAGAZINE 26

Approaching the elevated 14th green

OPPOSITE With a small target guarded by deep bunkers, the par three 15th is capable of taking shots from those golfers relaxing after a prolonged stretch of tough holes

Considered the nation's oldest athletic organization, San Francisco's Olympic Club was founded in 1860 and moved into golf following World War I, with the purchase of a struggling country club in nearby Daly City. Sandwiched between the Pacific Ocean and Lake Merced, the golf property was large enough for the creation of two courses, both initially designed by Willie Watson but in 1927 completely redesigned and rebuilt by course superintendent Sam Whiting.

The club's centerpiece is the Lake Course, a notorious championship venue built beneath its elevated clubhouse on a steep hillside that leans down toward the lake. Given the difficult nature of the terrain here, the routing was crucial, with Whiting mostly staggering his holes across the heavy slopes rather than heading up and down them. From the outset, the layout was intended to test the game's best players, its fairways planted with thousands of pine, cypress and cedar trees that now crowd the once sparse landscape and make this one of the tightest driving courses imaginable. Approach play is equally severe as the greens are small and quick; often slightly raised the putting surfaces are generally tilted sharply forward and flanked by deep bunkers.

The par five opening hole sets the tone for the round; it bends to the right with trees and thick rough ready to punish anyone straying offline. More impressive is the sideslope approach up into the steep 2nd green and the long, downhill par three 3rd with its fast target surrounded by nasty traps. The 4th and 5th are then real brutes, each bending one way around trees but with fairways that slant in the opposite direction and force you either to shape your ball from the tee or to hit your second from a long way back. There is a similarly torturous stretch of demanding 400-yard plus par fours around the turn, these holes straighter slogs but with trees and rough again waiting to catch anyone not precise enough with their driver. The closing run is equally stiff, ending with the club's most recognized hole, the short par four 18th, which is memorable for a treacherous uphill approach played into a tiny green cut into the hillside and angled cruelly to the front.

Although little structural change has occurred since it opened, Robert Trent Jones did lengthen several holes prior to the club's first US Open in 1955, as well as adding the track's one and only fairway bunker. Further strengthening and modification has continued to take place between subsequent championships, including the softening of the putting contours on the 18th green following the controversial US Open of 1998.

With plenty of room, tricky green sites and narrow fairways protected by trees and dense ryegrass, the Lake Course at the Olympic Club remains an attractive location for event organizers, particularly given its proximity to the city. In truth, however, the course lacks outstanding holes and its fairway corridors are really too narrow for great golf. In many ways this is an American equivalent to a place like Royal Troon, which is far from the best course in Scotland but unquestionably one of its most suitable tournament venues, especially for those who like to watch the game's champion professionals suffer.

Mayacama Golf Club

COURSE OPENED 2001

DESIGNER Jack Nicklaus

GOLF DIGEST 66

GOLF MAGAZINE 98

Cut into a rise, this series of attractive bunkers protect the 2nd green

OPPOSITE With its crested fairway and perched green, the opening hole is a particularly pleasant introduction to golf at Mayacama

Situated in the heart of the Sonoma Valley, north of San Francisco, the Mayacama Golf Club opened in 2001 as a prestigious golf, wine and residential retreat built for a small, discerning membership. Set attractively within the foothills of the Mayacamas mountain range, the club's sprawling property covers more than 650 acres and was once owned by *Peanuts* cartoon creator Charles M. Schulz.

Built within a series of peaceful hills and deep valleys, the golf course was designed by Jack Nicklaus with holes weaving across a forested landscape and skirting a grand collection of oak, madrone and manzanita trees. The whole development is very tastefully master-planned, with the housing mostly located on a high ridge and set well back of the rolling fairways. It seems clear that Nicklaus was given first choice of the available land for his design, and he incorporated various natural features into the holes, including dense ravines and smaller creeks and ditches. A number of the longer holes bend around trees and feature cross-hazard approach shots, while the shorter holes tend to have target areas set at the base of slopes and are fairly penal on those who miscue their tee shot.

The view out across the golf course from the Mediterranean-style clubhouse is a stirring introduction to Mayacama, with the excellence of the turf and the quality of the shaping apparent from the outset. Although there isn't an abundance of strategically stimulating holes, the course is beautifully built and carefully routed to ensure maximum drama and create a number of impressive backdrops. The greens are particularly effective. Bentgrass and lightning quick, they feature subtle rolls and ridges designed to feed weaker balls back off the putting surfaces.

Individual highlights include the strong par four 6th, sweeping right and crossing a gully protecting its contoured green, and the mid-length 7th, which bends almost 90 degrees in the other direction and features a fun pitch shot across a ditch. The best stretch of golf, however, comes through the middle of the back nine and includes the likes of the 14th, a short cross-valley par three with a small green built on a hillside ledge, and the fine dogleg 13th, its approach played into a shallow target set beyond a deep creek. With a wonderful view of the surrounding countryside from its elevated tee, the heroic par five 15th is also very good, its falling fairway turning sharply to the left and its green benched attractively beneath a hill and beyond a nasty ravine. The short par four 16th is another nice hole, despite offering little incentive for the average player to gamble from the tee.

There is a lot of competition in Northern California, and though Mayacama isn't the best course in this part of the state, it is a very commendable estate layout that modern golf fans, in particular, are bound to enjoy. Interestingly, the club is equally as devoted to wine as to golf, with members not only given their own private wine lockers but the opportunity to associate with some of the region's premier vintners, who are made honorary members here.

Desert Forest Golf Club

COURSE OPENED 1962

DESIGNER Robert "Red" Lawrence

GOLF DIGEST NR

GOLF MAGAZINE 78

Set in the scenic foothills of the Lower Sonoran Desert, the Desert Forest Golf Club was founded by ambitious real estate entrepreneurs as part of their plans to transform an isolated rural wasteland into a thriving residential hamlet. The course is situated within the town of Carefree, north of Scottsdale, and was designed by Red Lawrence, an East Coast architect who moved to Arizona in 1958 principally because of his wife's poor health. Lawrence previously worked with William Flynn, but had designed very few courses himself when given the opportunity to create what would become his most acclaimed piece of work.

Widely regarded as the first quality desert course in America, Desert Forest opened in 1962 and was built as a stand-alone golf club without country club facilities or any real estate intrusions. The layout was created with a modest budget and minimal earth moving, Lawrence simply carving his playing corridors through the rugged undergrowth.

Characterized by the complete absence of superfluous features, the design itself is quite simple, but the challenge presented is one of the toughest in the Scottsdale region. There isn't a single fairway bunker on the course, nor are there any water hazards or long forced carries, yet what makes the track so demanding are the narrow strips of fairway and the smallish greens, which are often pushed-up and flanked by deep traps. Straight driving is the only recipe for success here, as the fairways play even tighter than they appear, thanks to the firm turf and a number of crowned or undulating landing areas that are prone to feeding balls off the short grass and down toward the nasty desert vegetation.

To score well on this course, you must be on your game from the opening drive through to the final approach, as disaster can strike at any point in the round. The holes posing the greatest threat to par are probably the 5th and 7th, a pair of notorious doglegs that really define the Desert Forest experience. The 5th is the toughest par four on the course, as it bends almost 90 degrees to the left and forces you either to play a lay-up followed by a wood or to hit an aggressive drive over the desert and through a pair of saguaro cacti toward a distant fairway. Even more exciting for the long hitter is the 7th, a peculiar hole that doglegs at a right angle but can be played as a straight par five for those strong enough to carry the waste and flirt with a long diagonal dry wash that separates the final two landing areas. Unfortunately, on both of these holes there is only one route to the green for the shorter hitters, and a massive advantage for those able to drive the ball long and straight.

Surrounded now by hundreds of high-end clubs and luxury golf estates, Desert Forest remains a golfing pioneer in Arizona, as it was the course that inspired other developers to view this vast landscape as more than just an arid wasteland. Although the layout lacks the pedigree of America's best courses, the proliferation of desert golf over the ensuing decades has made it one of the nation's most significant.

OPPOSITE The 11th is the longest hole at Desert Forest, ending with this small and apparently straightforward putting target

San Francisco Golf Club

COURSE OPENED 1915
DESIGNER Albert W. Tillinghast
GOLF DIGEST 37, GOLF MAGAZINE 15

One of the most exclusive clubs in America, the San Francisco Golf Club was formed toward the end of the 19th century but golfing did not begin on its present A.W. Tillinghast layout until 1915. Located a few miles south of the Golden Gate Bridge, the Tillinghast course was a landmark in this country, as it was not only the legendary architect's first great piece of work, but also the first course of real quality anywhere on the West Coast.

Built across rolling pine-covered ground close to Lake Merced, the course is best recommended for its wonderfully creative design style and a property that features ravines and an array of interesting internal golf undulations. One particular ravine was the scene of the last legal duel in American history, when a California Supreme Court Justice shot and killed a United States Senator in 1859. Within this valley lies the club's renowned drop-shot par three 7th, appropriately labeled the "Duel Hole" and apparently Tillie's favorite among the many hundreds of holes he created.

Although the front nine features the most dramatic landforms, green contours across the entire layout are brilliantly conceived, while the fairways tend to head through boldly bunkered valleys, swing around sprawling traps or be routed along the edge of the ravines. Picking out highlights here is a hard task, because even the flattest fairways are superbly bunkered to present clear and intriguing strategic options and angles. The most obvious highlight is the 7th, a great par three dropping toward a small kidney-shaped green that falls on the right and is protected by sand on the left. Continuing down the valley and rising into a steeply leaning green, the 8th is also outstanding, as is the recently restored par three 13th and the gorgeous three-shotters that conclude each of the nines.

Although Tillinghast is renowned for the variety of his design work, there is something refreshingly unique about this club that sets it apart from the gems he created on the East Coast. Hidden to all but the fortunate few, San Francisco Golf Club is not only the clear golfing standout in the Bay Area, but among the top dozen or so classic layouts anywhere in the country.

The Preserve Golf Club

COURSE OPENED 2000
DESIGNER Tom Fazio with J. Michael Poellot & Sandy Tatum
GOLF DIGEST 95, GOLF MAGAZINE NR

Designed by Tom Fazio, with input from both Sandy Tatum and J. Michael Poellot, the Preserve Golf Club is the centerpiece of an enormous development in the hills outside Monterey known as the Santa Lucia Preserve. Previously used as ranching land, this vast, rolling property covers 31 square miles, yet less than 10 percent of the area is used for golf and housing, with the remainder preserved in perpetuity as untouched open space.

The golf course itself occupies a mere 350 acres, its holes arranged in a large loop and mostly set within a series of small hills and valleys at the base of the surrounding Santa Lucia Mountains. Fazio used the distant peaks to provide a dramatic backdrop to a number of the better holes here. He also integrated natural ponds and streams into the design and carved his fairways from a collection of timeless redwoods and ghostly live oaks. These oaks occasionally block golfers driving to the wrong part of the fairways, especially on the longer holes. Approach play is definitely the key to scoring well, however, as the fairways tend to be relatively spacious but the sizeable greens are built with sharp slopes that often kick inaccurate balls down banks or away to dangerous three-putt areas. Several targets feature subtle false fronts, while a number of others are shaped to allow shrewd golfers to use the contours to feed their shot toward tricky hole locations.

As secluded a place to golf as one would ever find, the Preserve experience begins with an eight-mile drive up the club's winding entrance road, which leads players to a historic Spanish-styled clubhouse that dates back to the 1920s. Although the course itself doesn't rival the best along the Carmel coastline, the development is a class act and most will find it hard not to be seduced by its pristine playing surfaces and first-class service.

OPPOSITE Set down within a pronounced valley, the mid-length 3rd showcases the beauty of the Santa Lucia Preserve landscape

Bel-Air Country Club

COURSE OPENED 1927
DESIGNER George C. Thomas Jr.
GOLF DIGEST NR, GOLF MAGAZINE 89

Home to a number of Hollywood A-listers, the Bel-Air Country Club was founded by an oil tycoon and designed by architect George Thomas, who, along with his partner William Bell, built the course across the hills and valleys of West Los Angeles. The pair began by shaping what is now the front nine, which opened for play in 1927. The back nine was added a few years later, once they had figured out how to overcome a particularly large canyon that split the property in two. Placing the clubhouse on a crest overlooking the hazard, they decided to build the 10th tee immediately beside the canyon and locate a green 200 yards away on the other side, connecting the back nine to the front via a large suspension bridge.

In its infancy, Bel-Air was regarded in the same league as Thomas's celebrated creations at Riviera and LA Country Club, but unfortunately the members have continually altered their layout over the ensuing years. Aside from removing several key design elements, they have rounded out most of Thomas's innovative bunker shapes and allowed trees to narrow the playing corridors. Thankfully, the original routing remains largely intact, and it is full of great variety and manages to tie the awkward landforms together in a cohesive and strategic manner. Traversing a series of valleys and linked by concrete tunnels carved through the hills, the front nine is best recommended for beautiful green complexes at the 3rd, 5th, 7th, 8th and 9th, while back nine gems include the par three 13th with its magnificent frontal bunker, the three-shot 14th and the downhill 17th, which turns right and tiptoes precariously along a narrowing ridge. There is nothing on this course, however, to quite match the 10th, and the pleasure one gets from marching across the club's iconic bridge knowing your ball rests safely on the distant green.

Despite substantial changes, Bel-Air retains the attributes of greatness and, thanks to its routing and preserved architectural features, is still a fabulous golfing experience. There is no doubt, however, that the restoration of more Thomas design would make the course even better, and elevate it back alongside his other LA masterpieces.

The Estancia Club

COURSE OPENED 1995
DESIGNER Tom Fazio
GOLF DIGEST 81, GOLF MAGAZINE NR

A prestigious gated community on the northern slopes of Scottsdale's distinctive Pinnacle Peak Mountain, The Estancia Club was opened in 1995 and its golf course designed by acclaimed architect Tom Fazio. Arranging the holes around the base of the rocky landmark, Fazio crafted his course from a spectacular 640-acre parcel of desert, incorporating stunning boulder formations, saguaro cacti and outlooks over the distant Sonoran peaks into much of the layout.

While early holes skirt the towering granite structure, much of the back nine meanders up into the dusty hills and through areas of great natural elevation change. The mid-length 10th starts the gentle rise up into the higher ground, the hole framed by massive boulders and followed by an exquisite short par three played into a green wedged within a giant rock amphitheater. Other moments of note include the drive from the back tee on the 12th, which forces players to hit across a canyon, and the falling approach through a narrowing valley into the 17th green. The uphill 13th is also very good, as are front nine par fours at the 2nd and 5th, the latter with a striking backdrop and sloping green banked into the base of a hill.

Although Estancia lacks world-class individual holes and the general standard of design is below courses like Shadow Creek and the Quarry at La Quinta, the golf is very stylish and Fazio's artistically shaped greens are both interesting to hit into and fun to chip and putt around. The course is one of the most enjoyable to play in the greater Scottsdale region, and its superior turf standards, general ambience and the rugged beauty of its surrounding mountains help to make the club particularly popular in the high-end golf market.

OPPOSITE **Sun sets over the stunning**
5th hole at The Estancia Club

Eugene Country Club

COURSE OPENED 1967
DESIGNER Robert Trent Jones
GOLF DIGEST 64, GOLF MAGAZINE NR

Located at the southern end of Oregon's Willamette Valley, the Eugene Country Club was founded in 1899 but moved to its present home during the 1920s, where a new course was designed by leading amateur golfer H. Chandler Egan. The Egan course survived until 1967, when Robert Trent Jones reversed the entire layout, switching green sites into tees and tees into greens, making the 1st the 18th and creating left-hand doglegs where right bends had previously existed.

Aside from changing direction, the routing remains largely intact, with only par threes at the 7th and 12th altered to allow both to play across ponds. A number of other water hazards were expanded, and pressed against the putting surfaces rather than lying wasted in front of the teeing grounds. The green sites were also enlarged and, typical of Jones' work, they were generally raised, pitched forward and defended by striking sand hazards cut into their banks.

Occupying a tightly compact property blessed with gentle undulations, the course is primarily recommended for its challenging target areas and magnificent collection of trees, some firs towering up some 200 feet. The holes themselves are all solid, but unfortunately few standout as exceptional. Longer holes tend to lack variety from the tee, while three cross-pond par threes is probably one too many, though all work reasonably well. What makes the course fun to play, however, are green complexes like the 15th, which is built on a small diagonal shelf, and shallow plateau targets like the 8th and 9th.

Firmly entrenched within *Golf Digest's* Top 100, the club has unquestionably benefited from the popularity of Bandon Dunes, as Eugene is conveniently located midway between Portland and the resort. Although it isn't in the same league as the Bandon courses, this is a beautiful place to golf and a fine detour option for those heading south down I-5.

Sahalee Country Club – South/North Course

COURSE OPENED 1969
DESIGNERS Ted Robinson, Rees Jones
GOLF DIGEST 76, GOLF MAGAZINE NR

The Sahalee Country Club was founded by members of two separate Seattle golf clubs who were determined to build a championship-caliber course. In 1967, they purchased 180 acres of rolling ground on the Sammamish Plateau, half an hour east of the city. Architect Ted Robinson was selected as course designer and given the task of crafting 27 holes through giant cedar and Douglas-fir trees native to this part of the continent.

Known for its magnificent evergreens and interesting ground gradients, the South/North tournament course is compactly routed and incredibly narrow, with tall timber cramping fairway corridors and often blocking approach shots for those only slightly off-center from the tee. The opening par four is an appropriate, though difficult, introduction to the challenge, trees pinching its fairway so tightly that finding the short grass with anything beyond a 4-iron is next to impossible. The green, like many here, is small and flanked by sand. The next few are equally cramped, but later holes at least offer golfers the opportunity to drive with their longer sticks. Most of the better moments come through the back (North) nine, which boasts the most pronounced ground contours and tends to have a little more width from the tee. It begins with a beautiful par four that heads across a saddled crest and then down to a peninsula target cut into a pond. The rising 15th fairway also crosses a narrow crest, the hole followed by a very effective mid-length par four, its small green set beyond a deep valley and either approached with a mid-iron from a level lie or with a blind wedge from down in the depression.

Although the Robinson routing remains unaltered here, in 1996 Rees Jones began an extensive program of redesign and modernization, stretching holes and altering a number of green and bunker shapes. His work has clearly made Sahalee an even more demanding tournament test, though ultimately it is still too tight to be considered quite top shelf.

OPPOSITE Water and sand protect the green at the dropkick 8th hole on Sahalee's North Course

Rustic Canyon Golf Course

COURSE OPENED 2002
DESIGNER Gil Hanse with Geoff Shackelford
GOLF DIGEST NR, GOLF MAGAZINE NR

An unassuming public facility built on land leased directly from Ventura County, the Rustic Canyon Golf Course was designed principally by Gil Hanse, with input from local golf writer Geoff Shackelford. The course opened in 2002 and is located within a rugged 300-acre canyon in Moorpark, about 50 miles northwest of Los Angeles. Though Hanse gets primary design credit here, Shackelford was heavily involved in the routing, working with Hanse and his team to find the best arrangement of holes and to ensure that construction caused minimal disturbance to the site's natural ground contours.

As a result of their minimalistic approach to design, this was one of those rare modern courses built on time and under budget, with construction taking just six months to complete and less than 20,000 cubic yards of earth being moved during the process. Arranged in two loops on either side of a central clubhouse, the layout is full of intelligent holes and cut by a natural sandy wash that is regularly incorporated into the design. Most holes feature wide-open fairways and sensibly generous greens, which boast plenty of interesting movement and are often fronted by closely mown apron areas that promote the running approach. Aside from the bunkering and some terrific green sites, early highlights include the pushed-up par three 8th, multiroute par fives at the 1st and 5th and clever short fours like the 3rd and 7th, their split fairways tempting aggressive golfers to take riskier driving lines. On the back nine the standouts are the Cape-style 14th, which bends dramatically around the wash, and the mesmeric par five 13th, its fairway strategically bunkered and its bean-shaped green wrapped around a central trap that creates dilemmas for those approaching from the wrong side of the hole.

With its high architectural standards yet affordable green fee, Rustic Canyon is a rarity for California and, not surprisingly, is a course that has become increasingly popular with public players who appreciate the charms of strategic design.

Princeville at Hanalei – Prince Course

COURSE OPENED 1990
DESIGNER Robert Trent Jones Jr.
GOLF DIGEST 39, GOLF MAGAZINE NR

Built for the Princeville development on the north shore of Hawaii's Kauai Island, the Prince Course was designed by Robert Trent Jones Jr. and built atop lush tropical cliffs that tower 300 feet above Kauai's picturesque Hanalei Bay. Cooled by Pacific breezes, the layout is one of Jones' most scenic creations and offers golfers rare panoramic views of both the sea on one side and green volcanic mountains on the other.

Loaded with dramatic elevation change, the course is routed in a large loop and briefly skirts along coastal bluffs while also heading through dense valleys and across deep canyons and meandering creeks. Despite the obvious glamour, the course has issues with playability, as the par threes are a little severe while a number of the longer holes are unnecessarily narrow from the tee. Greens are typically small, tiered and often built without safe areas to miss, meaning that the difficulty of the approach shot is often disproportionate to the quality of the drive.

The most interesting holes here tend to be those that are the most brutal, such as the signature par three 7th, which plays into the trade wind and requires a long carry across a massive canyon as surf crashes into an azure cove to your left. The 11th is another brutal high-wind par three, this time heading toward a narrow kidney-shaped target pressed against a densely vegetated ravine. Other holes of note include the tough, twisting opener, the par four 12th, plunging more than 100 feet along a slender valley, and the gorgeous 13th, split by a creek that crosses the fairway and then wraps around the side of the green.

It may seem unfair, but Trent Jones Jr. courses tend to be measured in terms of their aesthetic values rather than their golfing substance. The Prince Course, with its incredible backdrop and glorious coastal views, is visually one of his most pleasing layouts, though it is hard to endorse wholeheartedly a course that has so many extreme challenges.

OPPOSITE **The home hole on the Prince Course at Hawaii's Princeville Resort**

Torrey Pines – South Course

COURSE OPENED 1957
DESIGNERS William F. Bell, Rees Jones
GOLF DIGEST NR, GOLF MAGAZINE 74

A municipal golf facility owned and operated by the city of San Diego, Torrey Pines is set on a rocky bluff high above the Pacific and features two championship-length courses designed initially by William F. Bell in 1957. The more noted of the layouts is the South Course, which has changed substantially since first opening, particularly following a major renovation started by Rees Jones in 2001. Jones stretched the course by hundreds of yards, adding tees and moving greens but also reworking bunkers and pinching fairways to increase the difficulty of the holes.

Despite the coastal outlooks and the fact that much of the layout is routed around a deep ravine, the South course is mostly flat and quite repetitive. Fairways tend to be straight and either lined by thick rough or deep bunkers, with few strategic driving lines and little chance of playing challenging out-of-position recovery shots. Approach play is slightly more interesting, as the greens are attractive and well built, though again they lack variety as many are raised, titled sharply forward and protected on both sides by sand. The best holes here are the par threes, as the longer holes tend to be unpleasant bruisers that lack subtleties. Rare exceptions include the 4th, a decent two-shot test along the cliffs, and the par five 13th with its tiered greenside bunkers and exciting new back tee.

Unfortunately, for all its tournament pedigree, the sad truth about Torrey Pines is that from a design perspective neither course is outstanding. The most recent changes have made the South Course an ideal championship venue, but without its rough grown, its greens speeded up and its fairways narrowed, this track would not only fail to test the better golfer, it would struggle to hold the interest of regular players.

OPPOSITE The visual appeal of Torrey Pines
is apparent at the short 3rd

The Midwest &
Rocky Mountains

The Midwest & Rocky Mountains

Sand Hills
Crystal Downs
Ballyneal
Prairie Dunes
Chicago GC
Whistling Straits
White Bear
Colorado GC
The Golf Club
Oakland Hills
Victoria National
Kingsley
Muirfield Village
Interlachen
Lost Dunes
Erin Hills
Inverness
Sutton Bay
Camargo
Wolf Run
Olympia Fields

Double Eagle
Butler National
Medinah
Blackwolf Run
Crooked Stick
Cherry Hills
Hazeltine National
Castle Pines
Shoreacres
Scioto
Bellerive
Arcadia Bluffs
Canterbury
Sand Ridge
Milwaukee CC
Flint Hills National
Sycamore Hills
Tullymore
Rich Harvest Links
Sanctuary

W idely regarded as the Father of American golf, Charles Blair Macdonald was a frustrated part-time golfer when the World's Fair came to Chicago in 1893, and with it the opportunity for him to build a simple seven-hole course at Lake Forest to entertain the visiting dignitaries. Having returned to America from Scotland in 1875, Macdonald had spent the preceding years fruitlessly trying to interest his friends in the ancient game to which he had become so attached. The Lake Forest project gave him the impetus to establish the Chicago Golf Club and design what became the first 18-hole course in the United States.

Macdonald's next effort was on the club's new Wheaton property in 1895, and although the designer's later remarks about his work were far from flattering, the course attracted championship play and its profile helped the game establish a foothold in the Midwest. Following his departure for the greener golfing pastures of New York, men like Donald Ross and Seth Raynor took advantage of surging interest in the sport by building a number of fine parkland courses across the central American states. Perry Maxwell was also a significant figure prior to the Depression, working with Alister MacKenzie to create the treasured holes at Crystal Downs and designing the first nine at the wonderful Prairie Dunes course in Kansas.

Despite the presence of celebrated championship venues in major centers like Chicago, Detroit and Columbus, it's these Maxwell gems, Pete Dye's work at Whistling Straits and a group of modern dune superstars that now headline golf in the American heartland and best capture the ruggedness and appeal of this part of the world. The 1995 opening of Nebraska's remote Sand Hills Golf Club was the most significant development here since Macdonald's time, the course debuting near the top of every credible golf ranking list and focusing attention on the remarkable sand dunes that cut directly through the Great Plains of Central America.

Others have sought to exploit these same remote dunes, the most successful being Colorado's Ballyneal and a little-known public course in Nebraska called Wild Horse. Away from the sand, unheralded Midwest courses omitted from this book but worthy of commendation include the unique daily fee Lawsonia Links in Wisconsin, the Black Sheep Golf Club on the western outskirts of Chicago and Michigan's Dunes Club, a Pine Valley – inspired nine-holer developed by Bandon Dunes owner Mike Keiser and cut through wooded scrubland close to Lake Michigan.

OPPOSITE The par four 6th on the South Course at Detroit's celebrated Oakland Hills Country Club

Sand Hills Golf Club

COURSE OPENED 1995
DESIGNERS Bill Coore,
Ben Crenshaw

GOLF DIGEST 12
GOLF MAGAZINE 8

Arguably the most important American golf course since Augusta National, Sand Hills is set among the endless rolling dunes of north-central Nebraska. Its 1995 opening not only placed this remote and seemingly desolate region firmly on the golfing radar, but it almost single-handedly led to a rebirth in classic golf architecture in this country.

Set within an expansive valley and surrounded by some of the game's most impressive dune structures, the course was created by Bill Coore and Ben Crenshaw, who spent more than two years investigating possible ways to route their holes across this incredible landscape. Prior to selecting their final arrangement they had identified more than 130 quality holes, their toughest job being to work out which ones needed to be sacrificed for the sake of routing coherence. Aside from displaying unprecedented levels of variety and excitement, their selected holes were also simple and inexpensive to build, with soft shaping of some greens and tees but very little earth moved during construction.

The result is one of the most natural layouts in golf, the tee and green locations "discovered" by Coore and Crenshaw and the fairways simply draped majestically across Mother Nature's undulations. Although winds can whip through these Nebraska plains with great force, they don't come from a prevailing direction, so the designers were careful to ensure their holes were playable under all conditions. Fairways are sensibly spacious, while the target areas are mostly open to encourage chase-in approach shots. The diversity of the putting slopes is quite astonishing, as is the variety of the actual green locales, whether they be pitched in hollows, set atop plateaus or built beside exposed sand dunes that have either been tidied into formal traps or left in their raw state.

Dominated by huge, sandy blowouts, the 1st and 18th holes were apparently the first that Coore and Crenshaw discovered here, and much of the routing revolved around their retention. Sweeping through a series of rugged bunker shapes toward a small platform green nestled within a natural amphitheater, the par five opening hole is one of the best in the world. The 18th is even better and, remarkably, everything in between is just as good. While some holes do stand out for special mention, exquisite green contours at the 2nd and 3rd, lumpy ground undulations on the 9th, strategically placed fairway bunkers on the 5th and 10th and a cool skyline target at the 11th prevent any of the others from suffering by comparison.

More obvious glamour holes include the par four 4th, which tumbles almost 500 yards toward a sublime green perched on a shelf, a monster 30-foot crater guarding one side of the putting surface and a sharp fall-off protecting the other. Shorter but no less sinister, the 7th is already an American legend, its green reachable in the right winds but resting dangerously atop a tightly bunkered knob and more difficult to hold the closer you play your pitch. The 8th is another solid shortish par four, its clever horseshoe green wrapped around a nasty central bunker.

On the back nine, the two-shot 12th is an excellent test, its bulging fairway split by a vertical ridge that

OPPOSITE **Wild, windswept bunkering accentuates the gorgeous setting of the 17th green**

kicks inaccurate drives down into sunken hollows. The par three 13th, which heads into a green saddled atop a distant dune, and strategic bunkering on the uphill 15th, where golfers who can attack the right-hand bunker are given an optimum line into a crowned target guarded by another fearsome trap, are both outstanding. The finish is also first class. Following a gorgeous falling five at the 16th, which continually rewards those able to hit their first two shots close to sand, comes an impossibly beautiful short par three with a postage stamp – sized green surrounded by deep, shaggy bunkers. The 18th is then a magnificent uphill closer, its fairway running right-to-left across the tee and set immediately beyond an enormous sandy blowout. To reach the final green in regulation, the climbing approach has to negotiate a continuum of this hazard as well as a sharp false front.

Despite the success of Sand Hills, Bill Coore and Ben Crenshaw have resisted the temptation to stretch themselves beyond one or two new projects a year. The pair's growing body of work is extremely impressive, but this landmark creation remains their signature piece. Like so many great courses in America, the only disappointment with this club is that it is so private few passionate golf people actually get to play here.

ABOVE Looking across the tightly bunkered and sharply angled 7th green

OPPOSITE One of the first holes "found" by designers Coore & Crenshaw, the strong par four 18th highlights the natural golfing landscape available at Sand Hills

Crystal Downs Country Club

COURSE OPENED 1929
DESIGNERS Dr. Alister
MacKenzie, Perry Maxwell

GOLF DIGEST 10
GOLF MAGAZINE 14

Approaching the green at
MacKenzie's brilliant par five 8th

OPPOSITE Tumbling along an undulating
fairway toward a steeply pitched green site,
the 1st hole is a marvelous introduction to
"the Downs"

Located close to the western shore of Lake Michigan, the Crystal Downs Country Club was designed by legendary architect Dr. Alister MacKenzie, who was introduced to the site in 1927 following his work at Cypress Point. MacKenzie inspected the property with his partner Perry Maxwell, and was delighted by the prospects the wild terrain offered. He routed the course and designed the first nine holes, leaving Maxwell to oversee construction and apparently take on a more significant role during the design of the back nine.

Displaying all of the characteristics that make Maxwell and MacKenzie's best courses so widely admired, Crystal Downs has an extraordinary collection of short par fours, a great set of greens and a superb routing that makes full use of the land's natural attributes. The front nine is more open and arranged across a series of tumbling dunes, while much of the back nine is set within an elevated woodland. The transition between these areas is handled particularly well.

Aside from the imaginatively contoured greens, what makes the Downs so fascinating is that many of its better holes are so audacious that they have so far defied duplication. The entire outward half could fall into this category, the fun starting from the elevated 1st tee, which overlooks Crystal Lake and most of the windswept opening stretch. The hole itself falls sharply along a bouncy, crowned fairway toward a cruel left-leaning green at the base of a small dune. Innocuous looking but deceptively steep, the 2nd then tracks back uphill to a target angled forward and at least five feet higher at the back than the front.

The 4th is a strategic par four that doglegs around the tree-lined boundary and favors a fade from the tee and a draw into the green.

The next stretch is truly astonishing, starting with a unique par four that heads diagonally across a large bunkered ridge toward a hidden green tucked 350 yards away on the other side. Multiple options exist, but the angle of the putting surface and alignment of the split fairway encourages a dangerous drive as close to the edge of the upper shelf as possible. The 6th and 7th are also multioption short par fours, the 7th particularly memorable as its green is set in a hollow, shaped like a boomerang and wrapped around a bunkered knoll. Two further world-class gems conclude an absorbing nine. The 8th is one of MacKenzie's best par fives, its fairway full of heaving undulations and the hole rising into an inhospitable green site placed precariously atop a small ledge. It is followed by a quality uphill par three, which was apparently an afterthought and built because MacKenzie had miscalculated his front nine and only designed eight holes.

Largely arranged by Maxwell, the back nine has a totally different feel as the golf heads away from the open hills and into the more wooded areas. A beautiful par three played across a valley, the 11th introduces the golfers to the trees and features one of the cruellest back-to-front greens anywhere in the Midwest. So acute is the tilt here that some have hit this green in regulation but then taken an unplayable drop to avoid the prospect of putting off the front and back down the fairway. The par four 13th is another with a notorious green, this time angled away to the

right and featuring a high front tier, sunken back areas and contours that ensure the sloppy approach is followed by three or more putts. The star of the closing stretch, however, is the 17th, a bewildering short par four that first falls through a narrow dale and then rises into a beautiful target perched atop a distant peak. There are at least half a dozen ways to maneuver your ball from the tee to the green, as slopes off a large hill cut the fairway into smaller landing areas, each progressively more difficult to hit but leaving an appropriately easier approach.

Along with Augusta National, Crystal Downs is the most challenging of MacKenzie's surviving courses, primarily because the holes are so unique and modern putting speeds have made the sharply angled greens so terribly daunting. The thick native roughs are also effective hazards, as are the artistic bunkers, which are used both strategically and to enhance the shape of the ground. Strangely, despite the timeless quality of its architecture, for a number of decades the course barely registered on national golf ranking lists. Thankfully, a rediscovery was made several years ago that has seen this remarkable layout regain popularity as well as its rightful place in the upper echelon of American golf courses.

ABOVE **Options abound at the unique 300-yard 17th hole**

OPPOSITE **Squeezed between a pair of world-class short par fours, the mid-length 6th is an equally outstanding piece of design**

Ballyneal Golf & Hunt Club

COURSE OPENED 2006

DESIGNER Tom Doak

GOLF DIGEST NR

GOLF MAGAZINE 46

"Ballyneal is set upon a thousand acres of sand dunes, and our goal has been to take them as we found them and build a course which is a product of the land, rather than forced upon it."

TOM DOAK

OPPOSITE **The hand of man on Mother Nature, this picture of the 3rd hole shows how Doak's marvelous blow-out bunkering perfectly complements the slopes and natural dune formations at Ballyneal**

Founded by brothers from the small agricultural town of Holyoke in northeastern Colorado, the Ballyneal golf course was designed by architect Tom Doak and built upon some of the finest duneland in world golf. These dunes, almost four hours south of Nebraska's famous Sand Hills Golf Club, were ready-made golfing fields discovered by the brothers when they were small boys chasing cattle around their parents' farm. Years later, having established a small hunting club outside of town, they returned to the dunes they had discovered as kids and decided to develop them into a formal golf facility.

Quickly identified as the ideal architect, Doak was invited to visit their property and, not surprisingly, he fell instantly for the land and the opportunity it afforded him to create a course with timeless appeal. Unlike the sweeping dunes of Sand Hills, here the sand structures were more abrupt, yet with the same natural corridors that make the holes appear so untouched. The designer was given extraordinary freedom by his clients on this project, and after two years spent considering various routings he was able to produce for them a golf course of the highest order.

An old-fashioned walking layout that flows beautifully from green to tee, Doak caused minimal disturbance to the native terrain and created the sense that his holes simply emerged from their rugged surrounds. The jagged, blowout-style bunkering is superb, while the putting surfaces are incredible and feature dizzying internal undulations that are certain to be lots of fun for regular players and a real eye-opener for the first

time visitor. Positioned within a variety of settings, the targets often appear simply as an extension of the rippling fairways and come complete with ridges, tiers, basins, humps and large false fronts.

Although Doak built a number of real gems here, it is the lack of any awkward architecture and the originality of the holes that makes Ballyneal so special. Rarely on such a dramatic site does a course exist without black spots or dull areas linking better bits of land, yet here there is nothing even remotely dreary or uninteresting. The course opens with one of the great starting holes in golf, especially from the back tee, where it bends diagonally across an untamed hollow. Consistent with Doak's strategic principles, in places the fairway is more than 70 yards wide, but those bailing away from the dangerous side are left with an obscured and more difficult approach.

Each subsequent hole has great merit, but likely favorites include the attractively bunkered par three 3rd and the audacious par four 7th, a remarkable hole notorious for a skinny green set within a natural half-pipe. Devilish sand fingers eat into the right portion of this target, creating the need for golfers to use the steeply banked left side to feed their balls toward certain flag locations. The short par five 8th is an equally remarkable piece of design, or more accurately preservation, as the naturally occurring humps and hollows around and within this cleverly angled green are what makes the hole such an original. The massive bunker structure through the center of the bulging fairway is also beautifully located to create an element of doubt and entice players to take a tighter line from the tee.

Other huge highlights include the extreme putting contours on the 12th green and the glorious par three 15th, played across a spectacularly bunkered ridge and into a deep depression. Emerging from the heaviest dunes on the site, the finishing stretch is also outstanding and comprises a couple of super-tough par fours and a top-class par five that heads sharply uphill and turns through a narrow dune saddle. Here your second shot options are to lay back and leave a long uphill third or attack a pass between the dunes and try to get closer to the green.

Following the success of Sand Hills came the inevitable search for comparable golf land within America's remote central dunes, Doak's masterpiece the only course thus far that has been able to match the standard set by Coore and Crenshaw farther north. Aside from terrific land and terrific design, Ballyneal is full of fun, charismatic golf holes and blessed with an understated charm that fits perfectly with the old-world ambience of what feels like an ancient layout. Why any prospective member would look for more in a golf club remains one of life's great mysteries.

ABOVE Natural ground contours and an audacious green site make the approach into the 7th hole the most fun shot on the course

OPPOSITE Set in a depression beyond a bunkered crest, the 15th is another one of Ballyneal's spectacular par threes

Prairie Dunes Country Club

COURSE OPENED 1937

DESIGNERS Perry Maxwell,
Press Maxwell

GOLF DIGEST 30

GOLF MAGAZINE 16

The crowned, undersized green at
the par five 17th

OPPOSITE Prairie Dunes ends with
this difficult 380-yard par four; its
tight, undulating fairway cut through
shimmering fescue grasses

A genuine American treasure, the Prairie Dunes Country Club is located in the heart of central Kansas, but built among the sort of undulating sandhills that one would expect to find along the Scottish coastline. The club was founded by Emerson Carey, a prominent local golfer who discovered this natural wonderland five miles northeast of Hutchinson and immediately recognized its potential for great golf. In 1935, he commissioned renowned course architect Perry Maxwell to inspect the 480-acre property. Maxwell was apparently captivated by the exciting dune shapes and spent weeks on site before deciding how to arrange his course.

As far from a typical links environment as could be conceived, the site nevertheless retained a genuine links feel thanks to its exposed, sandy terrain and attractive dune structures covered in a dense weed and indigenous grass mix known here as gunch. The course was built using only horses, mules and wheelbarrows, with the native topography carefully fashioned into formidable fairways and green shapes mostly by hand. Maxwell apparently routed 18 holes for the club, but only nine had been built when the course opened for play in 1937. It took until 1957 for the full 18 to open finally, Perry's son Press adding the final nine holes after his father had passed away.

The original holes are spread through both nines and are mostly those nearest the clubhouse. There remains some debate as to whether Press Maxwell followed his father's intended plan in completing the layout or discovered the additional holes himself. Regardless, he did a terrific job, as the interplay between the holes works particularly well and the greens across the course are consistently contoured to an exceptionally high standard. Press's better holes include the par three 4th, with its target cut on a dune ledge, and the tough par four 5th, usually played into the teeth of the wind. The 11th and 12th greens are also worth mentioning, the 12th for its fascinating internal contours and the 11th for a cruel hump that guards the center of the putting surface and kicks weaker balls either side and into trouble. His most outstanding hole, however, is the par four 16th, which turns through sand toward a skinny green that is angled to only accept approach shots from golfers placed perfectly within the dogleg.

Picking out Perry Maxwell highlights would involve descriptions of each of the holes he built. The 1st and 7th may seem relatively simple affairs, but genius greens elevates each into the seriously good category. The par three 2nd is another stunner, its green set diagonally into a dune and protected by slick breaks and deep frontal bunkering. His other short hole, the 10th, is played uphill over a sea of gunch to a terrific target that falls on both sides. Outshining them all is the club's signature hole, the 8th, which crosses a bumpy crest before rising toward a green built into a hill and sloping severely off the front. The beauty of the setting as well as the wild undulations within both

fairway and green make this one of America's best, and most intimidating, par fours.

The final two holes are also world-class, the 17th a superb reachable par five that tumbles along a narrowing fairway toward a small domed target built atop a knoll. Apparently modeled after the finisher at Crystal Downs, the 18th then heads along a densely vegetated dune ridge, the angle of its green meaning that those who hope to make a closing par need to take on the rubbish with their drive to ensure a decent approach shot angle.

Prairie Dunes has as many knockout holes as any course in the Midwest and presents all players with a strong and comprehensive examination of their golfing prowess. The club gets full marks for keeping its turf keen and its native roughs healthy; aside from problems with the trees that cramp the 12th fairway, they have done a tremendous job preserving this wonderful Maxwell design. It is also worth noting that, unusually for a course of this quality, these caring custodians are happy to share their treasured layout with visiting golfers. Those who haven't yet had the pleasure of a round here, therefore, should make immediate plans. It won't disappoint.

OPPOSITE Maxwell senior left the members at Prairie Dunes with a number of brilliant holes, none better than the naturally rising 8th, one of the most unforgiving par fours in the Midwest

Chicago Golf Club

COURSE OPENED 1895/1923
DESIGNERS Charles Blair
Macdonald, Seth Raynor

GOLF DIGEST 28
GOLF MAGAZINE 17

"Raynor scarcely knew a golf ball from a tennis ball when we first met, and although he never became much of an expert in playing golf, yet the facility with which he absorbed the feeling which animates old and enthusiastic golfers to the manner born was truly amazing, eventually qualifying him to discriminate between a really fine hole and an indifferent one."

CHARLES BLAIR MACDONALD

OPPOSITE **Raynor and Macdonald built countless Redan par threes, the 7th at Chicago GC arguably their best**

One of the early pioneers of American golf, Charles Blair Macdonald was introduced to the game while studying in Scotland during the 1870s, and upon his return to Illinois became a key figure in helping establish golf as a mainstream sport. Aside from driving the development of the USGA, he also won the inaugural US Amateur Championship and designed the landmark National Golf Links on Long Island, America's first truly world-class design. His first significant contribution to the sport, however, was as the founder of the historic Chicago Golf Club.

Established in 1892, the club's first track was a basic nine-holer designed by Macdonald on a small farm west of the city. In the spring of 1893 he extended it to 18-holes, making it the first full-length course anywhere in the United States. The club's popularity grew so rapidly that the following year members purchased a 200-acre field near Wheaton, where Macdonald could build them a more substantial layout. His new course measured 6,200 yards and opened in 1895. Despite the success of the Wheaton move, Macdonald left Chicago for New York and began formulating plans to build what he regarded as the ideal golf course.

The creation of the National Golf Links elevated architectural standards in America, and Macdonald was soon asked to advise on improvements to his old Chicago layout. Rather than handle the work himself, he sent his associate Seth Raynor. Apparently armed with specific instructions from his mentor, Raynor rebuilt the course in 1922–23, retaining a couple of Macdonald holes and adding prototypes of others like the Redan, Road, Biarritz and Eden. He also designed several excellent originals, using the same strategic design principles as these famous templates. The greens, in particular, are memorable for their sheer size as well as for the steep internal contours and deep trenchlike bunkers that line the sides of the oft-raised putting surfaces.

There are almost too many outstanding holes here to review individually, but a couple of key stretches do stand out. The start is superb, the uphill opener a refined remnant of the 1895 course with its slanting fairway, strategic bunkering and huge green site leading to many a soft opening bogey. The 2nd is then a bruising uphill par four with a nasty Road Hole green complex, while both the Biarritz 3rd and the innocuous-looking, but deadly, par five 4th also feature frightening target areas. As does the par three 7th, one of the world's finest Redan's. Completing a stunning loop of holes, the 8th bends slightly to the left but is ingeniously shaped to encourage play out to a wide right field, leaving an approach from a falling stance and into a green angled across the golfer. Equally intimidating are the second shot into the Redan-like 11th green as well as the elevated par four 12th, with its unique part-punchbowl green, and the wonderful Eden par three at the 13th. The finishing fours are also brilliant, both the 17th and 18th heading uphill into huge, baffling green shapes that boast plenty of internal movement and surprisingly difficult central pins.

Despite a small and private membership, the development of the Chicago Golf Club is inextricably linked to the sport's increasing popularity in the United States during its formative years. Thankfully, the course has remained remarkably well preserved through the decades, a handful of well-concealed back tees about the only noticeable change since the 1920s. There are bound to be some that find these holes too short for modern play, but for purists, historians, architecture buffs or simply passionate golf people, Chicago GC is the absolute embodiment of a great day's golf.

Whistling Straits – Straits Course

COURSE OPENED 1998
DESIGNER Pete Dye

GOLF DIGEST 24
GOLF MAGAZINE 24

"Pete Dye has always made the most of the glorious possibilities that the land affords. He is nature's best collaborator and this time, he has truly outdone himself."

HERBERT V. KOHLER JR.

OPPOSITE **With the ambition and resources to continually host major championships, Whistling Straits is likely to remain a highly rated and prominent golfing fixture for many years to come. Pictured is the 3rd hole**

Whistling Straits was the brainchild of business magnate Herbert V. Kohler Jr., who in 1995 purchased a 560-acre parcel of land along the western shores of Lake Michigan that had previously been earmarked for a nuclear power plant. Apparently inspired by the big links of Ireland, Kohler recognized the potential for great golf in the site and employed renowned architect Pete Dye to collaborate on a 36-hole complex. In a few short years, Whistling Straits has grown to rival Pebble Beach and Pinehurst as America's favored golf retreat, with its Straits Course rightly recognized as the property's prize asset.

While the Irish Course was built away from the lake, Straits occupies a two-mile stretch of land along its shoreline and enjoys almost constant views of the water. Aside from a spectacular setting, Dye was also blessed with a generous budget and a client who allowed him to shift staggering amounts of sand during construction. Close to a million cubic yards of material were brought onto the site to create a series of towering dunes, while substantial quantities were also scraped away from the cliff areas to build ledges and allow holes to get as close to the water as possible.

Although these dune structures tend to overwhelm the property, Dye's vision and his ability to integrate interesting and original design ideas into such a big landscape is extraordinary. As is the sheer volume of hazards he carved into the sandhills. Whether simple scrapes or formal bunkers, there are more than 500 in total, with the majority shaped to complete a visual picture rather than complement a strategic situation. Those used within the design tend to be pot traps either dug into the sculptured green areas or positioned along the sides of the fairways. Coupled with humps and hollows, a two-loop routing and bouncy fescue surfaces they help to give the course a fairly authentic linkslike feel.

Following a tight opening hole that bends toward the lake and punishes anyone not immediately able to nail a straight drive, comes an exciting par five along an elongated ledge, its terrific chase-in green site protected by a cleverly positioned pot bunker. The next is the first in a remarkable set of par threes, each built directly on the water's edge and ranging from difficult to unplayable depending on the wind. The skinny 12th green, for instance, is virtually impossible to hold downwind, particularly its elevated right side, while the 17th falls steeply toward the water and features an obscured target tucked beyond a large knob. Best of the group is probably the 7th, which crosses part of the shoreline to a wonderful green complex banked into a hillside.

The longer holes also mix scenery with severity. The strong and skinny 4th is one of the hardest par fours in America, with extreme penalties for a miss on either side, while the 9th is memorable for the scale of its surrounds and the 8th for a thrilling second shot played off a shelf and down to a beautiful target positioned before the lake. On the back nine, Dye continues to show little sympathy for the misplaced stroke. The bunkers and bold fairway undulations of the par five 11th are especially intimidating, while the plunging approach into the 18th green is a fairly scary way to end your round, the shot hit over a creek and into a knuckle-shaped target set within a massive sandy amphitheater. More impressive are the heavily

bunkered, semistrategic 15th and the gently arching 13th, with its putting surface perched against the cliff and open to allow clever players a number of access routes to the pin.

Super long, narrow and exposed to strong winds, this is one of the toughest par 72s anywhere in golf, and although fun to play, it isn't recommended for golfers in a hurry nor for those in a fragile emotional state. Unless you are a world-class professional, there are likely to be many shots here beyond your capabilities, and in some instances your best method of success is working out how to limit the damage to a bogey rather than how to force a good score out of a particular hole. Regardless, there is no denying that the Straits Course is one of the most impressive construction achievements in modern golf and an apt tribute to the genius of designer Pete Dye, who somehow created a championship-ready beast that is both overdone and unforgiving yet at the same time utterly compelling.

ABOVE The 12th is the shortest of the par threes here, but the target is small and fraught with danger

OPPOSITE Like the preceding short holes, the 17th at Whistling Straits also heads along the Lake Michigan shoreline

White Bear Yacht Club

COURSE OPENED 1912

DESIGNER Donald Ross

GOLF DIGEST NR

GOLF MAGAZINE NR

View from behind the recently restored 9th green

OPPOSITE Full of dizzying undulation, the charms of White Bear are apparent from the very first hole

One of American golf's real charmers, the White Bear Yacht Club was formed as a sailing club for blue-blooded easterners on the banks of Minnesota's pristine White Bear Lake back in the late 1800s. Golf was not added until 1912, but Donald Ross's initial nine-hole course was such a hit that he extended the layout to 18 holes in 1915. The sport then quickly became the club's principal recreational activity.

Low profile and continuing to sneak under the radar of ranking panels, the course Ross designed here was one of his very best, and certainly the most interesting for golfers conditioned to believe that great terrain, rather than great turf, is the essential ingredient for great golf. Like at nearby Interlachen, Ross brilliantly incorporated all of the natural features of the site into a routing that moves across a series of radically undulating hills and ridges. With the exception of the 18th fairway, there is no letup from the natural bump and flow of the land, so for those who don't appreciate odd bounces, sidehill stances and hitting into obscured targets, the par threes will offer your only relief.

White Bear starts with a tremendous par four that first plunges downhill and then rises up into an elevated green set beyond a huge bunkered ridge. The 2nd and falling par three 3rd are also good, but it's the prolonged stretch of quality holes from the 5th to the 17th that really elevates the track into America's elite. Massive undulations and cool greens make the 5th, 10th, 12th and 15th exciting par fours to play, while the 7th is a classic par five with genuine three-shot options and an aggressive but dangerous two-shot strategy. Narrow and bumpy from the tee, its green is within reach but set on a spur and protected by a hump that kicks

most balls away to tricky chipping gullies. This hole, as well as other wild fives like the 9th, 13th and 16th, underscore the quality of Ross's routing and his ability to locate fun and interesting green sites. Generally small but with lots of natural shape, the targets here show tremendous imagination and are full of subtle variety. Both the 11th and 12th, for instance, are situated beyond a frontal crest, the 11th with a high backdrop to allow balls to feed toward the pin and the 12th, by contrast, falling away steeply at the rear. There are at least seven or eight other outstanding greens, as well as a number of approach shots that rank among the most enjoyable Ross ever conceived.

Interestingly, his original plans for White Bear were destroyed during the 1930s and the course suffered through an extended period of neglect thereafter. Thankfully, this neglect was addressed by the careful restoration work of Tom Doak's team during the 1990s. Reinstating fairway widths and green areas, they also removed inappropriately planted trees and unnecessary traps, including those near the 7th and 9th greens, which in turn allowed full restoration of some fascinating chipping areas. This project was an enormous success and has helped present-day members better appreciate the true quality of their precious layout.

Donald Ross designed some remarkable courses in America, but few that have managed to evade publicity as successfully as the White Bear Yacht Club. With some of the finest slopes for golf in the Midwest, there is no doubt that were the layout a little longer and the climate more conducive to growing decent golf grasses, passionate golfers from all over the world would flock to play here.

Colorado Golf Club

COURSE OPENED 2007

DESIGNERS Bill Coore,
Ben Crenshaw

GOLF DIGEST NR

GOLF MAGAZINE NR

*"The elements – the wind, the
roll of the land, the firmness of
the turf – shape how you will
play this golf course. There's very
little dictation in the design. That
makes for ongoing interest over
days, months and years."*

BILL COORE

OPPOSITE **A pleasant view of both the
split-tier putting surface on the short
11th hole and the countryside that
surrounds the Colorado Golf Club**

Set amongst the pine-covered hills and lush
meadows of Parker, southeast of Denver,
the Colorado Golf Club was designed by
leading architects Bill Coore and Ben
Crenshaw and opened for play in 2007. In
demand and notoriously selective with their
projects, the designers were clearly attracted
to the undisturbed nature of this 1,700-acre
property and the fact that the golfing part
of the development would be free from the
encumbrance of associated housing.

Coore and Crenshaw were given great
freedom here, choosing to arrange their course
across prime acreage through the center of
the site. The routing is broken into two loops,
each starting and finishing within the wooded
hills and flowing effortlessly up, down and
across the steady terrain. Both nines skirt the
expansive lower meadowland before rising
back into the more dramatic upper reaches,
incorporating ravines, streams and a natural
sandy wash along the way. Despite the size of
the golfing area, by keeping tees and greens
in close proximity the layout is easily walkable
and has a distinct sense of intimacy and flow.

Throughout the round, the undulating
playing corridors are generous, but the greens
are contoured to encourage golfers to flirt with
punishing bunkers for optimum angles. The
variety of green settings is exceptional, with some
targets set on small plateaus, others built within
shallow valleys, abutting hazards or benched into
hillsides and shaped with bold false fronts. All

rest comfortably within the surrounding terrain
and provide intriguing options for both approach
and recovery play. The bunkering is another
feature, the unkempt and naturalistic style of
the sand shapes resembling the famous traps on
Australia's Sandbelt. The strategic placement
of bunkers across the flatter ground and on
the short par fours is particularly impressive.

There are examples of outstanding design
all over this property. The par fives tend to
be strategically bunkered and offer multiple
routes to the green, while the two-shotters are
a mix of shorter fours with severe target areas
and generously proportioned longer holes that
cleverly provide advantageous lines to the golfer
who can plan, and then execute, the appropriate
drive. The par threes are also well constructed,
particularly the short 2nd with its exquisite
green benched into an attractive dune, and the
longer 17th, played across an elbow of a river
and into a picturesque right-to-left target.

Other areas worthy of special mention include
the tremendous green complex on the strong
par five 15th, its approach played from a falling
fairway across a deep gully and into a large
putting surface leaning steeply to the front.
The previous hole is a mid-length par four that
resembles the famous 8th at Sand Hills, your
line from the tee determined by which side of
the boomerang green the pin is placed. On the
front nine, the 3rd is an unusual par four with
a plunging diagonal approach across a sandy
arroyo, while the 4th and 5th, across the flattest

section of the course, are subtle holes with wide fairways that can lull sleepy golfers into soft bogeys. The pronounced ridge through the right side of the 5th fairway, and the shaping of a green partly obscured for those driving too safely from the tee, are especially good. The highlight of the outward nine, however, is the magnificent par four 9th, played initially across a crest and then featuring a downhill, sideslope second shot into a mighty green perched on a shallow rise. Like many targets here, this one is boldly contoured to reject the slight mishit, either via its shaved false front or by feeding balls toward gaping traps on either side of the putting surface.

Previously used to raise Arabian horses, the land this course was built on may have lacked the glamour and obvious raw appeal of a Sand Hills or a Friar's Head, but in the right hands it proved to be ideal for quality golf. Given the strength of the Coore and Crenshaw portfolio, it seems unlikely that the Colorado Golf Club will ever become their flagship layout, but it should further cement their reputation as one of the finest architectural firms of all time.

ABOVE Aggressive golfers hoping for an eagle putt at the 16th must attack the narrow right side of this dual-route fairway

OPPOSITE The 17th is a gorgeous par three played across a river toward an angled green raised beyond its banks

The Golf Club

COURSE OPENED 1967

DESIGNER Pete Dye

GOLF DIGEST 40

GOLF MAGAZINE 36

"I told Mr. Jones I liked the property, but actually I would have been tickled to death to build anything with the kind of money he was talking about."

PETE DYE

OPPOSITE **Approaching the tranquil 18th green at Pete Dye's early masterpiece in Ohio**

Frustrated by increased traffic at his local country club, businessman Frederick Jones started acquiring farmland near New Albany in Ohio during the 1960s with a view to creating a private golf course for his close friends and associates. Pete Dye was still working on the front nine at Crooked Stick and had yet to establish his reputation when Jones offered him the plum job of designing and building his course. The property he had acquired was now 400 acres, mostly woodland with a creek cutting through part of the site.

For Dye, this was a dream assignment, as there would be no requirement for housing and few budget constraints, and all Jones wanted from his designer was a course that appeared aged from the moment it opened. Dye obliged by devising a spacious, natural-looking layout and employing a range of grass types, bent for the fairways and tall fescues for the roughs, to give the course a classic feel. Built with minimal earthworks, the course opened in 1967, to be known simply as The Golf Club.

The holes here are routed across the broad landscape with great variety, the fairways rarely running parallel to each other and holes continually altering in both direction and character. The creek comes into play on a handful of holes, most notably the par four 6th, where both the drive and approach must carry the hazard. Six further holes feature lakes and ponds, but unlike other Dye courses, this one constantly surprises with its uncomplicated subtleties. There are some exceptional uses of angles, doglegs with ample width and multiple options of attack and water and cross-bunkers employed to create strategic driving lines. The 13th, for instance,

required substantial earthworks but is a wonderful hole that favors tee shots placed beside a manufactured wasteland, those bailing down the right having to hit their approach over sand and directly toward water.

Another artificial star is the par three 3rd, which heads over a pond but is famous for an unusual bunker complex that wraps around the rear and left side of the green. Here the sand is actually split into a series of bunkers that are staggered, tiered and fortified by sleepers. Some parts are so deep they are not visible from the tee. The genius of a hazard like this is that psychologically the hole becomes more difficult once you have played it and discovered all of its dangers. The rest of the par threes are excellent as well, as are longer holes like the 6th, with its strategic use of the creek, the 12th, 13th and long par four 15th, which features an obscured drive across a bunkered ridge. There is also a fine stretch of simple looking but complex holes through the middle of the round. Both the 7th and 8th are strengthened by steep targets, while the bunkerless 10th is short and wide open, but the approach is complicated by a small bank in front of its green.

Despite being one of Pete Dye's earliest designs, this course is one of the few that hasn't undergone major revisions over the years. Even the length from the back tees remains unaltered. The only modification of note was made when a large oak beside the 16th green died, which allowed the club to extend the putting surface.

Unlike anything else built during this period, The Golf Club is not just significant because it differs so greatly from Dye's other creations, but because it remains universally admired and appealing to both progressive and more traditional-minded golfers.

Oakland Hills Country Club – South Course

COURSE OPENED 1918
DESIGNERS Donald Ross,
Robert Trent Jones

GOLF DIGEST 17
GOLF MAGAZINE 18

OPPOSITE **The par four 11th hole**

OVERLEAF **The final approach, featuring the 18th green on the South Course and the magnificent Oakland Hills clubhouse**

One of the world's most recognizable championship venues, the Oakland Hills Country Club is located 20 miles northwest of Detroit and was founded by businessmen connected to the Ford Motor Company. It's first layout, the South Course, was designed by Donald Ross and opened in 1918. Ross later added a second track, but the South remains the club's favored and most significant possession.

Built with championship play in mind, the South Course was always long and featured the most severely contoured set of greens Ross had ever built. Despite successfully hosting many major events, by 1950 the club felt it was no longer an adequate test of leading professionals, and Robert Trent Jones was employed to modernize the layout. Jones strengthened the holes by growing thick rough, adding fairway bunkers and moving the greenside traps closer to the putting surfaces. Although he mostly left the tough green shapes alone, the fairways were narrowed considerably, as width and strategic angles of attack were replaced by relentless difficulty and a desire to continually punish the slight spray.

Labeled a monster by Ben Hogan in 1951, the new course proved popular with both the USGA and the PGA and continued to be tweaked and stretched in the subsequent decades. The opening holes are a great introduction to the challenge ahead; both the 1st and 2nd fairways are frighteningly tight and discourage a driver, even though each green was built to encourage a bold tee shot. The 1st green, in particular, is a superb piece of design, with the putting surface leaning from back-to-front and featuring a central bowl and a wicked

back tier all but impossible to hit from distance.

Another quality hole is the 5th, which is pinched tightly from the tee, cut by a creek and rises into a built-up target notorious for its large internal breaks. The hole marks the start of a fine stretch of golf, through to the 11th, with holes set across the best parts of the property. The climbing 8th and the sidehill 10th are both excellent tests, while the 6th, with its superb Ross green, is still a fine medium-length par four despite Jones's traps crowding the landing area and forcing a lay-up from the tee. The star attraction, however, is undoubtedly the 11th, which heads along a jumbled ridge but is best noted for a really cool approach shot uphill into a saddle green leaning steeply forward and set atop a plateau. The finishing run is also solid, particularly the cross-sand approach into the 18th and the long par three 17th, which is played over a bunkered embankment that obscures your view of a wide green and its deadly right ledge.

In many ways the South Course at Oakland Hills is the ideal modern championship course, as it is easily converted to a par of 70, has plenty of length and with modern green speeds the contours are tricky enough for even the cruelest tournament organizers. Any disappointment with the difficulty of the current setup is tempered by the fact that the routing remains mostly as Ross intended and the greens are still very good. The club could easily remove some unnecessary bunkers and revert holes back to their original widths in order to create a better members course, but this is unlikely and, indeed, of all the classic layouts hardened for the sake of tournament prestige, this remains one of the most pleasing.

Victoria National Golf Club

COURSE OPENED 1998

DESIGNER Tom Fazio

GOLF DIGEST 22

GOLF MAGAZINE NR

"I see a hundred great golf holes here, my challenge is to pick the best 18."

TOM FAZIO

OPPOSITE **Certain he could find dozens of great holes, Fazio tried to convince his client to build 36 at Victoria National, but he was instead instructed to focus on just 18. Pictured is the mid-length 4th**

One of the more fascinating inland courses from the 1990s, Victoria National is a private members club built on a reclaimed strip mine near the small southern Indiana town of Newburgh. Dominated by a complex system of lakes and ravines, the layout is among the best by architect Tom Fazio, owing to his intelligent use of the existing hazards and his ability to fashion some fairly severe features into exciting golf. These remarkable "natural" features were actually a by-product of almost 50 years of mining operations on the site, the lakes formed when miners reached underground springs and the excavated areas filled with water.

Running through the property with great irregularity, the lakes are a mix of widths and depths and often come complete with vertical cliffs crashing directly down into the water below. The ideal landscape for an eye-catching modern design, Fazio's great achievement here was to integrate the hazards into a seamless, walkable course that both thrills the average golfer and tests the better hitters. From the back tees, the layout is a little tighter than some will expect from Fazio, while the greens are also unusually steep and in many spots are built with effective chase-in areas that allow players the option of flirting with a hazardous side by bouncing in their approach shots.

The routing is Victoria National's real strength, however, as 12 holes touch water and the rest are blessed with enough elevation change to create interesting challenges. A river bending around the 2nd and 3rd fairways acts as a course boundary and feeds a large interior lake that the designer used to separate his two nines. The opening and closing areas are probably the most impressive parts of the course, the central holes not lacking for drama or visual excitement but the first six and final few being where most of the quality can be found.

Of the longer holes, early standouts include the strategic mid-length 2nd, played over and along steep cliffs and with its green bunkered to favor a tee shot placed down the dangerous left side. Another is the bunkerless par four 6th, dominated by a large triple-tier target collapsing to the front and built with a substantial left-to-right slope. The par fives are equally intriguing; the 3rd initially follows the perimeter river but turns sharply inland as you near a skinny front-to-back green hidden behind a large mound, while the 9th is a solid driving hole that heads over a bunkered crest and then down along a split fairway toward the main lake. On the back nine, the heavily treed 14th is an excellent two-shotter that rises steeply into a tiered green fronted by a large depression. The 15th is then an heroic risk/reward par five that demands an accurate drive through trees, followed by either an aggressive shot from a falling fairway over a pond or a really tight layback squeezed between water and thick native grasses.

The par threes are also outstanding. Aside from the 7th, each measures in excess of 200 yards and is dominated by water, the best being

the spectacular 5th, which crosses two fingers of water and has a third located behind its narrow peninsula green. The most frightening is the 16th, played downhill to a small putting surface almost totally surrounded by trouble. Completing a treacherous finishing stretch, the next two are long par fours bending right around lakes. The 17th heads into an elevated green guarded by sand on one side and clever swales on the other, while the 18th turns 90 degrees around a lake, meaning most approach shots are hit with a long-iron from the neck of the fairway to a nasty green that falls toward the water.

For an architect like Tom Fazio, Victoria National was an extraordinary opportunity, as it is hard to imagine any client allowing him the freedom and budget to shape such vast lake structures. Of all the *Golf Digest* Top 100 courses overlooked by *GOLF Magazine*, this is the highest ranked and, given its quality, one of the most surprising omissions, especially considering that other Fazio tracks like Sea Island and Trump National appear on their list. Victoria National is more impressive than both of these courses and, if given the opportunity, is a layout that readers will thoroughly enjoy playing.

ABOVE The 2nd is a wonderful par four that rewards golfers able to position their tee ball down the more dangerous left side

OPPOSITE Decades of mining left these dramatic pit lakes that Fazio was able to incorporate into the par three 5th hole

Kingsley Club

COURSE OPENED 2001
DESIGNER Michael DeVries

GOLF DIGEST NR
GOLF MAGAZINE NR

An exciting start, this picture shows the opening tee shot at Kingsley where golfers are forced to drive either left or right of an impressive cluster of bunkers

OPPOSITE Long, strong and with its green leaning to the left, the 16th is a terrific par three that favors those able to hit a precise fade shot

Located an hour east of Crystal Downs, the Kingsley Club was the first solo design project for architect Michael DeVries, who spent much of his youth at the Downs and even worked on the grounds crew for a number of years studying the elements that made the course so special. DeVries had previously worked for Tom Fazio and Tom Doak, but his selection as lead architect for this project was a big gamble. It took an endorsement from the head professional at Crystal Downs to convince the club owners of his suitability.

The young designer did not disappoint, recognizing the opportunity he had been given and working tirelessly to create a course that could stand proudly among Michigan's finest. Just as at Crystal Downs, the front nine here is dominated by sparse rolling duneland and the back nine is carved through steeper hills and mature hardwoods. By shaping his bunkers with rugged edges and locating his greens in a range of natural settings, such as in saddles and punchbowls or atop crests and into hills, the designer was able to massage the terrain into a classically styled golf course without moving much earth.

There is a great balance to the routing, although the more expansive undulations of the opening nine give it slightly more appeal. The round begins with an interesting split-level par five, central traps creating an upper and lower fairway and distinct routes into the distant green. The 2nd is an outstanding short par three, played along a ridge to a narrow, semiconcealed green that falls sharply into bunkers. Among the other memorable holes are mid-length par fours at the 4th, 6th and 8th. The 4th features a wild fairway but is best noted for a massive basin green set beyond a small berm, while the 6th heads first over a large bunkered ridge and then into a wonderful target situated on a natural shelf between two hills. The 8th is the most strategic; aggressive golfers can flirt with the right rough and a large central bunker in order to set up the best pitch into a small ledge green.

The back nine is also first-rate, the holes are more heavily treed and also more undulating. Particularly impressive are gems like the driveable par four 13th, which offers countless options of attack and one of the most bizarre greens in the Midwest, the target more than 12,000 square feet in size, almost 60 yards long and with a pronounced dip through its middle. The par three 16th is another beautiful hole, the green set within a gentle right-to-left slope that allows you to chase a ball off the right side or play a more aggressive fade shot. Less receptive is the 15th, which is the longest par four on the course but with the smallest green, its target precariously raised several feet above the fairway and tucked into the base of a hill.

Although there are a couple of problem spots at Kingsley, the architect's inclination to leave the ground contours alone—even the severe ones— has paid dividends, because the entire layout fits nicely into the terrain. Pleasingly, the club keeps the bumpy course firm and fast, which ensures the holes remain both challenging and fun to play. This was indeed a remarkable opportunity for someone starting out in the design business, and should DeVries carve out a long and successful career in golf, it will no doubt be in large part owing to the success of his efforts at the Kingsley Club.

Muirfield Village Golf Club

COURSE OPENED 1974
DESIGNERS Jack Nicklaus,
Desmond Muirhead

GOLF DIGEST 18
GOLF MAGAZINE 25

*"I set out to build not only
an outstanding golf course
for every level of player, but a
magnificent course for watching
a tournament"*

JACK NICKLAUS

OPPOSITE **Looking back down the
notorious par four 14th, its skinny
green a particularly difficult target to
hit from the right half of the fairway**

Co-designed by Jack Nicklaus in the prime of his extraordinary playing career, Muirfield Village is an exclusive private club situated a little northwest of his hometown of Columbus, Ohio. The club was modeled after Augusta National and Nicklaus, like Bobby Jones, was involved in its creation from the outset. Along with club founders, he undertook an exhaustive search of the outer reaches of the city for a suitable site, eventually settling upon a beautiful 220-acre property along the banks of the Scioto River.

With rolling ground, a trickling creek and a mix of mature trees, the chosen site was ideal for exciting golf, but Nicklaus was an inexperienced designer, so he partnered with architect Desmond Muirhead on the project. Muirhead was primarily responsible for the routing and did a terrific job arranging the holes across the sloping landscape. The pair apparently didn't get along, however, and Nicklaus became chief custodian of the course following its 1974 opening, spending the ensuing years continually refining and reshaping the holes into a fine modern championship test.

Dominated by water and constant elevation changes, the layout is visually stunning and full of variety from the tee as holes sweep both ways across the terrain. Muirfield Village is very much a second shot course, however, as the greens are small, quick and guarded by deep traps or pushed against ponds and creeks. Approach play is regularly complicated by false fronts and subtle breaks off the surrounding bunkers, which are both well placed and attractively built. Nicklaus regards these hazards as his primary defense against low-scoring professionals, and has regularly altered them to make them more challenging. After experimenting with furrowed rakes, in recent years he has made them deeper to ensure a genuine penalty follows a misdirected stroke.

Not surprisingly, the better holes here are those where the water and elevation changes are best utilized. Interestingly, the 1st fairway bends right against a gentle right-to-left gradient, while the 2nd hole moves slightly left but leans toward a stream down its right side. Both have excellent greens, as does the 3rd, which turns through trees toward a small target pressed hard against a pond. Similarly dominated by strategically positioned water, the 5th is a tempting split fairway par five dissected by a creek through the last half of the fairway. The shorter holes also work well; the downhill 8th has a tight green surrounded by sand, while the 12th resembles the 12th at Augusta National with its shallow target set diagonally across the tee and directly beyond a lake.

The mid-length 14th is another fine hole. Generally approached with a wedge, it features a seriously wicked green that is banked against a pond and angled sharply toward the trouble. The next is a narrow par five that rises and falls through trees as it heads into an attractive plateau green site. Consistent with the entire layout, the finish is also daunting, with few birdie opportunities and plenty of areas to make bogey. About the only oddity is the 17th, which is the only hole that deviates from the original routing and neither fits strategically nor visually within the rest of the course.

Muirfield Village was one of Jack Nicklaus's first major design projects, and many contend it is still his most significant piece of work. The course strongly resembles Augusta National, and although it may not quite reach the level of Bobby Jones's cherished Georgia creation, it shares similar traits and is an equally ideal venue for professional tournaments.

Interlachen Country Club

COURSE OPENED 1921
DESIGNERS Donald Ross,
Willie Kidd

GOLF DIGEST 62
GOLF MAGAZINE 72

Approaching Ross's wonderful
6th green

OPPOSITE Set beneath Interlachen's
striking clubhouse, the par five 9th was
immortalized when Bobby Jones accidentally
skimmed his ball across this pond en route
to winning the 1930 US Open

One of America's most historic golf clubs, the Interlachen Country Club had humble beginnings when founded on rolling farmland in Minneapolis's southwest during 1909. Members originally golfed on a Willie Mason course, which was built in 1911 and survived until the 1919 arrival of Scottish architect Donald Ross. Ross's visit changed Interlachen forever, as he devised plans to totally rebuild the golf course, keeping none of the original layout and routing his holes across two plots of land divided by Interlachen Boulevard. Immediate acclaim followed its 1921 opening, with the course best remembered as the venue of Bobby Jones's 1930 US Open triumph, the third leg of his famous Grand Slam.

The current layout remains remarkably faithful to the original design and features 11 holes on the main property, with the 11th through 17th routed across the road on a heavily wooded tract of land adjacent to a lake. The most significant alterations made to the Ross plans occurred in 1928, when Willie Kidd, the club's professional, converted the 17th into two holes and removed the par three 11th because it was positioned too close to the road. Many years later, the 1st green was pushed back beyond a small pond, changing the opener from a straightaway hole to a narrow dogleg through trees.

Maturing trees have also caused a few issues around holes such as the 11th and 12th, but most of the layout remains relatively open and is recommended for Ross's intelligent use of the site's natural undulations within his design. The fairways fall beautifully across the land, while the generously sized greens are often set on raised plateaus and cleverly angled to make you wary of hitting past the pin but frightened of coming up short. Short to mid-length par fours such as the 2nd, 6th and 7th, are among the highlights of the outward nine, each fitting snugly into the sloping ground and giving aggressive options to a range of players. The best is probably the 6th, which crosses two ridges and dares brave drivers to slash beyond the farthest ridge for a clearer view of an elevated target that falls sharply into a deep bunker. Equally memorable is the second shot into the par five 4th hole, the fairway sloping left-to-right with a pond on the right and an obscured view of the green from the left.

The back nine starts with a terrific-looking par four played from beneath the clubhouse, the hole heading into an elevated green sitting atop a crest. The par threes are also very effective, the 13th featuring a stunning lake backdrop and Kidd's 17th falling toward an excellent left-to-right target area receptive to a chasing tee shot. Although the landing area on the 15th may be a little dated, it remains a beautiful driving hole, as does the 18th, which features a semiblind tee shot into an obscured fairway valley followed by a rising approach into a dangerous green with a steep false front.

Although not quite as sporty as that of White Bear Yacht Club, the land here is ideal for good golf and the quality of the original design remains largely preserved. Oozing history, and with a magnificent clubhouse structure and first-class amenities, Interlachen is the envy of other clubs in Minnesota and is a course that traditionalists, in particular, are sure to enjoy playing.

Lost Dunes Golf Club

COURSE OPENED 1999

DESIGNER Tom Doak

GOLF DIGEST 63

GOLF MAGAZINE NR

The view from the 12th tee, with golfers able to hug the right-side bunkers given the best approach angle into the green

OPPOSITE The home hole at Lost Dunes is another challenging yet highly strategic par four from designer Tom Doak

An apparently natural marriage between a young minimalist architect and the sand dunes of the Michigan shoreline, the Lost Dunes Golf Club was, in reality, one of the most complex and unlikely success stories of the 1990s. Founded by businessman Jeff Shearer, the club is located in the southwest corner of the state, less than a half-mile from Lake Michigan but built within an abandoned sand mine and split by a busy Interstate highway. After considering a number of more experienced architects, Shearer chose an enthusiastic local named Tom Doak as his designer. The decision was the making of the golf club.

Doak arranged the first seven holes on the inland side of the highway, with the remainder of the course set on the main property, where three pit lakes are a prominent feature. Although the site had a fertile, sandy base, the mined areas were mostly flat and far from ideal for golf. Unperturbed, Doak skilfully managed to route a unique yet intelligent and coherent layout across the difficult and disjointed landscape. The greens, in particular, are excellent and fascinating both for their daring contours and the manner in which they were created. Formed in partnership with Mother Nature, Doak roughly shaped his targets but then let the wind blow the topsoil around for a few weeks before he grassed them. Some slopes may seem a little extreme, but they all fit nicely with the shot required and the variety of recovery options is first class. As at Ballyneal and Barnbougle Dunes, here missed greens are often followed by a sideways pitch or chip with the ball fed back off a slope toward the hole.

Early highlights include superb fairway bunkering on the first two holes, the heavy undulations of the 3rd

and 4th greens and strong, strategic two-shotters at the 6th and 7th. On the main paddock, water holes are well integrated into the layout, particularly at the reachable par five 10th, where a cascading green shape is guarded by a pond but still tempts players to take a gamble from back in the fairway. The most exciting approach, however, is the one played into the split-level 11th green, which falls steeply to the left and rests in a naturally elevated saddle. The next hole drops more than 50 feet and features subtle green contours that create clear choices from the tee. The par five 15th, which sweeps around a lake and up into a heavily bunkered hillock, and the multiroute 17th, are also noteworthy.

Throughout the round there is a nice flow, with the birdie opportunities and torture tests spread evenly across both nines. Fairway widths are generous, yet driving into ideal areas generally means taking a risk from the tee. The classically rugged bunker shapes are also strategic and varied, with the small trap standing sentinel short of the brilliant 6th green proving just as effective at creating uncertainty as the deep beast guarding the target on the 11th.

Tom Doak has established an enviable reputation for producing memorable courses that are playable to a range of skill levels, and again at Lost Dunes he rewards good shots with birdie putts and only punishes those that are poorly planned or executed. Although the course is unlikely to win the sort of accolades bestowed upon his more spectacular creations, this is a tremendous achievement which, given the restrictions, must rank among the most impressive built by this architectural Renaissance man.

Erin Hills

COURSE OPENED 2006

DESIGNERS Dana Fry,
Dr. Michael Hurdzan,
Ron Whitten

GOLF DIGEST NR

GOLF MAGAZINE NR

Dense meadow grasses, deep bunkers
and a small ledge green complicate
play on the short par four 15th

OPPOSITE The home hole at Erin Hills
is a mighty par five that sweeps right
and then left through sand and fescue

Despite its small-town setting, the 2006 opening of Wisconsin's Erin Hills golf course was one of the most eagerly anticipated of recent years. This was not due to the event being carried out with any great fanfare, but rather because the unopened layout had already been awarded a National Women's Amateur event and was being touted by the USGA as a future US Open venue.

Covered in fescue grasses and surrounded by rolling meadows, Erin Hills occupies a vast 650-acre site blessed with a series of dunelike hills and ridges that had apparently been created by glacial deposits made during the last Ice Age. The course was designed by Dr. Michael Hurdzan and Dana Fry with assistance from golf architecture critic Ron Whitten. Given the nature of the terrain and the plateaus, hollows and internal undulations that existed on the property, the design team tried hard to find as many natural settings for their greens, tees and fairways as possible. A number of tees are located atop ridges, with greens often built in saddles, up on plateaus or cut into the hillsides. Earthworks were only required on a handful of holes, with the majority of the playing corridors simply discovered and grassed for play.

Despite its obvious appeal, Erin Hills is quite a controversial course, with several areas of concern. First there is the routing, which forces front tee players to walk substantial distances between greens and tees. Second, the layout is very long and difficult, which is great for championship play but at times it does get a touch severe for the average public course golfer. On the positive side, approach shots into the large, sloping 3rd green and the elevated 7th are both exceptional, as is the punchbowl target and bunkering on the shorter par four 4th. The 8th is also good, the nasty left-turning two-shotter rising sharply as it nears a dangerously pitched putting complex.

Next is the beautifully bunkered 9th, which was initially built as a "Bye" hole but is now part of the course proper and arguably the best short hole on the property. This fine, falling par three, links the outward half to a back nine that begins with an unusual par five, its 650-yard fairway rising all the way through to an 80-yard-long Biarritz-style green that comes complete with a deep central depression. Further moments of note on this side include an obscured approach into a basin green on the 12th and the attractive one-shot 13th with its putting surface leaning toward a deep greenside bunker. The short par four 15th is another hole with a fine green site, its elevated target cut into the side of a hill and demanding pitch-shot precision from those back in the fairway.

While there is no doubt that the majority of readers will enjoy tackling Erin Hills, some will feel there are a few too many forced carries for such a linksy-style layout. It's true that some of the longer uphill shots are brutal on the weaker hitter, but this is a gripping experience and not only are the best holes here outstanding, they are manageable for a wide range of skill levels. The good news for all public course golfers is that there are sure to be more of them in the years ahead, for Erin Hills is one track that is certain to mature and improve over time and become even more exciting to play, especially for low markers.

Inverness Club

COURSE OPENED 1919
DESIGNERS Donald Ross,
George Fazio, Tom Fazio

GOLF DIGEST 41
GOLF MAGAZINE 41

The Inverness Club was formed in 1903, when a number of Toledo's prominent businessmen financed the purchase of 80 acres of farmland a few miles west of the city. They began by golfing on a nine-hole course, which was later expanded to 18 and then redesigned by the great Donald Ross in 1919.

The Ross course was noted for its brutal green complexes and a compact routing arranged around a series of ridges and two key ravines that cut across the site. Perhaps owing to the initial confines of the property, Ross built some of his smallest greens here, although they lack none of the creative contouring. The elevated targets are especially nasty, their crowned shapes and falling fronts placing an even greater premium on precise iron play.

Despite its design pedigree, Inverness has been altered continually since completion, first by A.W. Tillinghast, and then by Dick Wilson during the mid-1950s, both men lengthening holes, rebuilding some greens and adding bunkers in preparation for major tournaments. The most significant change came in 1976, when George and Tom Fazio were hired to make revisions to the 17th green. The pair felt areas of the course were too cramped and suggested part of the front nine be rerouted to assist spectator circulation for big events. The club agreed and converted three holes into the long par five 8th, removed the short 13th and then added the 3rd, 5th and 6th on adjacent land it owned.

Regrettably, these changes did little to enhance the golfing experience, but fortunately there are still enough high-class originals on the main property to more than compensate for any disappointments within the newer section. Sharing a crested ridge and central fairway bunkers, the adjacent 1st and 10th holes both head across a brook into excellent green sites, the 1st located atop a ridge and the 10th set down into the ravine. Rousing long par fours across bold ground contours at the 4th and 7th are also magnificent. Initially played back-to-back and among the toughest two-shotters Ross ever built, a combined score of nine on these adjoining holes is generally considered about par. Routed back and forth across the primary ravine, a five-hole stretch from the 13th is equally impressive. Again the strong fours dominate, the 15th narrowing through a falling valley and then heading toward a small green beyond the creek and the 17th featuring a small, steeply angled target set into the base of a hill. The heavily bunkered 18th is a famous finisher that is best played with a fairway wood and a wedge, the severity of the traps and the fast, contoured green making par on this mid-length hole more than acceptable.

Inverness isn't a goliath of world golf by any means, but it is one of the better parkland clubs in the Midwest and does command respect from all who play it. Major men's championships have probably moved beyond the layout, but there is no doubt that were top-line professionals to return someday, they would find the green contours, together with the high-lipped bunkers and thick roughs, a more than adequate examination of their skills.

OPPOSITE **Characterized by small greens with plenty of break and Ross's intelligent use of natural features, like this shallow gully housing the 17th green, Inverness may be short by modern standards but remains a stern test of the championship player**

Sutton Bay Club

COURSE OPENED 2003
DESIGNER Graham Marsh

GOLF DIGEST NR
GOLF MAGAZINE NR

Looking from the tee toward the gorgeous 2nd green and beyond to the shores of Lake Oahe

OPPOSITE The green at the 9th is enhanced by Marsh's rugged bunker shapes and its panoramic water views

One of the more remarkable developments in modern times, Sutton Bay is an exclusive hunting, fishing and golfing club built on an isolated cattle ranch more than 40 miles north of the South Dakota capital, Pierre. The club was founded by a coyote state native and built on stunning glacial bluffs that overlook Lake Oahe, a vast body of water that was formed when the Missouri River was dammed during the 1960s. Course architect was Australian Graham Marsh, who first saw the land in 1999 and was immediately awestruck by the size of the lake and the sight of endless dunes tumbling down toward its shoreline. Interestingly, he designed much of the course without detailed architectural plans, preferring instead to stay on site and personally supervise the shaping of each hole during the 18-month construction period.

Despite obvious comparisons with remote cousins like Sand Hills and Ballyneal, Sutton Bay is an entirely different creature altogether. For a start, the dunes are not sand-based, while the routing is arranged in a large out and back loop that stretches more than two miles along the lakefront. The most significant difference, however, is the manner in which the "discovered" holes are tied together. As at Sand Hills, these heaving dunes offered up hundreds of potential golf options, yet instead of focusing on developing a tight, cohesive collection of holes, Marsh chose to select 18 separate entities that are often considerable distances apart. As a result the course is difficult to walk and doesn't flow as smoothly as it might have otherwise. On the positive side, it is

loaded with drama and blessed with that special sense that its holes are mere extensions of the ancient, rustic landscape.

Boasting tremendous views from all corners of the property, Sutton Bay starts with a plummeting par five that overlooks the lake and falls more than 100 feet as it winds its way through a series of tall mounds. The 2nd is then a short par three that also falls toward the water, with the next 14 holes looping along the lowland portion of the site. Throughout the round, Marsh's use of native prairie grasses and sprawling bunker shapes to create unique scenic contrasts and define the generous landing areas is especially effective. As are his green complexes, which are generally well contoured, varied and fit comfortably within the rugged surrounds.

Among the better holes on the outward nine are the par four 3rd, with its wide, inviting fairway and tight skyline green, and the attractive one-shot 5th, played toward a target sliced into a dune shelf. The downhill approach into the shallow green on the 7th is another high point, as is the par three 9th, arguably the most spectacular hole on the course thanks to its deliciously perched green and uninterrupted backdrop. Aside from a couple of uncomfortable driving visuals, the back nine is also very good, its holes set higher into the hills and noted for a number of excellent green settings. Particularly memorable is the uphill pitch shot into the par five 15th and the rolling par four 16th, dominated by fantastic lake vistas and an open green set on the edge of a plateau.

This part of South Dakota is famous for its pheasant hunting and great fishing, and for a private club to work in such a remote locale it was essential that the golf be of a standard to complement the other world-class activities available to potential members. To his credit, Marsh did an excellent job shaping such an exciting and natural-looking layout out of these irregular and unpredictable landforms. Although the general lack of fluency within the routing keeps Sutton Bay from reaching the loftier heights of Sand Hills and Ballyneal, the views are unsurpassed on an inland course anywhere in America, and the design is of sufficient quality to ensure that the arduous journey to get here is well worthwhile.

OPPOSITE A grand sweeping view of the lake, the endless undulation and a perfect South Dakota sunset from Sutton Bay's impressive par four 16th

The Camargo Club

COURSE OPENED 1927

DESIGNER Seth Raynor

GOLF DIGEST 55

GOLF MAGAZINE 43

The 5th at Camargo is a copy of the Eden hole at St. Andrews and part of the most underrated set of par threes in US golf

OPPOSITE The uniquely contoured 16th green, with a relatively flat front but a twin-tier back portion

Formed in 1925, the Camargo Club was initially developed to provide alternate golfing facilities for members of the land-locked Cincinnati Country Club. It was later established as a separate entity, however, and built on an expansive tract of countryside in the Village of Indian Hill, northeast of the city. On the advice of Charles Blair Macdonald, Seth Raynor was employed by the founding members to survey the site and begin preparing plans for their golf course. As was his practice, Raynor modeled his design on the work of his mentor, planning replica versions of existing holes that had been identified by Macdonald as outstanding. Despite Raynor's sudden death in early 1926, the layout was ready for play the following year.

Interspersed with dramatic valleys and ravines, Camargo is mostly built across a series of gently sloping hills and noted for the quality of its replica holes and the nature of Raynor's bunkers and enormous greens. The trenchlike traps are up to 15 feet deep, while the square-edged targets are consistently more than 10,000 square feet in size and steeply canted to leave those hitting too safely away from side flags, or leaving their ball above the hole, with nightmare putts. The course is not long, but it still provides a stern examination of your game as the uphill approach shots can be difficult to judge and the greens are so large that back pins can add 30 yards to many of the holes.

Aside from the scale of some of these impressive green structures, the highlight here is unquestionably the sterling set of one-shot holes, which are collectively the finest on any Raynor course. Modeled after the short holes at St. Andrews, the 5th and 11th greens are both set on steep plateaus, the 5th noted for its

incredibly deep bunkering and the 11th for a cruel depression through the middle of its vast putting surface. The obligatory Biarritz and Redan holes are also terrific, the latter the equal of Chicago's famed version and beautifully shaped atop a soft rise and with a clever spine running through the green surface.

Although the par threes tend to capture most attention here, there are also a number of intriguing par fours. The 3rd, for instance, is almost reachable but played along a sharp upslope toward an inviting target that tempts big hitters to flirt with danger in order to set up a birdie chance. The mid-length 6th, played across a series of small hills, is another fine four, as is the strategically bunkered dogleg 10th, this time dominated by a deep frontal trap that has an uncanny knack of gathering poorly struck approach shots. Another daunting approach is into the 7th, an Alps hole with its immense square green set beyond a blind cross-bunker in a sunken punchbowl. Other interesting green sites include the hog's-back 12th and the triple-tier 16th, which features a large back plateau split in two by a swale.

Classy and quietly understated, Camargo is a special club and a real treat for those with a keen eye for classic golf architecture. A lot of credit for the current state of the course must go to Tom Doak, who has helped preserve Raynor's design intent by converting bunkers back to his original style and returning the shrunken greens to their appropriate proportions. Despite comparing favorably with other Raynor courses, somehow this one continues to slide under most golfing radars. For the unaware, therefore, a game here is a most pleasant surprise.

Wolf Run Golf Club

COURSE OPENED 1989

DESIGNER Steve Smyers

GOLF DIGEST NR

GOLF MAGAZINE NR

Pressed hard against water, the green at the difficult 14th hole

OPPOSITE The long, all-carry par three 13th is one of the most daunting holes at Wolf Run

One of the most relentless tests of golf in the Midwest, Wolf Run is situated 20 miles north of Indianapolis and was founded by a local dentist wanting to build a demanding golf-only club for accomplished players. His selected site for the course was a partly forested tract of land blessed with both a large ridge and the aptly named Eagle Creek cutting through the property.

Designed by a relatively unheralded architect, the course opened in 1989 and immediately raised eyebrows, both for its difficulty and for the quality of Steve Smyers's design. Routing much of his front nine across an open cornfield, Smyers set the back nine partly within a wooded bluff, with the creek popping up regularly throughout the round to add strategic and visual interest. His main method of protecting par was to build narrow fairways surrounded by punishing native fescues and to create small, contoured greens. The bunkering is also quite striking. Rugged and generally deep, the traps are positioned to punish those who stray, but hitting away from sand leaves tricky recovery shots, as short grass and steep slopes create a great variety of short game challenges.

The sense that Wolf Run is pretty special hits from the moment you step onto the 1st tee, the hole played from atop a large hill down onto a valley fairway defined by waving fescue grasses and a series of wonderful bunkers arranged diagonally along the left side. A tee shot played safely to the right leaves an awkward approach angled across further traps and into the shallow part of a small target. The 2nd hole is a long par three played to a green placed directly over the creek. This same creek wraps around the side of the minuscule dropkick 16th green and cuts across the 15th and 7th fairways, the approach on the 7th played from an upper shelf to another tiny target beside the water.

Away from the hazard, memorable holes include the par four 9th, which turns left from a crowned fairway and rises into a tiered green surrounded by pot bunkers, and the brutal stretch from the 12th to the 15th. Visually intimidating from the tee, the 13th is a cracking par three played from an abrupt ledge out across a deep valley and into a green resting perilously beyond a heavily bunkered hillside. The 14th is just as nasty, with the drive bending around a small mound and the falling approach an all-carry shot across water to an undulating green with plenty of sand trouble. The narrow drive and elevated green site on the 15th are also seriously challenging, as is the final approach shot into the 18th, played with a mid-iron across a deep ravine.

The strength of Wolf Run is the consistent quality of its holes and Smyers's stylish bunkering and creative green complexes, which, although small, effectively test both approach play and the golfer's powers of recovery. The layout is perhaps a little too severe on players with mid-to-high handicaps, but given the degree of difficulty, it is surprising that major magazine's have overlooked this fine course in their ranking lists.

Olympia Fields Country Club – North Course

COURSE OPENED 1922

DESIGNER Willie Park Jr.

GOLF DIGEST 42

GOLF MAGAZINE 69

At one point America's largest country club, Olympia Fields was the brainchild of prominent businessman Charles Beach, who in 1915 recognized the growing popularity of golf and a shortfall in quality courses around the Chicago area. His search for a suitable site upon which to develop a multicourse, megaclub brought him to a large tract of forested farmland 25 miles south of the city. Covered in flourishing oaks and a series of steep ridges and meandering streams, the land was ideal for golf. Beach and his founding members then purchased 670 acres and, incredibly, within just seven years had attracted more than a thousand members, completed four courses and built one of the grandest clubhouses in existence.

The fourth course opened in 1922 and was designed by dual British Open champion Willie Park Jr. Now referred to as the North Course, Park's track was the centerpiece of Olympia Fields and when financial hardships forced the club to sell half its property during the 1940s, it was the land for this course, as well as an 18-hole composite from the three earlier courses, that were retained.

Designed with the same simple, strategic principles employed on his British masterpieces, the North Course has become a tighter driving course than initially intended, but Park's back-to-front green sites are still the dominant feature of the layout. The routing is also impressive; much of the course rolls softly across the terrain, but a number of wonderfully natural holes were built amid the heavier undulations. Among the best is the par four 3rd, which plummets over a crest toward a hidden fairway, the approach then rising again into a gorgeous green site resting on a plateau and

set beyond a creek and a group of imposing bunkers. The 14th also hits up high into a dangerous hilltop target, this time across a gully from a flatter lower ledge. Bending left around bunkers, the 11th is another wonderful hole, its fairway leaning right to encourage a bold left-side drive and the approach played through sand to a green falling away at the back. The gently bending 2nd and the short par four 4th, with its large saucer-shaped fairway leaving an obscured second shot for those unable to smash their drive beyond a distant ridge, are also fun to play. As are skillfully bunkered par threes at the 8th and 13th, along with the uphill approach into the two-shot 17th.

Aside from a number of back tees, the only significant change from Park's plan is an awkward new par three, the 6th, which drops from an elevated tee down to an angled, tiered green that is quite out of character with the rest of the targets. The other blow for traditionalists and keen students of classic architecture is the unfortunate extension of a pond beside the 18th green. The finishing hole is still a terrific long par four, but the pond now eats into the front of a steeply pitched target which leans forward and was clearly designed to allow weaker hitters to play a longer, running approach shot.

These changes aside, the North Course at Olympia Fields continues to provide a tremendous challenge and the club has done well to preserve a classic feel yet remain a relevant tournament venue. The course is probably a few outstanding holes away from being regarded among the greats of American golf, but this is one of the most pleasing championship layouts in the Midwest, and unquestionably among the top few in Illinois.

OPPOSITE Once the largest country club in America, Olympia Fields was reduced from 72 to 36 holes in the 1940s, Willie Park Jr.'s wonderful North Course the only one of its layouts to have survived intact. Pictured is Park's tremendous 3rd hole, where a blind drive is followed by this thrilling approach

Double Eagle Club

COURSE OPENED 1992

DESIGNERS Tom Weiskopf,
Jay Morrish

GOLF DIGEST 70

GOLF MAGAZINE 79

The nature of the Weiskopf/Morrish shaping on display here at the 3rd green

OPPOSITE The par five finisher at Double Eagle is a terrific gambling hole with plenty of options and an exciting cross-pond approach

Double Eagle is a small private club developed by golfing enthusiast John H. McConnell, the founder of a multibillion-dollar steel company established back in the 1950s near the Ohio capital of Columbus. McConnell built his club a little north of the city, on farming grounds he had initially purchased to be used as a fishing retreat for friends and staff. Later, when golf became his primary passion, he approached Ohioan Tom Weiskopf to first inspect the site and then help him convert the land into a quality course.

With more than 300 acres of land at their disposal, Weiskopf and his partner, Jay Morrish, set about creating a golfing experience to rival the premier private clubs of the region. Shielded from the outside world by dense woodland, the interior of the property was ideal for golf, as it was mostly cleared of trees and had some nice natural ravines and ponds. Leaving the slopes and contours largely as they found them, the designers arranged the course in two loops either side of a clever dual-tee 19th hole, the layout having a spacious feel with trees really only an issue during the mid part of the front nine.

The strength of the Weiskopf/Morrish course is its variety, both in the length and nature of the holes and the use of flashed-up bunkers and subtle green shapes. After a solid opener played from an expansive fairway across a gully to a shallow target, the course settles into a soft rhythm with a series of attractive holes that are unlikely to terrorize those thinking clearly and hitting well. Things start to heat up at the long par four 5th, with its daunting approach heading over a gnarly ravine and into a tight green. The reachable par five 6th is a classic gambling hole, the fairway turning through trees toward a dangerous but tempting target set beyond a small ditch. The cross-gully approach into the 7th green is also impressive, as is the multioption 9th hole, noted for its split-level fairway and large, spectacle bunkers that prove particularly cruel to those approaching its contoured putting surface from the safer lower fairway.

The back nine features more water and a series of gently bending holes, the best being the Cape-style 15th, which doglegs around a lake toward a small green bunkered to favor those who drive bravely beside the water. There are also a couple of cool heroic holes at the death, both the 17th and 18th offering real prospects of an eagle putt to those taking an aggressive line into the green. The 17th is a driveable par four along a lake, with the option of playing dangerously along the hazard or using the two-shot route and bailing to the wide side of the hole. The 18th fairway is then split by a central bunker, which creates distinct landing areas and at least three paths from tee through to the peninsula green.

Weiskopf and Morrish did a first-class job here, creating a pleasant environment for the game and carefully extracting some exciting golf holes out of the subtle landforms. Although Double Eagle isn't quite up to the standard of the pair's course at Loch Lomond in Scotland, it nevertheless has plenty of quality and a simple elegance that is hard not to admire.

Butler National Golf Club

COURSE OPENED 1972

DESIGNERS George Fazio,
Tom Fazio

GOLF DIGEST 21

GOLF MAGAZINE 97

The par three 13th, with its putting surface leaning strategically toward the lake

OPPOSITE Butler's beautifully sculpted 5th hole is no place for the fainthearted or those prone to hitting their tee shots fat

An exclusive male-only enclave, Butler National was one of the earliest collaborations between George Fazio and his nephew Tom Fazio, and remains one of the pair's most notable creations. The club is located in Oak Brook and was founded by Paul Butler, a local entrepreneur and the man responsible for developing the village into an affluent and thriving Chicago suburb. Butler's brief to the Fazios was to build a course that would be difficult enough to test the world's best professionals, the designers obliging by creating a track that rates among America's hardest.

The land provided for the layout was well treed and had some decent elevation change, though nothing overly drastic. The Fazios enhanced the site by building a series of water hazards, then fashioned a course that was long from the tips and had fairways lined by roughs and bunkers that are especially severe on stray balls. What really give Butler National its teeth, however, are its undersized greens, which are generally set at an angle across the fairway, making target areas even smaller and allowing pins to be tucked behind bunkers on tiny wings. The putting surfaces are also contoured and kept very slick, making both approach and recovery play even more challenging.

The round opens with a series of solid holes and a number of tight green sites. Played over a lake to an attractive peninsula green, the par three 5th is the start of a nasty run that includes the long and narrow 6th and the tricky par five 7th, a hole that bends so sharply around a creek and trees that it discourages aggressive tee shots. The short 8th then heads along the rim of the creek, while the 9th is an unforgiving four with a small green and a slender fairway pinched by trees.

The back nine is even more demanding. The 11th and 13th are tough par threes with cleverly angled greens, while the rising cross-pond approach into the 10th and the lakeside drive on the 14th are both particularly difficult for tentative players. Hardest of all, however, is the 12th. Converted from a par five into a par four, its long and narrow fairway is lined by trees, bunkers and rough and gently rises toward a three-shot green with a tiny, crowned front entrance. Completing a very thorough examination of your skills are long fours at the 17th and 18th, the final hole forcing golfers to negotiate a huge oak guarding the right side of the fairway by either driving left and carrying more water on the approach or bending their second shot around the limbs.

Despite their aging reasonably well and continuing to provide a stiff test of golf, in recent years Tom Fazio has been involved in a program to refresh and strengthen the holes in the wake of modern advancements in the game. His most significant work was to rebuild the bunkers, digging them deeper and crafting traps with flashed-up sand faces that are visually striking. Although there are a number of holes here that still seem unduly harsh, Butler National was founded as a championship venue and is a club that remains determined to humble the highly skilled golfer. It may no longer serve as a regular tournament host, but with plenty of solid holes and supreme grooming, this is a layout that most readers would thoroughly enjoy playing.

Medinah Country Club – No. 3 Course

COURSE OPENED 1928

DESIGNER Tom Bendelow
with revisions by
Rees Jones and others

GOLF DIGEST 11
GOLF MAGAZINE 35

One of America's most highly rated tournament venues, the Medinah Country Club was founded by Shriners from Chicago's Medinah Temple, who in the early 1920s purchased enough land in northern DuPage County to build a world-class country retreat complete with three full-length golf courses. Tom Bendelow was retained as golf architect, his famed No. 3 course opening in 1928. Initially considered too easy, the layout was overhauled a few years later with the strengthened version quickly establishing itself as the club's championship test.

Routed through a rolling oak forest and crossing Lake Kadijah several times, the modern No. 3 still follows Bendelow's general plan, although the practice of lengthening and toughening holes has become more frequent and rigorous as the decades have passed. Aside from the tees continually being pushed back, the fairways have also been narrowed and a number of greens relocated. This work has been done by a number of consulting architects, including most recently Rees Jones who, in 2002, stretched the track beyond 7,500 yards from the tips. Jones also rebuilt the bunkers and redesigned a number of key greens, including each of the cross-lake par threes.

Although it does provide a supreme test for professional events, for average golfers No. 3 lacks the subtlety and variety of really elite championship courses. With the exception of the 8th, each of the par threes plays directly across the lake, and in much the same manner, while most of the longer holes are claustrophobic and uncomfortably narrow. Fairway bunkers are employed sparingly and rarely used strategically, generally only appearing in places where the tall oaks don't pinch landing areas tightly enough. The course basically tests your ability to continually hit straight, precise shots. There aren't really tactical angles to consider nor is there much chance of playing fun, out-of-position recovery shots as any slip up here, however marginal, is intended to cost you a stroke or more.

Holes like the 9th, 11th, 14th and 16th are horrendously cramped by trees and terribly unfair on players unable to move the ball both ways with length and precision. The hardest is probably the 16th, which horseshoes around huge trees, then heads up a very steep incline into a small target with a severe front that feeds weak balls 40 yards back down the fairway. Of greater interest are more forgiving holes like the gently rolling opener and the uphill par four 4th, which is as severe on short approaches as the 16th, but much more playable from the tee and with a larger back-to-front green. Another quality hole is the long two-shot 12th, its green guarded by a huge oak on its left side and the approach played from a left-to-right sidehill stance. The 6th, 7th, 8th and 15th holes are also fairly solid.

Despite areas of mediocrity, there is some decent ground movement here, and with a better routing, more imaginative green complexes, some strategic bunkering and heavy tree clearing this could be a terrific layout. The founding fathers of Medinah, however, aimed to create America's premier country club and they have continually sought and hosted high-profile tournaments. This focus on retaining championship prestige has ensured ranking list prominence for No. 3, though, in truth, the course is a notch below many of those ranked beneath it.

OPPOSITE Redesigned by Rees Jones, who added the back bunker and moved the green closer to the water, the 2nd is one of three short holes at Medinah No. 3 that play directly across Lake Kadijah

Blackwolf Run – River Course

COURSE OPENED 1990

DESIGNER Pete Dye

GOLF DIGEST 69

GOLF MAGAZINE 82

View from the tee on the
par five opening hole

OPPOSITE The par four 9th hole,
conservative players likely to lay-up down
the left while aggressive golfers will take
aim at an inviting green 300 yards away

Situated on the outskirts of the quiet Wisconsin village of Kohler, about an hour north of Milwaukee, Blackwolf Run is a 36-hole resort facility set beside the constantly winding Sheboygan River. Named after a prominent chief of the indigenous Winnebago Indians, the property was developed by Herbert V. Kohler Jr. and the golf holes designed by his collaborator at Whistling Straits, Pete Dye.

The first 18 holes at Blackwolf Run were opened in 1988, with the remainder added over the following two summers. The pick of the golf is the River Course, which features nine originals (1–4 and 14–18), and nine that were built in 1990. Arranged in a large twisted loop, the layout follows the snaking river with several greens pressed against its banks and other holes set down in an attractive internal basin. Common to a number of Dye courses, the fairways are quite spacious but the greens are tight and treacherously contoured. Across the property there are plenty of risk/reward-type moments as well as other areas where the strategic use of water, trees or artificial mounding complicates otherwise straightforward approaches.

The round starts with a strong par five opening hole, which is built beside the river and bunkered to encourage aggressive golfers to seek that starting birdie. The other three-shot holes are also very interesting, the 8th with its split-tiered fairway and the 11th and 16th both bending dramatically around the river. Worthwhile front nine par fours include the strong 5th, its target benched into a steep hill, and the almost reachable 9th, which offers golfers multiple routes to the green, including a shortcut through tall trees and directly across an elbow of the river.

Better holes on the back nine include the par four 12th, where a driving pond and central fairway bunker create two avenues into a dangerous waterside green. The 13th is another key hole, if only for the fact that it may be the most difficult par three in America for slicers. Heading up the length of the river, the left side of the hole is blocked by trees forcing you to play either a draw out over the stream or a high lofted shot directly over the towering trees. Also worthy of note is the par four 14th, its slender fairway bending hard right around a lake and its green hidden beyond a pronounced berm for those who hit too far away from the water. Typical of many Dye layouts, the round ends with a strong three, tough four combination, the 17th complicated by a skinny green angled toward the river and the 18th bending around an occasionally flooded waste bunker and featuring a charming green that it shares with the final hole on the Meadow Valleys Course.

Although there are some aesthetic differences between the original holes and those added downstream a few years later, the River Course at Blackwolf Run comes recommended for its design coherence and the number of exciting holes dotted across both nines. The layout isn't quite in the same league as Whistling Straits, but for fans of destination golf the fact that it is far less taxing and time-consuming than the Straits Course has to add to the appeal of this increasingly popular region.

Crooked Stick Golf Club

COURSE OPENED 1967
DESIGNER Pete Dye

GOLF DIGEST NR
GOLF MAGAZINE 95

"I keep going back to Crooked Stick and wondering how I ever came up with it so early in the game. I'm absolutely amazed I ever put it together."

PETE DYE

OPPOSITE **The lengthy one-shot 17th hole at Crooked Stick, Pete Dye's earliest headline-grabbing creation**

A modern golfing heavyweight, Pete Dye was little more than a part-time architect in 1963 when he embarked on an odyssey across the Atlantic to play the classic old links of Scotland. Inspired by what he saw, Dye returned to his home in Indianapolis determined to build a local course that paid homage to these ancient gems. He managed to convince 60 friends and associates to form a golf club and contribute the funds required to build their course. Rather than seeking comparable terrain for his layout, he instead decided to recreate natural golf movement on a flat cornfield north of the city.

With financial backing secured, the enthusiastic but inexperienced designer set about transforming his 200-acre blank canvas into a believable and enjoyable golf test. This involved building a mix of sprawling bunkers and smaller pot traps as well as swales, mounds, undulating fairways and hazards supported by wooden bulkheads. Dye had the back nine finished in 1964 but had exhausted all of his construction funds. It took him a further three years to raise the additional capital required to complete the front nine.

Although the routing hasn't altered substantially since the 1967 opening, Dye lives on site during the summers and has made regular changes to the course, replanting and recontouring the greens more than once, lengthening holes and continually tinkering with trees, bunkers and mounding. He also converted the front trap on the 16th into a pond, and shifted the 15th tee away from what is now a road, eliminating a dangerous dogleg across private property.

There is tremendous variety to Dye's routing and design here, players needing to be on their game from the start as holes are visually challenging and continually alter in their orientation. From the tee, there is enough width to allow for various routes into greens that are intricately contoured and effectively able to punish the careless or overly ambitious. The back nine is slightly more impressive than the front and features more gradient variations and a more interesting collection of holes. These include the 12th, bending first around diagonal traps and then rising into a superb green site, and the side lake 18th, which is cleverly shaped to benefit the bolder driver. The shortish par five 15th is another really good hole with a remarkable boomerang green wrapped around a deep trap. The par threes are also solid, particularly the long and open 17th, which is bunkered to encourage a right-to-left chasing approach. On the front nine the standout is the 6th, a picture-postcard par three across a pond that is dominated by a gorgeous old oak tree standing beside the green.

Pete Dye is a fascinating character, and although he had dabbled in golf design prior to Crooked Stick, this was the first substantial project in his portfolio and its success helped launch what became a generation-defining career. These are no longer his greatest holes, but the course remains dear to his heart and is consistent, tremendous fun to play and continues to provide a solid test for all levels of golfer.

Cherry Hills Country Club

COURSE OPENED 1923

DESIGNER William S. Flynn

GOLF DIGEST 53

GOLF MAGAZINE 63

Surrounded by some of Denver's most expensive real estate, the Cherry Hills Country Club was opened in 1923 and designed by prolific Philadelphia architect William Flynn. Flynn was employed by the club to build them a championship-length course, to be laid out across an attractive meadow south of the city. Despite the presence of a couple of winding creeks, much of the land here was flat and rather uninteresting, yet the designer managed to create a strategic layout that, until recently, was unchallenged as the premier course in the state.

Flynn's supreme achievement at Cherry Hills was an intelligent, balanced routing that combined exciting holes on great land with solid holes across the flatter ground. His use of the creeks and the natural contours that were present on the virgin terrain is also outstanding. Although construction is fairly basic, the green shaping and general use of bunkering is quite sophisticated. The design itself is very subtle, with the firm greens angled to ensure that driving your ball into the correct part of the fairway is essential, particularly on the more undulating holes, where out-of-position approach shots are fraught with danger.

Despite its modest length and the fact balls tend to travel farther at Denver altitudes, Cherry Hills has a tough reputation and continues to provide all players with a great test of golf. After a reasonably soft start, the first stern challenge is the pitch into the heavily bunkered 3rd green, followed soon after by another superb pitch shot over massive frontal traps on the par five 5th. In terms of difficulty, the layout steps up a gear from the super-hard par three 8th, protected by a deep trap and a tricky green with plenty of cunning breaks. The 9th then heads uphill along a narrow fairway that offers a huge reward to those able to drive long and straight, as it is crowned to kick anything not flighted precisely down into bogey areas. The downhill, right-to-left 10th is another beautiful par four demanding a cautious approach.

Next outstanding hole is the 14th, which is a brutal two-shotter turning hard left toward a nasty green squeezed between sand and a creek. Marking the start of a fine finishing stretch, it is followed by a tight par three that backs onto this same creek and another strong four cut diagonally by the hazard. Flat and seemingly straightforward, the 17th is then a shortish par five complicated by a low-set island green. The first two strokes here may be simple, but the third can be nerve-racking, as the firm putting surface is set immediately beyond a lake that will catch anyone getting too cute with their pitch. Ending the round is a stirring Cape-style finishing hole, heading uphill along this same lake and into the most severe green on the course. Hitting away from the water not only leaves an awkward sidehill stance but a horrible angle across a deep bunker and into a target sloping cruelly away.

The measure of Cherry Hills is how solid its unspectacular holes are, and the fact that the continued tweaking and lengthening of the course has failed to adversely affect the character of the original Flynn design. Best remembered for Arnold Palmer's barnstorming final-round charge to the 1960 US Open title, this storied course is not an obvious American classic, but its subtleties have helped the layout remain relevant and continue to provide golfers with a terrific examination of their game.

OPPOSITE **The 18th at Cherry Hills is a wonderful finishing hole that rewards those brave golfers able to drive their ball aggressively down the left side of the fairway**

Hazeltine National Golf Club

COURSE OPENED 1962

DESIGNER Robert Trent Jones

GOLF DIGEST 89

GOLF MAGAZINE 77

The par five 15th, its narrow fairway
lined by deep bunkers

OPPOSITE Heading toward the 10th
green, with Lake Hazeltine and the
club's famous 16th green in the distance

Developed specifically to host championship play, the Hazeltine National Golf Club was founded by Totton Heffelfinger, a former president of the USGA and a member of Minneapolis's Minikahda Club, which in the 1950s had become threatened by the development of a local freeway. Heffelfinger sought an alternate site for the club and found what he believed to be an ideal piece of land beside Hazeltine Lake in rural Chaska. When members of Minikahda rejected the move, he decided to proceed with plans for a new club of his own.

Heffelfinger's choice of course architect was Robert Trent Jones, who was in the prime of his career and building the sort of long and demanding layouts that tournament organizers were starting to prefer. Hazeltine opened in 1962 and, though it quickly established its tournament credentials, there were serious shortfalls with the layout and Jones was forced to make regular alterations. These changes included straightening several doglegs, adding countless back tees, shifting a few green sites and, most notably, converting the 16th from a par three to a famous par four alongside the lake. The green on the par three 8th was shifted to the other side of a pond, while the creation of the 16th fairway meant the two-shot 17th had to revert to a par three. In later decades Rees Jones made further adjustments, adding new bunkers and back tees prior to major events in 1991, 2002 and 2006 and, interestingly, restoring some original hazards and landing areas that had

become relevant again with the increased length.

Some of these extensions have made parts of the course a little confined, as back tees and greens are often squeezed in close proximity. That said, the current layout is an excellent test of golf, with plenty of length, a good mix of well-bunkered holes and some fine back-to-front angled greens. The property has gentle undulations, which allowed Jones to build tight, flowing fairways through the trees and, as was his style at the time, to locate several targets on elevated areas.

Not surprisingly, the best part of the course is down by the lake. The approach shot into the 10th green is beautifully framed by the water, while the signature 16th is a wonderful spot for a golf hole, its drive crossing part of the hazard to a narrow fairway partly obscured by trees and reeds. The approach shot then heads into a dangerous green cut into the lake and falling away on all sides. Other solid holes include the left-bending opener, long par threes at the 4th and 13th, the nice drive and pitch 5th hole and the strong, uphill par four 9th. The finishing stretch is also good. The 17th is an attractive par three with a tight target, while the small green on the newly stretched 18th is tilted steeply forward and does seem a fairly harsh end to the round for those playing from the tips.

Although not quite in the class of White Bear Yacht Club or Interlachen, Hazeltine National is firmly established as Minneapolis's premier championship venue and is a polished layout with a number of good holes, excellent conditioning and plenty of difficulty.

Castle Pines Golf Club

COURSE OPENED 1981

DESIGNER Jack Nicklaus

GOLF DIGEST 36

GOLF MAGAZINE 85

"I am as proud of our course as I am of the people who have been so instrumental in making the dream come true."

JACK VICKERS

OPPOSITE **Looking back down the uniquely shaped 18th fairway from the luxurious Castle Pines clubhouse**

Nestled in the foothills of the Rocky Mountains, Castle Pines is an exclusive gated community located in Douglas County, some 30 minutes south of Denver. The development was founded and financed by oil entrepreneur Jack Vickers, who purchased a large tract of ranching land in the 1970s and employed his longtime friend Jack Nicklaus to help him bring world-class golf to the region.

At the heart of the subdivision are two private courses designed by Nicklaus, who also prepared the preliminary routing for a public course that was later finished by Tom Weiskopf. The most significant of the three courses is the Castle Pines Golf Club, which opened in 1981 and is personally controlled and managed by Vickers.

Built more than 6,000 feet above sea level, the course is mostly carved through a forest of ponderosa pines and scrub oak, with a number of the early holes enjoying picturesque views across wildflower meadows and out toward the mountains of the Front Range. Arranged in two loops on either side of an elevated clubhouse, both nines start by plunging downward and end with holes tracking back up the hill. This is not an easy walking course, as some of the climbs are substantial. The holes are also very long, and although altitude helps your ball fly farther through the air, controlling your distance is vital, as the targets are protected by some of Nicklaus's most severe bunkering. On a handful of greens there are actually areas that collapse into deep traps, making precision on the approach shot even more important.

The most prominent holes here are the heroic water par fives and those with the controversial collection bunkers. The 5th is probably the nastiest example. A long par four playing steadily uphill, the green is shallow and angled steeply forward but most notorious for a concave front section that feeds flag-bound balls down into a difficult bunker. The 6th also features a collection bunker in its front, but sensibly the hole is shorter and the putting surface more generous, especially as many will have a wedge in their hand. Another infamous hole is the 9th, a strong two-shot test played across and then along a creek and featuring a steep uphill approach into a tiered green guarded by a yawning frontal trap.

The plunging par four 10th is also very good; this time the approach is played from a gently leaning fairway into a green that is not only quick and full of breaks but set immediately beyond a pond and guarded by back bunkers. Other tricky targets include the 12th green, wedged tightly between a mound and a pond, and the triple-tiered 13th. Aside from a penal and overly complicated green site on the long par three 16th, the run home from this point is quite solid and offers all level of player the chance to take risks and end with some birdies.

Although structurally Castle Pines has remained largely unaltered, in the years since it opened the layout has been regularly modified and lengthened to retain its championship status. Appealing to low markers in particular, the holes here are attractive and memorable, with the conditioning, views and general club atmosphere also weighing heavily in its favor.

Shoreacres

COURSE OPENED 1921
DESIGNER Seth Raynor
GOLF DIGEST 88, GOLF MAGAZINE 42

Founded on Chicago's North Shore in 1916, Shoreacres is a wonderful old golf club that boasts both a clubhouse by famed architect David Adler and a course by his golfing contemporary Seth Raynor. While Adler's stunning building overlooks Lake Michigan, the Raynor layout is built away from the water on a rolling property interspersed by a number of creeks and deep ravines.

The club's founding members had initially wanted Donald Ross to design their golf course, but his failure to respond to letters led them instead to the emerging Raynor, who did a superb job routing his holes across the site. The ravines are expertly used throughout the design and incorporated into holes in a variety of ways, as are the ditches and creeks that meander across the property. Raynor's course is also noted for its wonderfully intricate green complexes. Generally broad and sloping to the front, they feature wide areas that force players to either flirt with side pins or face massive putts across the greens if they bail too safe. A strength of Shoreacres is the short to mid-length par fours—the 2nd, 4th, 11th, 13th and 17th all fine holes under 400 yards with tricky, strategic greens. Also memorable are the replica par threes and the short par five 15th, noted for second-shot complexities created by an unusual split fairway.

Aside from some terrific individual holes, what makes Shoreacres such an interesting course is its evenness and Raynor's clever use of the topography. His greens and bunkers are well positioned and the fairways flow with enough variety to keep players on their guard. The layout is a little short for today's star golfer, but for the average guy able to look beyond length and slope ratings this is one of Chicago's premier places to play.

Scioto Country Club

COURSE OPENED 1916
DESIGNERS Donald Ross, Dick Wilson
GOLF DIGEST 58, GOLF MAGAZINE 47

Located in a leafy suburb of Columbus, Ohio, the Scioto Country Club was established with the 1916 opening of its Donald Ross golf course, but was made famous decades later when a young Jack Nicklaus decided to take up the game here.

Despite its rich golfing heritage, Scioto has suffered considerable change during the years, and unfortunately the current layout barely resembles the original Donald Ross plans. Virtually all of his bunkers have been moved, removed, enlarged or simply converted to a more modern style, while his putting contours were lost during a redesign by Dick Wilson in the 1960s. Wilson is also responsible for a divisive change made to the 8th, a par five over beautiful rolling ground that plays to a target now resting on an island surrounded by a moat.

The routing itself remains almost intact and is the strength of the course, Ross using the trickling stream and the site's natural ground movement to great effect within his design. Interesting fairway contours and elevated green sites are especially effective on holes like the 2nd, 5th, 13th and 16th. The par four 10th is also very strong, the drive played toward a crested fairway and the downhill, sidehill approach into a large green set beyond the creek and flanked by sand. The other notable holes here are the front nine par threes, the 4th a long shot into a tightly bunkered plateau and the 9th an excellent mid-iron across sand into a green perched atop a ridge.

Although recent attempts have been made to restore some lost Ross elements, the renovations have not been wide-reaching and seem more focused on retaining championship pedigree than returning clever design elements. The Nicklaus legacy has all but ensured Scioto of a special place in the annals of American golf, and it continues to do very well on various ranking lists. In truth, however, the present layout is a considerable distance behind the quality of Ross's best-preserved classics.

OPPOSITE Scioto's controversial par five 8th, Dick Wilson moving Ross's green beyond a shallow canal during the 1950s

Bellerive Country Club

COURSE OPENED 1960
DESIGNERS Robert Trent Jones, Rees Jones
GOLF DIGEST NR, GOLF MAGAZINE 91

A proud and storied centurion, the Bellerive Country Club was originally founded in north St. Louis back in 1897 and moved to its present home west of the city in 1960, where a new layout was designed by Robert Trent Jones on a pleasantly undulating property he had helped the club select.

Dubbed the Green Monster, the Jones course was uncommonly long and demanding when it opened and noted for its massive, often elevated, green complexes. For decades the course remained a fierce test of golf, but the need to keep pace with the modern game and issues with flooding on its low-lying areas forced the club to undertake a substantial upgrade with Jones's son Rees. Completed in 2006, the program involved regrassing fairways, greens and tees, upgrading the drainage system, adding a number of back tees and reducing the size of several targets. Rees also enlarged the pond on the 2nd hole to create both a driving and second shot-hazard and added fairway undulations and a nasty new green to the 7th.

The immense targets remain the key feature of this course, the greens generally guarded by large bunkers cut into the surrounding slopes and built with ridges that divide the putting surface into distinct areas. This is the sort of course where Greens In Regulation only tell part of the story, three-putting a very common frustration for those sloppy with their approach play. Better holes include the nicely undulating 5th and the steeply rising 9th, which is noted for an uphill approach played into a wide target dissected by a valley. On the back nine, solid par threes like the 13th and the dangerous, all-carry 16th stand out, as does the two-shot 15th, a stiff driving test over a slight crest that then heads down to an attractively bunkered green.

With its difficult greens and long, tightly treed fairways, Bellerive is a ready-made tournament venue, though it isn't really in the same league as America's best championship courses. The ambience and wonderful facilities, however, make it a highly desirable club for those living in this part of the country.

Arcadia Bluffs Golf Club

COURSE OPENED 1999
DESIGNERS Warren Henderson, Rick Smith
GOLF DIGEST 46, GOLF MAGAZINE NR

Less than 20 miles south of Crystal Downs, Michigan's Arcadia Bluffs is a modern daily-fee facility built among huge clifftop dunes alongside the Lake Michigan shoreline. Designed by Warren Henderson with help from teaching professional Rick Smith, the course is located almost directly across the lake from Wisconsin's Whistling Straits, and similarly boasts awesome water views and some extreme design features. The big difference between the two layouts being that here the bulging landscape is mostly natural.

Occupying almost 250 acres along the lakefront, Arcadia Bluffs is arranged in two loops around an elevated clubhouse, the opening nine built on steadily leaning ground and the back among larger sandhills that crash more than 200 feet down along the bluffs. Although the terrain is spectacular, in truth much of it is too severe for good golf holes, particularly on the back nine. The 11th, for instance, falls so steeply that 400-yard drives are possible while the 10th, which does not drop as sharply, is even more severe as it heads blind over a dune and then through a wild valley that seems far too tight for such an exposed site. More impressive is the spectacular 12th, routed directly along the shoreline, and the one-shot 13th played toward the water and across a deep ravine. The other par threes are also good, as are front nine par fives like the uphill 3rd, notable for a series of staggered traps that need to be carried with either your second or third shot, and the falling 5th, which features a massively shaped waste area short of its green.

Given the extreme nature of this site, both the fairways and greens are generously sized, although skinny target areas do make some pin locations quite severe. The outlooks and playing characteristics, however, are first-rate, and most who play Arcadia Bluffs are likely to walk away from a round immensely satisfied.

OPPOSITE **Plunging dramatically off the dunes and then turning toward this spectacular green complex, the par five 11th is one of Arcadia Bluff's real glamour holes**

Canterbury Golf Club

COURSE OPENED 1922
DESIGNERS Herbert Strong, Jack Way
GOLF DIGEST 94, GOLF MAGAZINE 94

Founded by a group of prominent Clevelanders in 1921, the Canterbury Golf Club is located in the city's eastern suburbs on a compact property blessed with plenty of natural elevation change as well as a couple of flowing brooks. The course was originally designed by Englishman Herbert Strong, but reshaped shortly after by club professional Jack Way in preparation for the Western Open.

Full of strong, strategic golf holes that bend gently across the tumbling ground, this course is noted for its narrow fairways, punishing bunkers and nasty green sites that are generally angled back-to-front. A regular tournament venue in its early years, unfortunately the club is now landlocked and some of its better holes suffer from a lack of space. The opening hole, for example, heads blind over a central fairway ridge and used to be noted for a daunting long-iron approach played from a hanging lie. Today, good players are able to drive down onto the flat area for a much simpler second shot. The small, rounded plateau green at the 8th is another target that would benefit were an additional 30 yards added to the approach. Less affected are fun holes like the short but crowned par five 6th and the long par three 7th, played into a green resting atop a knoll. The finish from the wildly undulating par five 16th is also very strong. Requiring three precise shots for any chance at par, the 16th is followed by a bruising one-shotter heading into a two-tiered plateau and a deceptively steep uphill finishing four whose green is heavily guarded by sand.

Although many feel that Canterbury lacks modern championship length, it is still a wonderful members course with fine golfing ground, some really solid holes and plenty of variety. Aside from trees, the odd back tee and changes to the bunkering, this charming parkland layout remains very much as Strong and Way first conceived it and is a real American sleeper.

Sand Ridge Golf Club

COURSE OPENED 1998
DESIGNER Tom Fazio
GOLF DIGEST 60, GOLF MAGAZINE NR

Located near the small town of Chardon, 30 miles east of Cleveland, the Sand Ridge Golf Club was founded by the chairman of a large industrial sand company, who employed Tom Fazio to build him a course right beside his main Ohio quarry. Although the 370-acre property made available for the layout was relatively flat and infertile, it did include a large, attractive wetland area and Fazio was given the freedom to use as much of the neighboring sand as required to build his golf holes.

Routing his front nine through the site's mature hardwoods, Fazio then arranged his more open back nine in a large loop around the protected wetlands. The abundant available sand allowed him to ensure the highest possible turf standards and to shape and create hazards and fairway contours as desired. Some of the better holes include the twin-target 5th and the eye-catching par three 8th, played across a pond and into an angled green. The 11th and 13th are both strong and well-conceived par fours and the finishing stretch, which most directly incorporates the wetlands, provides a spectacular end to the round. Bending left around a lake, the mid-length 16th is a clever hole that offers multiple options of attack, while the 17th is a long but appealing one-shot hole that plays across part of the marsh.

Unfortunately, the rest of the course is fairly uninspiring. Most of the shaping is well handled, but a number of holes are unnecessarily overbunkered and the continual use of gently crested fairways does tend to get a little repetitive. In 2006, the Sand Ridge Golf Club merged with the older Mayfield Country Club, and while the amalgamated entity now has access to two very pleasant courses, neither is a genuine Top 100 candidate.

OPPOSITE The 16th hole at Tom Fazio's pristine Sand Ridge golf course

Milwaukee Country Club

COURSE OPENED 1928
DESIGNER Charles H. Alison with Harry S. Colt
GOLF DIGEST 48, GOLF MAGAZINE 73

From humble beginnings on a six-hole course on the East Side of Milwaukee, the Milwaukee Country Club developed into the state's most prestigious private club when it moved to its present home north of the city in 1910. Set on the upper Milwaukee River, its first 18-hole layout was designed primarily by committee members but was redesigned by Walter Travis when an additional 77 acres of land were purchased. Opening in 1926, the Travis course was not well received, and the very next year Charles Alison was employed to build it again.

Alison convinced the club to acquire an additional 10-acre parcel of land beyond the river, which enabled him to devise an entirely new routing. Noted for its flowing doglegs and strategic greens and bunkers, the new layout was an instant hit and extended across, and briefly along, the Milwaukee River. Better holes include those on the back nine around the river, the one-shot 8th, with its small, pushed-up target surrounded by sand, and the driveable par four 9th, played uphill toward a brilliant green built on a ledge with a cruel false front. The closing set is also very strong, the 16th is a great par four that heads over a slight crest and then into a green cleverly bunkered to deceive approaching golfers. The 18th is an outstanding uphill finishing hole featuring a tiered target that is not visible if you drive too safely down the right side.

Alison's design at Milwaukee remained largely intact until Robert Trent Jones lengthened the course and removed a number of his fairway bunkers during a 1974 modification program. He also rebuilt the cross-river par three 12th. Arthur Hills later redesigned the 3rd and 14th holes, but the club is currently working on a program to return much of the course back to what Alison had intended. There is no doubt that properly restored this course would improve greatly.

Flint Hills National Golf Club

COURSE OPENED 1997
DESIGNER Tom Fazio
GOLF DIGEST 49, GOLF MAGAZINE NR

Frustrated by the quality of golf around the Wichita area, businessman Thomas Devlin decided to build his own high-end private golf club and scoured the outskirts of the city in a helicopter looking for prospective sites. Outside Andover, he discovered a 640-acre tract of land that had natural ponds and wetlands, established foliage and some decent elevation changes. The picturesque site was ideal, and once acquired he employed architect Tom Fazio to design his golf course.

Despite the holes requiring little earth moving, Flint Hills National cost $18 million to build, as some of the wetland areas were expanded and Devlin insisted upon the finest playing surfaces. The tees and fairways were sodded with zoysia grass, the large greens seeded with bentgrass and a bluegrass mix was used for the roughs. Aesthetically the course is first rate. The shaping is also good and the holes structurally quite sound, but those familiar with Fazio's work may be disappointed to find little new or interesting to digest. There are also some frustrations with the green shaping, as putting contours at times appear contrived to make certain pin locations inaccessible rather than to fit with the strategy of the hole.

The best stretch of golf comes late in the round, from the par four 15th, which is a terrific hole into a wide green that has a central hump helping to direct good shots to either left or right flag locations. The 16th is another strong two-shotter, while the 17th is a pretty par three that heads toward a lake. The par five 18th then sets up like a Cape hole around the lake, but the green is placed beyond water, sand and a large cottonwood tree that blocks the direct route for most golfers and makes it a definite three-shotter. Earlier, the 10th is a pretty par three played directly over murky wetlands, while the short par four 6th cleverly has its landing area shaped toward the green to encourage an aggressive play from the tee.

Kept in fantastic condition, exclusive and with all the peripheral trimmings that ranking panels seem to demand, Flint Hills National is a nice golf course and an obvious candidate for the Top 100, though it's a long way from Fazio's best.

OPPOSITE **The par three 10th hole at Flint Hills National in Kansas**

Sycamore Hills Golf Club

COURSE OPENED 1989
DESIGNER Jack Nicklaus
GOLF DIGEST 92, GOLF MAGAZINE NR

Opening in 1989, the Sycamore Hills golf course was designed by Jack Nicklaus as part of a residential development on the western outskirts of Fort Wayne, Indiana. Building on a large rural estate, Nicklaus fortunately had enough space to keep home sites mostly away from the golf and was further blessed with a fabulous collection of mature sycamore, oak and spruce trees and a naturally twisting river that ran through the property.

Water is a dominant feature throughout the course, with several large lakes and a number of holes routed along or across the river. The designer further protected par by building small, undulating greens that are often shallow, set across play and fronted by hazards that force golfers into an aerial approach route. The best holes tend to be the strong par fours, starting with the strategic 6th, which crosses water twice and features a clever green site that favors aggressive drivers. On the back nine, quality fours include the tight 10th and the 16th, which bends into a raised green set beyond the river. The 18th is also good, as it first hugs the river and then heads across the hazard toward a nice target framed by flowers. Unfortunately, the par threes are fairly unremarkable while, aside from the 2nd and its central driving bunkers, the par fives are strangely bland. The doglegging 12th, for instance, is poorly conceived and a straightforward prospect for strong players able to drive across the lake and into a vast landing area. Cut by the winding river several times, the split landing area 15th is much better, although the undulating green is excessively skinny and disproportionately long. A number of other green areas are unnecessarily severe as well, such as the left side of the boomerang 17th green, which is an impossible target to aim at given a huge tree guards this side of the green.

Sycamore Hills has all the hallmarks of 1980s Nicklaus design and, despite some problem spots, is a course that has matured well over the years and provided its small membership with much enjoyment.

St. Ives Resort – Tullymore Golf Club

COURSE OPENED 2001
DESIGNER Jim Engh
GOLF DIGEST 83, GOLF MAGAZINE NR

Set within the woodlands of central Michigan's Canadian Lakes region, the Tullymore golf course is a highly unconventional public access facility designed by architect Jim Engh and part of the St. Ives Resort development.

Dotted with lakes, marsh areas and a creek that trickles across the enormous site, the artistically shaped layout has some memorable holes but is most noted for its skinny greens and curious bunkering. Buried deeply into the ground, the bunkers here are mostly flat but lined by deep, grassy fingers that jut in from the sides to obscure the view of sand. Although they look great up close and in photographs, from a distance they appear to be lush depressions, and as a result fairways and greens tend to lack definition.

Another oddity are the heroic par threes, four demanding fearsome all-carry tee shots over hazards into severe targets. The most bizarre is the 12th, especially from the back tee, where you need to drive more than 250 yards across a swamp to have any chance of reaching a hidden green that is set in a hollow and squeezed between two ridges. More noteworthy are holes like the 17th, with its concave target lined by deep traps, and the back nine par fives, which all sweep left but use hazards and narrow greens more effectively than some of the earlier holes. The reachable par four 3rd, for instance, has a tiny green that would tempt most to play an aggressive shot were it not for the tall oaks and large frontal bunker that force an awkward layback and conspire to destroy any semblance of strategy that may have existed.

With its eye-catching architecture, fine turf conditions and dazzling water carries, Tullymore is an appealing option for many golfers, and is certainly worthy of a side trip for those on their way through to Crystal Downs.

OPPOSITE The distinctive bunkering style employed by Jim Engh at Tullymore is on display here beside the 6th green

Rich Harvest Links

COURSE OPENED 1999
DESIGNER Jerry Rich
GOLF DIGEST 51, GOLF MAGAZINE NR

The most surprising inclusion on any golf course ranking list, Rich Harvest Links was created by wealthy computer entrepreneur Jerry Rich on vast farmlands he owned in Sugar Grove, west of Chicago. Apparently denied membership at the Augusta National Golf Club, Rich decided to create his own private course for friends and invited associates, designing and building three holes on his property in 1989 and extending this to 18 holes ten years later.

Although the amenities here are first-class, Rich's design and routing are poor and the construction mediocre. There is simply no logic to the sequence or arrangement of holes, while the use of nonstrategic split fairways is, at best, confusing. The course is also badly bunkered and horribly over-treed, the likes of the 3rd and 13th among the most cramped golf holes anywhere on the planet. Both turn hard left through tall oaks, meaning that even if you fluke a fairway you'll probably have to take the second shot straight over or around further trees. The 13th is so overcrowded that no grass will grow on the tees, synthetic turf being used instead. Anyone who can hit this fairway without bouncing off limbs is a seriously straight driver.

Unfortunately, these holes aren't the only black spots. Par threes at the 4th and 14th are also ordinary, while most of the longer holes are ineffective, particularly the 16th and 18th, which have two tees and two distinct fairways that just happen to meet at the same green. The par five version of the split-par 16th is an awful driving hole, the tee shot marginally more appealing from the par four tees.

For the purposes of completing *Planet Golf USA*, Rich Harvest was as important to see as Pine Valley and Cypress Point, as it helped provide the parameters within which all other golf courses in this book are assessed. The club itself is ultra-private, immaculate and surrounded by lavish facilities, yet the course would struggle to break into Illinois's Top 50 and is perhaps proof that red herrings exist on golf ranking lists.

Sanctuary Golf Course

COURSE OPENED 1997
DESIGNER Jim Engh
GOLF DIGEST 73, GOLF MAGAZINE NR

Located in the tranquil hills of Castle Pines, the Sanctuary golf course was built by the philanthropic chairman of the RE/MAX real estate company as a not-for-profit facility he would use personally but also donate regularly to charities for their fundraising events. Designed by Jim Engh, the layout occupies an elevated ridge that overlooks the snow-capped peaks of the Front Range of the Colorado Rocky Mountains.

Carving his holes through soaring pines and working hard to preserve the scenic outlooks, Engh's work at Sanctuary is dominated by some steep fairway gradients and an unusual routing that features a plethora of downhill holes but offers strangely little incentive for aggressive play. The first five holes are all downhill, as are at least six others, yet landing zones are continually pinched or cut to prevent players from hitting their driver. Falling more than 200 feet from the back tee, the par five opener sets the tone for the round, as its landing area is so tight that the hole is typically played with a couple of mid-irons followed by a wedge. More effective are the likes of the par five 4th, the only long hole to really entice a driver from the tee, and the 5th, a beautiful par three that drops around 100 feet across a forest. Horseshoeing around a huge ravine, the 12th is a little severe on the average hitter but a cool hole to play for those able to contemplate a drive toward the green.

There is certainly much to admire about the Sanctuary, but unfortunately its site is a little extreme for sensible golf, the shaping is somewhat overdone and the big risk/small reward design philosophy will frustrate those interested in more than just pleasant scenery. Although these negatives fail to detract from the honorable merits of the facility, they do prevent it from being a true top 100-caliber course.

OPPOSITE **Looking down upon the 10th green at the Sanctuary from its elevated tee, views of the Rockies in the background**

The South

OPPOSITE The notorious par three 17th hole
on the Stadium Course at TPC Sawgrass is
a genuine Southern icon that alone attracts
thousands of golfers from all over the country

The South

Augusta National

Seminole

Pinehurst

Pete Dye GC

TPC at Sawgrass

Wade Hampton

Kiawah – Ocean

Yeamans Hall

Kinloch

Long Cove

Black Diamond Ranch

The Honors

Harbour Town

Peachtree

World Woods

Dallas National

Southern Hills

Jupiter Hills

Valhalla

The Bear's Club

Calusa Pines

Holston Hills

Colonial CC

The Homestead

Ocean Forest

East Lake

Grandfather

Sea Island

Sage Valley

Hawks Ridge

Kiawah – Cassique

Briar's Creek

Shoal Creek

Trump International

E ncompassing the entire southeastern and south-central sections of the US mainland, the American South is an enormously diverse golfing region that is perhaps best known as the birthplace of legendary players like Bobby Jones, Ben Hogan, Byron Nelson and Sam Snead.

Although there is evidence of golf in Charleston and Savannah during the 1780s and '90s, the oldest continuous club in the South is Georgia's Glen Arven Country Club, which was established in 1892. Many of the subsequent pre-Depression courses were founded by wealthy northerners, as seasonal retreats that allowed them to continue with their hobby into the colder winter months. Those who weren't members of clubs could get their fix at resorts like Pinehurst, which is now the largest golfing facility in the United States, with eight courses to choose from. The resort's best-known and most revered track is Donald Ross's beloved No. 2, which he crafted from the North Carolina sandhills over a period of several decades but grassed and completed in 1935.

Ross began his design career at Pinehurst and continued to run a prolific business from there until his death in 1948. He apparently only ever solicited two design contracts during this entire period, Seminole and Augusta National. The loss of the Augusta project to Dr. Alister MacKenzie is said to have motivated him to shape Pinehurst No. 2 into the best course in the region. Whether he achieved that goal depends on your perspective. Augusta obviously has its fans, as do Seminole and some of Pete Dye's more audacious creations, such as the Stadium Course at TPC Sawgrass and those on the South Carolina holiday islands of Kiawah and Hilton Head.

Despite the presence of such outstanding golf, there are probably more underwhelming courses here than anywhere else in the nation, particularly in Florida, where a high percentage of its 1,000 plus layouts were essentially built to sell real estate. Those that are worthwhile appear to have gone to great lengths to avoid being typecast as Floridian in style, spending vast sums of money to manufacture large undulations and natural-looking water hazards. Some of the better developments not featured in this chapter include The Concession near Sarasota, The Medalist and McArthur courses in Hobe Sound and Tampa's Old Memorial. Elsewhere, Diamond Creek and Forest Creek, both designed by Tom Fazio in the Carolinas, are superior to the much-loved backup courses available at Pinehurst while MacKenzie's Palmetto Golf Club, the Chechessee Creek Club near Hilton Head and Greg Norman's TPC Sugarloaf course, northeast of Atlanta, are also very good.

OPPOSITE Pete Dye's celebrated finishing hole at Harbour Town, a popular resort course on the South Carolina island of Hilton Head

Augusta National Golf Club

COURSE OPENED 1933

DESIGNERS Dr. Alister
MacKenzie,
Robert Tyre Jones Jr.

GOLF DIGEST 3

GOLF MAGAZINE 3

"Augusta National provides shots which the greatest of all golfers has the utmost difficulty in carrying out successfully, and yet it has only twenty-two bunkers, no rough, and is a paradise for the average golfer."

DR. ALISTER MACKENZIE

OPPOSITE **Despite the fact that Augusta is totally inaccessible to average golfers, and too difficult for them anyway, a round here remains the ultimate fantasy for most of the golfing public; pictured is the green at the par five 13th**

Owner of the most revered golfing grounds in America, the Augusta National Golf Club was co-founded by the great Bobby Jones, who retired from competitive golf in 1930 with ambitions of creating a world-class course that a small group of his friends and associates could enjoy during the winter months. Along with Clifford Roberts, Jones purchased an old tree nursery in the city of Augusta and appointed Alister MacKenzie to assist him with the design of his dream layout. Full of rolling hills, creeks and a great variety of flowering plants and trees, the site was ideal for inland golf, and the pair worked closely to build a strategic masterpiece that formally opened for play in 1933.

While MacKenzie devised the routing scheme and basic outline for each of the holes, Jones spent hundreds of hours testing approach angles, putting contours and adding his own design ideas. Holes were draped naturally across the bulging slopes and the greens angled to reward accurate driving and constructed with some of the most creative internal undulations ever seen. Despite opening with no rough, few bunkers and wide-open fairways and greens, their remarkable course not only provided a stout challenge to a man of Jones's ability, but brought pleasurable enjoyment to the average club member.

The layout at Augusta is routed around its beautiful colonial clubhouse, the two nines looping out and back from the highest point on the property. The outward holes tend to be dominated by tight, unforgiving green complexes, while the more exciting back nine is noted for watery hazards that come into play on each of its par threes and fives.

There is also a pond hard against the green on the 11th, the most celebrated parkland par four in all of golf. The other truly world-class holes here are the 12th and 13th, the 12th inspired by a par three that MacKenzie's friend Harry Colt built at Stoke Poges in England, and the par five 13th bending left around a brook that famously cuts in front of its putting surface. Here the challenge is driving long and as close to the hazard as possible in order to set-up a relatively level stance and an optimum angle into a green leaning sharply toward the water.

While none of the remaining holes quite rival those around Amen Corner, the outrageously shaped putting area on the bunkerless 14th and the crowned green on the reachable par five 15th are notable for the drama they provide during the Masters. The reworked par three 16th, built by Robert Trent Jones in 1947, also seems to extract great theater, as does the monstrous par four closer, which heads through a narrow chute of trees before turning and rising steeply uphill into a tiered green. The biggest surprise for visitors used to seeing such holes on television is just how steep these elevation changes are. The drop from tee to green at the 10th, for instance, is more than 75 feet, while the climb back up the 18th fairway is almost as severe.

MacKenzie took great pride in his work at Augusta, believing it was destined to become the premier inland course in the world. He died in 1934, without having seen the finished holes and only months before the club's first invitational tournament. The following year, Jones reversed his nines and in 1937 pushed the 10th green back to its current location.

These were the first in a series of deviations from the initial plans, other modifications including the new 16th hole, the shifting of the 7th green and the doubling and tidying of the original 22 bunkers. There have also been hundreds of yards added to the layout in recent years and trees and rough grass grown to narrow the playing corridors. Modern green speeds have also had an affect on the design, the slick surfaces making high-spinning approach shots preferable to the bounce and run type these greens were constructed to accommodate.

Although it would be naive to assume that MacKenzie wouldn't have approved of any alterations to this course, there is no doubt that the loss of fairway width and general playability for the average golfer would concern him greatly. The reality, however, is that Augusta National has shifted from a members course to a tournament venue, and those who question whether the present layout would please the famous designer are overlooking the fact that his holes no longer need to accommodate a range of skill levels. They simply have to keep the world's best professionals at bay for one week a year.

OPPOSITE There are few more famous holes in golf than the short 12th at Augusta National, which MacKenzie actually modeled after a Harry Colt par three near London

Seminole Golf Club

COURSE OPENED 1929

DESIGNER Donald Ross

GOLF DIGEST 9

GOLF MAGAZINE 12

The strong, slanting par four
finishing hole, played directly along
the Atlantic dunes

OPPOSITE **Although many who visit
Seminole will miss its subtleties, the layout
remains one of America's finest from the
Golden Age; pictured is the brilliant 6th hole**

A landmark American classic, the Seminole Golf
Club was formed during the late 1920s and its golf
course designed by Donald Ross in the prime of his
extraordinary career. Set beside the Atlantic, the
land allocated to Ross for this course was unique for
this part of Florida, as it featured a small dune ridge
separating the holes from the sea as well as a larger
40-foot ridge running almost parallel through the
western part of the property. The ground between is
unremarkable, yet Ross cleverly arranged his holes
so that as many as possible could take advantage of
the main sand structures. A number of flat fairways
head up into elevated ledges, while other holes plunge
down from sandy peaks, skirt along the top of crests
or are arranged around the edge of the dunes.

Ross spent a great deal of time on site here, and
his ingenious routing system not only fully exploits
the natural terrain but also the ever-present coastal
winds by continually altering the direction of play.
Like at Pinehurst, the greens are the course's primary
defense, and most are steeply angled and generally
narrower toward the rear, meaning the farther the pin
is pushed, the tighter the actual target area becomes.
The bunkering is another key feature: The fairway
traps tend to be quite shallow, but the flashed-up
greenside bunkers are deep and punishing.

Although Seminole appears short by today's standards,
the combination of continually shifting winds and
brilliantly conceived putting areas ensures that birdie
chances are rare for those not striking precise irons.
Each of the nines begins on flat ground before heading
into the western dunes, standout early holes including
the rising par four 2nd and the magnificently bunkered

4th, which traverses the crest of the ridge and crosses
a series of deep traps strategically positioned short of
its putting surface. Even more outstanding is the mid-
length 6th, which measures less than 400 yards from the
tips and has both a generous fairway and a large green.
What makes this hole such a work of genius is the angle
of the green and the gentle left-to-right slant of the
landing zone; any drive pushed too safely away from
left-hand fairway bunkers leaves a nasty approach across
diagonal traps and into the shallowest part of the target.

The inward nine has more obvious showstoppers
as it skips between the ridges and ends along the
beachside dunes. Highlights include uphill approach
shots into the steep 11th and 14th greens, the
strategically bunkered 16th and the precise all-carry
pitch into the par four 12th, which is surrounded by
sand and noted for its tiny pinable areas. The par
threes are also first class, particularly the crosswind
17th, while the 18th is a finishing four of the highest
order, its fairway following the beach and its narrow
green leaning sharply toward a deep right bunker.

Like many clubs of this vintage, Seminole has suffered
extended periods of neglect, most notably during and
after World War II. In the 1960s, Dick Wilson was hired
to repair some of this damage and to restore the lost Ross
features. There has been much subsequent debate as to
whether he structurally rebuilt the greens and bunkers
as Ross had intended, but there is no question that
philosophically the course remained true to his strategic
principles. Without moving many driving bunkers or
adding copious back tees, the club has done well in the
ensuing years to ensure the layout has retained both
its classical appeal and modern golfing relevance.

Pinehurst Resort – No. 2 Course

COURSE OPENED 1907
DESIGNER Donald Ross

GOLF DIGEST 19
GOLF MAGAZINE 11

"I sincerely believe this course to be the fairest test of championship golf I have ever designed."

DONALD ROSS

OPPOSITE **With its cruel domed greens and deep bunkers, Pinehurst No. 2 has become the quintessential Donald Ross experience, though, in truth, it is unlike most of his other creations; pictured is the green complex at the short 15th**

An American icon, Pinehurst was created as a holiday village and winter health retreat by Massachusetts entrepreneur James Tufts, following his 1895 purchase of thousands of acres within the vast North Carolina sandhills. Capitalizing on the growing popularity of golf, he soon added a rudimentary golf course to his property and then, in 1900, appointed Scotsman Donald Ross as its head professional. For golfers, this is where the Pinehurst story really begins, as Ross remained in the village for almost half a century and not only reshaped these barren sandhills into a world-class golf destination but grew an architectural practice that was responsible for more than 400 completed projects across the country.

Since his death in 1948, volumes have been written on Ross and his influence within the US golf industry. Pivotal to the telling of every tale is Pinehurst and its legendary No. 2 Course, which he first designed in 1907 and initially built with sand greens that were flat, square and uncontoured. He then spent many years experimenting with the layout, moving greens and testing internal putting contours. It wasn't until 1935 that he completed the routing and grassed all of his greens, finally satisfied that he had a Bermuda strain capable of surviving the harsh Carolina summers.

With some exceptions, the course is laid out across fairly unremarkable terrain, but in a strange way this allowed Ross to enhance his holes by building features that he may have been reluctant to create on a more natural piece of ground. Very much a second shot course, from the tee No. 2 doesn't look or feel like one of the game's top layouts, but around the famous turtleback greens it has an unmistakable aura of greatness. Pushed up and generally falling away on all sides, what makes these targets so formidable are the small ridges, humps and crests that cut across the putting surface to make the actual target areas even tighter. The mental battle here is continually about balancing the penalty awaiting a long approach shot with the desire to hit beyond the raised frontal areas. For those conditioned to hit at pins and slightly off their game, it can seem a brutal and repetitive test, as a miss generally leaves a nasty chip or putt back up a sharp slope and onto a quick green that is tilted away from play.

Despite the fact that a few of the driving holes are a touch underwhelming, No. 2 doesn't really have any major flaws, as the distinctive targets help to rescue anything potentially uninteresting. Better holes include the mid-length 3rd, its shallow green requiring real finesse to hit and hold, and the difficult par four 5th, which climbs a ridge and then features an awesome second shot into a rising green angled across the fairway and with a narrow central pinable shelf. The next stretch is also very strong, the highlight being the approach into the 7th and the cross-valley par three 9th, with its elevated target split by a pronounced tier. On the back nine, clever mid-length par fours like the 12th and 13th are

outstanding, as are the two par threes, the short 15th defended by the smallest green on the course and the beautifully bunkered 17th by an angled target that narrows the farther back the pin is pushed. Following this gem is a classic closing four, the hole leaning and turning a little to the right and featuring a green site with a clever diagonal swale and plenty of sharply breaking putts.

Although there have been few structural alterations made since Ross's passing, whether today's course would totally please him is unclear, as some significant aesthetic changes have taken place over the years. Most notable has been the grassing over of his bunker lips and the sad loss of native sandy roughs along the sides of fairways. There is also a strong suggestion that, owing to topdressing during those earlier decades, the distinctive dome-shaped greens are more pronounced than Ross had intended. It is also important to note that the putting surfaces were first converted to bentgrass in the early 1970s, and that Ross certainly never designed them with modern green speeds in mind.

These points aside, Pinehurst was one of the pioneers of early American golf and the success of its No. 2 course, as well as the story of its revered creator, are inextricably linked. Although Ross was the man who put the resort on the golfing map, without Pinehurst we may never have seen his eye for design materialize into architectural genius.

ABOVE The contour and angle of the green site are what make the strong 5th hole one of Ross's finest par fours

OPPOSITE Shrouded in pine shadows, this picture captures the imposing target at the par three 17th hole

Pete Dye Golf Club

COURSE OPENED 1995
DESIGNER Pete Dye

GOLF DIGEST 99
GOLF MAGAZINE NR

"It is eighteen of the most exciting and memorable holes that I have ever built on one course."

PETE DYE

OPPOSITE **The 18th hole at Pete Dye bends around the river and features this sunken target, which is hidden from most approaching golfers**

OVERLEAF **The boldly shaped par four 10th hole**

Named in honor of its iconic creator, the Pete Dye Golf Club is built upon an abandoned 500-acre coal quarry northeast of Clarksburg, West Virginia. The club was founded by a mining family which employed Dye to shape their coal-scarred landscape into a quality high-end golf establishment. Course works began in 1978, but delays and disagreements meant the full 18-hole layout was not completed until 1995.

Set down within a dramatic tree-lined basin, the property itself features remnants of the mines as well as several deep pit lakes and a river that winds its way across the site. Although built to modern specifications, in a way this is a throwback to Dye's earlier work, as the course has a quiet rustic elegance and its generous playing areas are full of strategic subtleties. One of the more pleasing aspects of design is the abundance of short to medium-length par fours, and the incentive they offer aggressive players to take risks. The mid-length 3rd, for instance, is wide enough to encourage driver from the tee, but the green is so devilishly contoured that a three-quarter pitch from an awkward angle can be next to impossible.

Making full use of the river and the site's best undulations, the outward nine is studded with fascinating golf holes and some rather unconventional design. The 1st tee gets the golfing juices flowing immediately, its split-tier fairway snaking toward a partly obscured green and featuring a tempting lower level that bold golfers looking to make a fast start can attack. The par four 2nd then heads obliquely across the river, its fairway running alongside the water as it approaches a severe green benched between bunkers and deep collection areas. The other strong par four on this side is the 9th, built with a central fairway bunker that splits its landing area and creates a tight right corridor for those after the best angle into the green. Following the river and gradually rising toward a target built atop an elevated bluff, the long 5th is another cool hole that seems to draw the golfer closer to trouble, as does the uphill 6th, a cunning short par four that follows a small creek. Here the driver zone does feel quite narrow, but the rewards for a strong tee shot are substantial, as laying back leaves a tricky uphill pitch that is difficult to judge correctly.

By contrast, the back nine begins and ends with wonderful cross-river par fours, but in between the golf is more open and less naturally dramatic. Notable holes include the shortish par five 15th, which bends around a lake, and the long, falling par three 16th. The audaciously shaped putting surface on the extreme 17th is also memorable. The undoubted standout, however, is the 18th, a mighty finishing four that heads along the water toward a green pressed against a fortified riverbank and partially hidden by large fairway contours.

Although some of the shaping at the Pete Dye Golf Club is a little overdone, Dye worked wonders on this property and did well to blend the softer, strategic holes with his more outrageous creations. A fitting tribute to a legendary architect, this memorable course can be both charming and cruel, lucid and at times difficult to completely understand—much like the designer himself.

TPC Sawgrass – Stadium Course

COURSE OPENED 1981

DESIGNER Pete Dye

GOLF DIGEST 79

GOLF MAGAZINE 33

The ultimate "signature"
Sawgrass's par three 17th hole

OPPOSITE Precision from the tee and
with your pitch shot are both essential
to make par on the dangerous 4th hole

The Tournament Players Club at Sawgrass was the brainchild of former PGA Tour commissioner Deane Beman, whose idea was to build a stadium-style course for the tour's annual Players Championship. In 1978, he purchased 415 acres of swampland in Ponte Vedra Beach for a single dollar and instructed Pete Dye to design him a tournament layout. Flat, sludgy and covered in dense palmetto scrub, the site was far from ideal for golf, but Dye created an appropriately demanding test by digging a series of deep lakes and using the fill to create mounding for the spectators and more intricate playing contours for the golfers. Interestingly, his original plan for the 17th included only a small pond, but sand was discovered around the green and the excavated area grew. Eventually the pit became enormous, and Dye's wife suggested the hole become an island par three. The rest, as they say, is history.

The Stadium Course at Sawgrass opened in time for the 1982 Players Championship, but dissatisfaction from the professionals forced Dye to soften a number of holes and make a series of other changes over the following years. Despite its teething problems, the layout eventually became widely accepted within the industry and was one of the most influential courses of the 1980s.

Aside from a number of wonderful holes, there is a tremendous balance to the routing here, as hole lengths vary and direction and doglegs change continuously. Dye also worked hard on angles of play, shaping holes to present golfers with clear strategic choices both from the tee and into the greens. Despite the target-style nature of the test, most greens are open at the front, so if in control of your golf swing and thinking clearly, it is possible to avoid disaster and post a respectable score. There is no let-up for poor play, however, as penalty areas are severe—a mix of traditional sand bunkers, grassy depressions, moguls, thick rough and water.

Surprisingly subtle in places, Sawgrass is a beautifully built course with narrow fairways and small, contoured putting surfaces. The round opens with a really tight driving hole, its angled green a particularly harsh target for those unable to hit close to a large fairway bunker. The next gem is the short 4th, featuring a daunting cross-water pitch into a gorgeous green breaking sharply off its safer right side. A number of par fives also feature cool shots into difficult greens. The 9th, 11th and 16th are all cleverly designed to ensure that only precise lay-ups can prevent complicated pitch shots. The 11th is split by a lake and a long waste bunker that forces golfers to choose either a tight left shot over water or a tight right shot close to water. The 9th turns left near the target and features a narrow landing zone for the second shot and a tiny green guarded by tall trees and sand. The 16th is then a classic gambling hole turning around pines and running against a lake, conservative player's needing to hit their second shot near water or risk being blocked by a large tree for their third.

The next is, of course, an American legend. Suspended on a bulkheaded podium in the middle

of a lake, the hole is one of the most significant par threes in golf and works largely because the green contours make the target appear smaller than it really is. Most will use a 9-iron or wedge here, so unless presented in tournament condition, you have to hit a pretty poor shot to find the water. The genius, if you like, of the hole is its location near the end of the round, golfers stand on the tee knowing that one bad swing can spoil their entire day. The 18th is another signature hole, this time bending left around the largest lake on the property and wonderfully shaped to somehow draw your eye closer to the hazard. The hole is brutal on those unable to hug the lake, as bailing away leaves you with a nasty second shot into a green angled toward the water.

The Stadium Course has become a modern icon, thanks largely to the infamy of these cruel finishing holes. Its success, and the explosion of copycat courses, has made it increasingly difficult to make such holes interesting, yet these have somehow retained their sense of fun and originality. Despite the fact that it was built for the best players in the world, thousands of golfers flock to Sawgrass every year to be beaten up by a ruthless and penal adversary which must surely rank among the most outstanding versions of this much-loved golfing genre.

ABOVE The dilemma for most golfers at the 11th is whether to lay-up short of the lake, or try to carry the ball over the water and sand

OPPOSITE The 16th is another fun par five, though its green is an unreceptive target for those leaving their second shot too far from the water

Wade Hampton Golf Club

COURSE OPENED 1987
DESIGNER Tom Fazio

GOLF DIGEST 15
GOLF MAGAZINE 53

The short, picture postcard
17th hole

OPPOSITE The 18th at Wade Hampton
is a terrific finishing five with the ability
to continually lure aggressive players into
attempting a heroic approach

Named after a celebrated Civil War general who spent his summers in North Carolina's Blue Ridge Mountains, the Wade Hampton Golf Club was founded by William McKee, a landowner near the small town of Cashiers whose family had purchased property from the Hampton heirs during the 1920s. Surrounded by national park and dramatically framed by granite-faced mountains, the course was opened in 1987 and designed by the experienced, but at that stage relatively unheralded, architect Tom Fazio.

Set within a pair of enclosed valleys almost 3,500 feet above sea level, substantial earthworks were required to flatten fairway areas and create landing zones, but importantly Fazio was able to arrange his holes in such a manner that there is little more than 100-foot of elevation change within the entire layout. Fairways are often downhill and were carved through a magnificent collection of giant pines and deciduous hardwoods, with many holes aligned to directly face the distant peaks. A number of naturally wandering creeks and ponds were also incorporated into the routing.

The elevated opening tee provides a breathtaking view of the mountains and of the twisted valley where the first five holes are set. The rest of the course is then arranged within a larger and more expansive basin. Aside from the scenery and turf excellence, the strengths of Wade Hampton are the opening and closing stretches and picturesque par threes, like the 3rd, 6th and 17th, the first with a waterfall backdrop and the latter two dropping over streams toward gorgeous green sites.

Strangely, the central section is rather subdued. The 11th is the only ordinary par three on the course, while longer holes like the 8th and 10th tend to fight the shape of the terrain a little. Tempting length par fours like the 7th and 12th are also fairly ineffective, the 12th an attractive-looking hole but one that rises along a narrow ridge that is too steep to entice most players from using more than a 3-iron from the tee. The run home from here, however, is very good, particularly plateau green complexes at the 13th and 15th, and the long par four 16th, which bends around trees, then slowly rises into a large target bunkered strategically to reward golfers able to take the inside line with their drive. Completing a fine finishing stretch is the reachable par five 18th, which features an enticing green entrance and a trickling hazard that runs the entire left side of the hole to catch those pushing too hard for that closing eagle putt.

Greens across the course are typically quick and undulating, while the fairway landing areas are regularly framed by Fazio's bold bunkering. As befits a national club of such esteem, the grooming here is first rate, although the climate really only allows for a couple of months of firm and fast conditions. The course, however, is a visual feast year-round, but most especially during fall, when the forest comes alive with color.

Completed a couple of years prior to Shadow Creek, Wade Hampton was the course that really sent Fazio's career soaring, and he has built few better since. With its stunning scenery, great grass and beautiful holes, it is unlikely that many golfers walk away from a round here disappointed.

Kiawah Island Golf Resort – Ocean Course

COURSE OPENED 1991

DESIGNER Pete Dye

GOLF DIGEST 38

GOLF MAGAZINE 28

**Kiawah's contentious cross-pond
par three 17th hole**

OPPOSITE **The final third of the par
five 2nd hole, its green angled across
play and protected by deep bunkering**

Made famous as host of the 1991 Ryder Cup, the Ocean Course at the Kiawah Island Golf Resort was designed by Pete Dye, who overcame extraordinary obstacles to complete his masterpiece in time for the event. Occupying a narrow two-and-a-half mile slice of land between saltwater marshes and the Atlantic coastline, the layout was built in the aftermath of Hurricane Hugo, which tore apart the site's coastal dune ridge shortly after construction began. Dye was forced to recreate most of the ridge, but worse, he was also forced to forego a large chunk of prime seaside land between the two nines after a surveyor mistakenly defined the area as environmentally off limits. The error was later realized, but the course had already been completed, so this land is now used as a driving range.

Arranged in two loops on either side of this large practice area, the Ocean Course runs mostly adjacent to the shoreline but is full of variety and subtle directional shifts. The sea is a constant companion, as ten holes touch the beachside dunes while the inland fairways were slightly elevated to allow golfers full view of the ocean as they play. As the wind blows fiercely and equally out of the east and west, the holes were built with great elasticity to allow them to be stretched or shortened according to the day's conditions. They were also designed with reasonably generous landing zones, great sprawling sandy waste bunkers and large greens, their contours and adjacent chipping areas beautifully tied in with the sweep of the surrounding terrain.

Although the front nine doesn't quite match the glamour of the later coastal holes, it isn't far behind. The opening stretch, in particular, is great fun, starting with a relatively friendly par four along a waste bunker followed by a beast of a par five that doglegs twice, crosses two marsh areas and features a harrowing plateau green angled across the fairway and pinched between deep bunkers. The 3rd green is even nastier; generally approached with only a short-iron, it sits atop a steep dune and falls sharply on all sides. Other features of note include strategic fairway bunkering on the 6th and 7th, an elevated but narrowing green on the short 8th, and the contours and collection areas around the putting surface on the excellent par four 9th.

Squeezed between the shoreline and a series of wetland hazards, the back nine winds its way through the most substantial dunes on site and begins with a string of great driving holes that head out to the course's western boundary. Tempting hazards and superb approach angles are features on the 10th, 11th, 12th and the 13th—which plays across and then alongside a tidal canal and requires a brave drive for a decent shot into the open green site. The remaining holes turn and follow the Atlantic dunes back to the clubhouse. The 14th is the standout par three on the course and features a target sitting on a large shelf and sloping toward the rear, while the 15th is a tremendous two-shotter with a gorgeous green site beneath the coastal ridge. The 18th, which bends around traps toward the sea, is outstanding as well. The

only black spot on the inward nine is the 17th, a frightfully difficult all-carry par three across a pond that would fit perfectly within Dye's other Low Country courses but is sadly out of place on a beachside track of this quality.

Dye has fine-tuned the Ocean Course since its opening, adding gullies and tricky contours to a number of greens, reshaping some of the sandy wastelands into formal bunkers and, most significantly, shifting the 18th green alongside the main seaside dunes. There has also been some softening done to ensure resort guests can handle the challenge. Although it isn't quite the monster that some have made it out to be, especially with a sensible choice of tee markers, there are a couple of areas that remain a little severe on the average player. The coastal practice range and subsequent distance between the two nines are also disappointing by-products of the unfortunate surveyor blunder, but these are really the only complaints of a rare gem that thoroughly deserves its reputation as South Carolina's premier track.

ABOVE Played toward the sea and across a wasteland bunker complex, the short 5th is a nasty assignment when the wind blows

OPPOSITE Perched atop a ledge and exposed to the elements, the 14th is a gorgeous par three and the start of a strong run home back along the dunes

Yeamans Hall Club

COURSE OPENED 1925

DESIGNER Seth Raynor

GOLF DIGEST NR

GOLF MAGAZINE 60

The putting surface at the short 3rd, complete with Raynor's sinister central ridge

OPPOSITE Approaching the charming 10th green

Formed by wealthy New Yorkers as a discreet winter retreat, Yeamans Hall was built within secluded woodlands on the northern outskirts of historic Charleston, South Carolina. The 900-acre site was selected for its proximity to the railway line linking the north of America to the south, and initially the club founders planned to build two golf courses here, as well as more than 200 homes and a hotel. The first course, designed by Seth Raynor, opened in 1925, but the Depression soon slowed development and eventually left the club with just 18 holes and fewer than 40 homes spread across its enormous property.

An intensely private club, for those fortunate enough to make it through the gates the Yeamans Hall experience starts with a long and glorious drive along an unsealed entrance road. Like stepping back in time, the drive winds through an idyllic collection of mature trees before crossing the 1st fairway, directly in front of its bizarre double-plateau green. This remarkable target had actually shrunk almost in half during the decades that followed World War II, but mercifully it was rebuilt, along with the 17 others, by Tom Doak during the 1990s. Doak's team did an outstanding job returning greens to their original specifications, increasing their size and restoring Raynor's false fronts, square corners and an array of interesting putting shapes that had been flattened over the years. They also reinstated a number of lost bunkers and cleared trees to open up vistas across the course.

Bordered by a tidal marshland and laid out across a surprisingly undulating savannah, Yeamans Hall is a clever and unpretentious delight that features wide playing corridors cut through a magnificent collection of moss-draped oaks and towering pines.

Predictably, Raynor's design houses a number of famous replica holes as well as enormous green sites that are protected by some of the deepest bunkers in the South. While most targets are angled abruptly forward, a couple have unique horseshoe-shaped ridges through their middle, occasionally forcing those in bad areas to have to putt away from the hole.

Aside from an immense opening green with a five-foot false front and steep back tier, outward nine highlights include the approach across trenchlike traps into the sunken 5th green, the sharply leaning Redan 6th and large back-to-front greens at the 7th and 8th. The short 3rd is also fantastic, the hole dominated by a horseshoe depression through the middle of its green. Although hard on those caught on side flanks, Raynor gives golfers every opportunity to get their ball close to the pin here, as the putting surface is large and most will be hitting little more than an 8 or 9-iron. The back nine starts with a mid-length par four that features another fearsome target; this time the green is raised, smaller and protected by deep traps, a narrow front and a central concave ridge. The immense plateau green on the 14th is equally memorable, as is the huge, square putting surface on the Biarritz 16th and the unusual punchbowl green on the 17th.

Despite the quality of such holes and the ferocity of these individual green sites, some dismiss Yeamans Hall for its modest slope rating and lack of length—particularly bigger hitters who generally find themselves playing lots of short-iron approach shots. That said, the par of 70 here is no pushover, and when presented in firm and fast condition, the layout still manages to provide a really thorough and utterly engrossing test for any golfer.

Kinloch Golf Club

COURSE OPENED 2001
DESIGNERS Lester George,
Marvin Giles

GOLF DIGEST 29
GOLF MAGAZINE NR

The effective split-fairway
par four 2nd

OPPOSITE The wonderful
approach shot into the 16th green

Situated among the tranquil pine-covered hills of central Virginia, the Kinloch Golf Club is an exclusive high-end facility that was developed, in part, by local amateur legend Marvin "Vinny" Giles. The club is located about 20 miles northwest of Richmond on a 270-acre property that had previously been earmarked for a residential subdivision. When the developer decided to build a golf course instead, Giles became a partner in the project and, together with local architect Lester George, helped design the holes.

The layout features two distinct nines, built on either side of a 70-acre lake, the front nine occupying a series of tree-lined ridges and the back set mostly beside the water. Aside from tree and brush clearing, building the course was relatively simple as very little earth was moved and enough natural features existed for good golf. From a design perspective, the holes are well conceived, highly original and attractive to play. The only concern is the continual use of split fairways to challenge better players, at least five holes offering aggressive alternate routes from the tee. These split fairways are much more effective on the par fours, when bold drives are followed by an easier approach or a possible eagle putt, as opposed to a par five like the 9th, where jumping the first hurdle only places a second, even greater, obstacle in your way.

Although far from standouts, the early holes do provide a solid introduction to the course. Both the 2nd and 4th are dual-fairway par fours, the 2nd a well thought out longer hole where the tight drive down the left side leaves a better angle into the green, and the 4th a reachable risk/reward challenge divided by a ditch. More interesting is the mid-length 6th, its approach shot crossing a nasty ravine toward a target cut into the side of a hill. The longer 8th is also very good, the drive bending around a slight rise and the approach played from a falling lie down to a shallow green positioned diagonally beyond a pond. Ending the nine is a unique par five that heads along a small brook and then across a large ravine, its fairway cut by the first hazard and the green set high beyond the wall of the second. For those seeking birdies, the right fairway is the aggressive line, but this side is awfully tight, and even when found it still leaves a long and frightening uphill shot that needs to be shaped around a tree.

The multiroute holes on the back nine also have their issues, particularly the width of the right fairway on the 11th and the use of a tall tree to block weaker hitters on the short par four 15th. Better are the nicely shaped plateau green on the 12th and the straight lakeside par four finishing hole. The 16th is also very strong, the hole bending around the lake and boasting a dramatic approach shot played across the corner of the hazard and into a tiered green perched spectacularly atop the bluffs.

Despite its infancy, Kinloch has done well to entrench itself among the upper echelon of *Golf Digest*'s Top 100, scoring highly in the categories deemed most important by the magazine's ranking panel. The standard of turf maintenance is incredible and the holes are attractive, memorable and difficult enough to test the most accomplished players. The level of service and general club ambience is also very high, which helps explain why many now regard this as Virginia's premier golf experience.

Long Cove Club

COURSE OPENED 1981

DESIGNER Pete Dye

GOLF DIGEST 78

GOLF MAGAZINE 88

One of Pete Dye's more crazed creations, the 5th is a short four with a blind green set beyond a large mound and pushed hard against the water

OPPOSITE The par three 13th is Long Cove's signature hole, the all-carry tee shot played toward a peninsula green framed by a coastal inlet

The Long Cove Club on Hilton Head Island was developed in the early 1980s as a resident-only golf club that would be the exclusive domain of homeowners within the 630-acre development. The course was designed by Pete Dye, who built a series of distinctive lowland holes around lagoons, wetlands and through a forest of stately sentinel pines and live oaks.

Unlike nearby Harbour Town, Long Cove was not created as a championship venue and Dye's focus throughout was on the residential player rather than the Tour-caliber golfer. As a result, he made his greens more spacious and his fairways wider. He also built natural-looking bumps, humps, mounds and moguls within his fairway areas, both to add to the strategic interest of certain holes and also to disguise the flat landscape. Importantly, the shaping is rarely overdone here, the only major exception being the large ridge Dye built along the side of the 6th, 7th and 8th holes to screen the course from power lines and a nearby road.

Arranged in two clockwise loops on either side of a central clubhouse, most fairways are cut through homes and trees, though the avenues of play are much less cramped than at some equivalent developments. Built around the same time as the TPC at Sawgrass, the opening hole here is a strong par four that bends around a lake. Unlike the famous 18th at Sawgrass, however, the green is bunkered on the water side to discourage an aggressive drive close to trouble. Dye built it this way simply to make it different. The next is a pretty par three over a pond, while the 3rd is a clever three-shotter that

doglegs around water and a large waste bunker. What make this hole so effective are the believable bumps and undulations that lead toward its nasty diagonal target. By contrast, the 5th is the most obviously sculptured hole on the course, and also the most controversial. Less than 320 yards from the back tee, the fairway is set obliquely against a lake, with a large mound blocking the view of a sunken green for those unable to tightly hug the water off the tee. Most face the terrifying prospect of playing a blind pitch for their second over the hill and toward a green pressed beside the lake.

The rest of the course is less divisive and, in places, more conventional than golfers may expect from Pete Dye. The most exceptional stretch is through the middle of the back nine, which reaches an open marshland area and overlooks an attractive inlet of the Calibogue Sound. The 13th is an all-carry par three that heads across a swamp toward its peninsula green, the hole followed by a tough par four that bends left around the tidal marsh and punishes those driving away from the hazard with a long, difficult approach shot over all the trouble. The remainder of the holes head back through the trees and are also very strong, particularly the 18th with its huge contoured green sloping steeply to the front.

Long Cove is a surprisingly subtle design full of creative green sites and really fine golf holes. It marks a pleasant break from some of the more torturous resort layouts around the region and is also more playable and enjoyable than some of the beasts that Dye created during this period.

Black Diamond Ranch – Quarry Course

COURSE OPENED 1988

DESIGNER Tom Fazio

GOLF DIGEST 67

GOLF MAGAZINE 81

"Every course is special, but I guess you could say the Quarry Course was one of the milestones in my career."

TOM FAZIO

OPPOSITE **Across the abyss, the short 13th is the first of the quarry holes at Black Diamond Ranch, and a daunting challenge for most players**

OVERLEAF **Set down within the site's largest crater, the 14th is one of the most memorable par fours in the South**

Black Diamond Ranch is a remarkable 1,300-acre central Florida development located a few miles inland of the Gulf Coast and just 90 minutes north of Tampa. The brainchild of computer pioneer Stan Olsen, who discovered the disused site while on a sailing trip, the club made headlines with the 1988 opening of its Tom Fazio–designed Quarry Course, built partly around abandoned limestone quarries. Fazio later added another 27 holes, but it is unquestionably these original Quarry holes that remain the club's main attraction.

Despite the presence of hundreds of home sites, golf has been the primary focus here from the outset, and Fazio was given his pick of the best available land for the first course. Determined to build something memorable and unique to this part of America, the land chosen included softly rolling pastureland as well as the elevated quarry areas, which were integrated into a dramatic five-hole stretch through the back nine. Routed across, along and then down into the two large quarries, these holes are incredibly exciting, yet what makes this course so impressive is the quality of golf away from these rocky hazards.

Full of ideal elevation changes, the lower land is uncommonly attractive for Florida and dotted with majestic trees and a mix of native vegetation. The design throughout this section of the course is also surprisingly subtle, holes incorporating sprawling sand traps, well-shaped green complexes and strategically positioned live oaks. Better holes include the split fairway 2nd and the classic par five 5th, which sweeps right and slowly rises into a small green set across the fairway and falling cruelly at the back. The 7th is another good driving hole and features a nice pitch into an elevated green, while the last half of the uphill par five 9th is notable for a shallow target best approached from a small right area protected by large cross-bunkers.

The back nine begins with excellent approach shots into the 10th and 11th, though the preceding holes are all soon forgotten for the sheer exhilaration of standing on the 13th tee and staring out over the corner of an enormous pit that must be carried in order to reach a distant green site. The next three holes occupy an even larger and more abrupt quarry. The par five 14th horseshoes along its rim, narrowing as it falls and approaches a green benched into the cliff. Skirting along the opposite clifftop, the 16th is a spectacularly difficult hole that is unfortunately a tad narrow, but sandwiched between is a wonderful short par four that drops dramatically into the quarry and runs alongside a crystal clear lake. The final quarry hole is the 17th, a long par three plunging back across the initial crater toward a nasty green set at the base of a rock wall.

The Quarry is clearly one of Tom Fazio's best design efforts and probably his most exciting course to play. Although the glorious quarry holes will dominate your memory of Black Diamond Ranch, it is the quality of the overall design and the balance between severe and sensible golf that makes this a landmark track in Florida and such a special treat for those lucky enough to play here.

The Honors Course

COURSE OPENED 1983

DESIGNER Pete Dye

GOLF DIGEST 35

GOLF MAGAZINE 65

Looking back down the fairway
from the green at the par five 2nd

OPPOSITE Among the most popular holes
at the Honors is the mid-length 9th, its
green pushed against a pond and hidden
to those bailing right from the tee

Created to honor and preserve the traditions and spirit of the amateur game, the Honors Course was founded by Coca-Cola bottling magnate Jack Lupton, a member at Augusta National and friend of the late Bobby Jones. Lupton had acquired land in a secluded wooded valley to the east of Chattanooga and employed Pete Dye to build him a championship-caliber golf course. Dye at the time was shaping some of his wildest modern creations, yet he was instructed to design this track in line with the traditions of early 20th century architecture.

With a spacious landscape and plenty of appealing ground movement, the layout was built with minimal disruption to the natural terrain, save for an irrigation lake through the middle of the property and some rather extreme shaping around the greens. Holes are generally cut through an attractive collection of oak, ash, dogwood, hickory, persimmon and willow trees with a superb variety of unkempt native grasses helping to provide contrast and define the playing areas.

Designed to challenge the game's great amateurs, the Honors is one of the more demanding layouts in the region, particularly since recent lengthening has stretched the back tees beyond 7,300 yards. Although the entire course is a strong and consistent test of your game, the front nine shades the back slightly in terms of the individual quality of its holes. The heavily contoured par three 3rd is the first significant test, followed by a pair of strong two-shotters that bend in opposite directions, the 4th with a lovely raised false front green and the 5th with a severe target area strategically angled to favor those able to hug the dogleg from the tee. The talking point on this side,

however, is the mid-length 9th, which features a narrow green leaning steeply toward a pond pressed hard against its putting surface. Complicating the hole for those driving too safely down the right side is a mound that obscures the target and makes the sideslope pitch directly toward the water even more daunting.

The back nine begins with a brutal par four, which has been stretched more than 50 yards since opening and had the downhill tendency of its fairway neutralized to reduce run for bigger hitters and make it play even longer. Fortunately things ease up a little from here, with better sections including the tiny crowned 12th green, which is set on a gentle ridge beyond a series of traps, and the strategic par four 15th, which bends around the lake and features a more generous bail-out area than some may expect from Dye. The tightly treed 18th is an excellent closing hole while the short 14th, originally played over a sandy waste, is now a really pretty par three across rugged native roughs to a skinny green set beyond a deep frontal bunker.

The Honors Course has done a tremendous job establishing its championship credentials over a relatively short period. The fact that the average club golfer has little chance of ever getting through the gates is disappointing, but the club ought to be commended for focusing on the amateurs and for successfully bringing top-line golf to Tennessee. For those fortunate enough to play here the complete absence of nongolf distractions, as well as the rich textures and colors of the landscape and the sounds of a site alive with nature, combine to make it a pretty special experience.

Harbour Town Golf Links

COURSE OPENED 1969

DESIGNER Pete Dye with
Jack Nicklaus

GOLF DIGEST 93
GOLF MAGAZINE 40

The green on the 13th is
surrounded by a sea of sand

OPPOSITE Part of Harbour Town's
famous finishing run, the 17th is a
tough one-shotter played across sand
and wetlands to a small, nasty target

Situated on the secluded South Carolina island of Hilton Head, Harbour Town is significant as the venue where Jack Nicklaus got his taste for course design and where Pete Dye was first thrust into national prominence as an architect of note. The course was actually the third at the Sea Pines resort, its first designed by George Cobb in 1962. Cobb had also prepared plans for Harbour Town, but Nicklaus apparently convinced the developer to use Dye instead, offering also to make strategic suggestions of his own. Although Nicklaus made several trips to the island during construction, Dye routed the golf course and was the creative genius behind its unique architecture.

The success of the inaugural Heritage tournament, won by Arnold Palmer, helped establish the Harbour Town brand, as did the spectacular closing holes along the sea and the fact that the course was unlike anything previously seen. Dye made a conscious decision during the project to move away from the popular Robert Trent Jones style of design in order to develop his own identity. Jones was building a course nearby and Dye wanted his to be different. He achieved this largely by building low-profile features and using railroad sleepers to shore up lagoons and define his bunkers. Significantly, he also built smaller greens that were still heavily contoured.

Despite opening with a sense of spaciousness, the course hasn't aged as well as some of Dye's other gems, primarily because the trees protecting homes now intrude farther into the fairways than is ideal. A tale of two parts, the first 16 holes are narrow and lined by pines, palmettos and giant live oaks, while the final two play alongside the marshes of the Calibogue Sound.

Mostly flat and heavily treed, the front nine builds nicely after a couple of relatively soft openers. Its better holes include the 4th, a demanding par three across a sleepered pond, and the short 9th, which features a cool approach for those able to navigate through the pines from the tee and leave themself a clear shot at the tiny kidney-shaped green. The rest is narrow and demanding, but the back nine is even more hostile, as the later holes are exposed to violent winds off the Sound. Bending left beside a lake, the long 10th is a tough start; its skinny green really needs to be approached from near the water. The 11th is then a super-tight two-shotter with a shallow target, while later in the round the 15th is a horrendously over-treed par five that demands length and accuracy from the first two shots for a clear view of a microscopic green for the third.

More enjoyable is the par four 13th, designed by Pete's wife Alice and featuring a fabulous pitch shot across a huge fortified trap. The highlight, however, is undoubtedly the closing stretch, particularly the short 17th, played directly across a tidal marsh toward the ocean, and the gorgeous par four 18th, which also crosses marshland and then follows the shoreline. The hole can be brutal on those unable to hit professional lengths—the small seaside green is a pretty unforgiving target when approached from distance.

Although some of the longer holes are now too tight for amateur players, most prominent Tour stops in the US seem to thrive on being overly difficult and Harbour Town is no exception. The island itself is one of the most enjoyable places to holiday in the American South, and this revered layout remains the best known and, for the majority, the most memorable of all the golf courses in the region.

Peachtree Golf Club

COURSE OPENED 1947
DESIGNERS Robert Trent
Jones, Robert Tyre Jones Jr.

GOLF DIGEST 87
GOLF MAGAZINE 57

"To be asked to build a golf course with Robert Tyre Jones Jr. in his hometown is an honor and responsibility."

ROBERT TRENT JONES

OPPOSITE **Peachtree is a beautiful course that was founded by Bobby Jones near his hometown of Atlanta; pictured is the view from atop the fairway on the par five 2nd, looking down toward the green**

Frustrated by crowds and the pace of play at the East Lake Golf Club, Bobby Jones and a handful of his associates decided to build their own private club within Metropolitan Atlanta. Like Augusta National, which is closed from May to October, the new Peachtree Golf Club was formed to allow them to golf in privacy and to let Mr. Jones enjoy a friendly round without spectators flocking to watch him play.

The search for appropriate ground upon which to build their new course brought the club's founders to a 250-acre parcel of woodland in an undeveloped part of town. Like Augusta, the site was a nursery and blessed with both broad golfing slopes and a stately mix of pine and hardwood. Once the land had been secured, attention turned to design, Bobby Jones this time using Robert Trent Jones as his architectural collaborator. Trent Jones was very much guided by the design principles at Augusta National and similarly had Bobby hitting hundreds of balls during construction to test playing angles and shot values. The first nine holes were opened for play in October 1947, but soon afterwards Bobby Jones became crippled by a spinal disorder. Sadly, he was never able to play his completed course.

Naturally, there is a strong Augusta influence here, and comparisons between the courses are almost unavoidable. With the sun streaming through the tall pines, the azaleas and dogwoods in full bloom and flashed-up sand bunkers dominating the flowing landscape, Peachtree has a similar aura of greatness without having quite as many knockout holes. Trent Jones's routing is most notable for the use of terrain and the number of elevated green sites and long runway teeing areas. Fairways tend to flow with the natural slopes, but have few driving bunkers, while by contrast the putting surfaces are enormous, generally steep and often entirely surrounded by trouble.

Early highlights include the wonderfully bunkered opening hole and the multiroute par five 2nd, which first heads along a rumpled shelf before dropping quickly over a creek toward a split fairway and a green guarded by a further pond. A mound within the green and the buried elephants along the 3rd fairway are further standouts. As is the par three 4th, played over a pond to an elevated but shallow green leaning sharply to the front. On the inward nine, the par five 10th falls and rises into a huge back-to-front target said to have been the largest in the USA when it was built. No less impressive, the 12th features a terrific uphill second shot into a beautiful target framed by sand, while the 15th is memorable for an approach played across a deep gully from a sidehill lie.

Although few design changes have been made since Peachtree opened, over the years the site became overplanted and as a result conditioning for a long time was scratchy. A recent restoration program has very successfully improved turf quality, particularly on the fairways, which were converted to a fine blade zoysia grass. Best of all, trees were cleared to open up vistas and restore the sense of spacious grandeur that the layout once enjoyed. Lost green areas were also restored and some back tees added, many positioned to force good players to shape tee balls around trees to keep them in play.

Though not as strategic as some other classics from this era, the fundamental design elements of the layout are sound and the setting, clubhouse and general ambience are all outstanding. Peachtree is a charming club and a round here truly is one of the genuine golfing pleasures of the South.

World Woods Golf Club – Pine Barrens Course

COURSE OPENED 1993

DESIGNER Tom Fazio

GOLF DIGEST NR

GOLF MAGAZINE 80

The last third of the tempting
par five 14th hole

OPPOSITE Tom Fazio's Pine Barrens
course at World Woods is one of the real
surprise packets of Florida golf. This picture
shows the bunkers and pine trees that need
to be avoided en route to the 18th green

The World Woods Golf Club was developed
by a Japanese corporation that purchased more
than 2,000 acres of forested land in west Florida
and commissioned Tom Fazio to build a pair of
distinctive championship-length golf courses.
Both opened in 1993, with the Pine Barrens
layout housing some of the most outstanding
design elements in the Fazio portfolio.

The native terrain here is similar to that
at Pine Valley and Fazio paid homage to the
Jersey giant with boldly undulating playing
corridors cut through swaths of pine and sand.
The design itself is daring and ambitious, but also
full of real class. Utilizing the property's natural
ground movement, Fazio mixed strategic alternate
route holes with thrilling all-carry shots into
distant target zones, generally building fairways
and greens that rest comfortably within their
surrounds. Interestingly, a number of the wider
targets are open on one side but fiercely protected
by steep banks, false fronts or deep bunkers on
the other. The Pine Barrens experience, however,
is really defined by a series of expansive sandy
hazards that dominate the pine forest setting and
make a big visual impression on the golfer.

The layout itself is arranged in two large
adjoining rectangles, with the front nine mostly
skirting the perimeter of the property and the latter
holes built through the interior. The opening is
solid but relatively subdued, things starting to get
exciting at the 4th, a heroic par five that allows the
aggressive player to blast a tee shot over a waste
bunker, leaving the elevated green well within range

but dramatically set beyond a huge frontal trap.
The 8th is also exciting, its fairway bending right
around sand that runs the length of the hole and
cuts in front of the green. The 9th is then a lovely
rolling par four with great bunkering and a fabulous
green that sits on a knob and falls away on all sides.

Full of awesome natural features and some terrific
green sites, the back nine begins with a series of
outstanding approach shots and a par five, the 14th,
noteworthy for a massive diagonal bunker that splits
the landing area for its second shot. The real stars,
however, are the 12th and 15th. The long par four
12th may be brutal on the shorter hitter, but good
players will love the challenge of an approach played
from a falling lie up over a massive bunker and into
a green placed within a natural bowl. The drive here
is actually played to a falling fairway, meaning that a
good whack from the tee can run nearer the green,
but the farther the drive, the higher the second
shot needs to fly in order to carry the sandy ridge.
The 15th is much shorter, its fairway strategically
split by an expanse of sand and its putting surface
resting within an undulating basin that is partly
hidden for those driving down the safer left plateau.

Rare for Fazio's better work, World Woods is
publicly accessible and moderately priced, but
best of all, the Pine Barrens course is fantastic
entertainment. There is no doubt that some of
the holes are overly difficult for longer markers,
but the land pitches and falls beautifully through
the pine and scrub and Fazio gets a big tick for
creating a visual feast that the vast majority who
golf here are bound to thoroughly enjoy.

Dallas National Golf Club

COURSE OPENED 2002

DESIGNER Tom Fazio

GOLF DIGEST 59

GOLF MAGAZINE NR

The par four 9th hole

OPPOSITE The 5th is a beautiful
par three that crosses one of
the property's deep ravines

Opening in 2002, the Dallas National Golf Club is a distinctive modern facility built on rocky ground less than ten miles from downtown Dallas. The steep and heavily wooded property contains almost 400 acres, but for years it had sat dormant because zoning issues prevented both mining and urban development. That was until 1999, when a local golfer, John MacDonald, purchased the land and managed to get it rezoned to allow him to develop an exclusive high-end private golf club.

Covered almost entirely in rock, the site had more than 170 feet of elevation change and essentially consisted of three large plateau areas, each split by deep, densely vegetated canyons and the occasional stream. Architect Tom Fazio was awarded the job of transforming this difficult terrain into an 18-hole layout, and his construction team spent their first 12 months crushing rock and using the debris to shape the holes. He then covered the entire course with sand prior to grassing the playing corridors. Aside from filling in part of a large ravine fronting the 18th green and building up the 14th and 16th fairways, the actual contours on the course are largely as Fazio found them. Some areas are quite steep, and things do get cramped from the 12th to the 14th, but otherwise there is a nice flow to the routing and more than enough good holes to keep most members satisfied.

Much of the course is routed atop or along the edge of the plateaus, while several holes on the back nine are cut through impressive limestone canyons. The green sites throughout the round are quite impressive, with the contoured targets generally either raised and flanked by traps or set down and open to a running approach. As one would expect from a high-end Fazio course, the turf quality is first class. The bentgrass greens are pure to putt on, while the fairways, tees and rough areas were sodded with a fine leaf zoysia grass that presents golfers with wonderful playing surfaces.

The better holes tend to be those around the broken terrain, including a couple of par threes on the front nine that either play across or slope gently toward the gullies. On the back nine, the standout hole is the dramatic 15th, a long two-shotter that first heads along and then directly across a large ravine. Away from the natural hazards, the 4th and 6th feature nice shots into slightly raised targets, while the lengthy par three 17th is an attractive hole played through exposed rock. The most strategic hole on the layout is the mid-length 7th, its open fairway dominated by a bunker down the right that leaves the best angle into a green falling sharply at the back and very tough to hold from the left side.

The landscape at Dallas National is unique, and Fazio's sensible approach to the design enabled him to extract maximum golfing enjoyment from the harsh environment. With neither ideal terrain nor suitable soil for golf, this was always going to be a difficult assignment, but he did a wonderful job creating such a good course on such unsuitable ground.

Southern Hills Country Club

COURSE OPENED 1936

DESIGNER Perry Maxwell

GOLF DIGEST 32

GOLF MAGAZINE 30

The steep, uphill approach
into the 18th green

OPPOSITE Among the sternest tests in
championship golf, the 12th at Southern
Hills is a long par four that ends with
this small, heavily protected, green site

Founded by a group of successful Tulsa businessmen amidst the gloom of the Great Depression, the Southern Hills Country Club was built on land owned by oilman Waite Phillips, who donated his 300-acre property to the club on the provision that his friend Perry Maxwell design the golf course. Maxwell, one of the most accomplished architects of the Golden Age, is said to have totally immersed himself in this project, even living in a tent on site during much of the two-year construction phase.

His layout is predominantly routed across the property's lower ground, with the clubhouse and tees on the 1st and 10th set atop a large ridge overlooking the holes below. Aside from some gentle rise and fall, the only substantial elevation is back up this main ridge into the 4th, 9th and 18th greens, which are among a group of targets renowned for their difficulty. Generally angled steeply from back to front, the putting surfaces are guarded by deep traps and particularly cruel on those leaving their balls above the hole. Although the greens are consistently menacing, driving accurately is the key to scoring well here, as rough and trees ensure that most missed fairways result in at least a bogey. The trees have unfortunately grown so much over the years that fairway target zones have shrunk substantially, meaning strategic approach shot angles are no longer as relevant as Maxwell would have intended.

Setting the tone for the challenge ahead, the round begins with a difficult stretch of narrow par fours. The opening tee shot plunges more

than 50 feet and needs to find the short grass for any chance at par, while both the 2nd and 3rd are cut by a creek and especially severe on those who take a few holes to warm up. The rest of the front nine is rock solid, but the best golf at Southern Hills comes mostly through the back half. Featuring more of the interesting ground movement, it begins with a mid-length hole that falls and bends sharply around the main ridge before rising up through trees into a tightly bunkered target. An excellent short hole at the 11th is followed by a bruising par four that demands an accurate drive and then a sidehill second shot toward a built-up green that is set beyond and beside a winding creek. The 15th and 17th are also strong par fours; each has wonderfully angled targets and would be even more outstanding with some width off the tee. As would the brutal closing hole, which rises steeply from a tight fairway toward a back-to-front green protected by deep bunkers.

Southern Hills is a fantastic establishment with terrific amenities and a strong championship history. The course itself is probably a little too demanding for the average golfer, especially as the trees intrude so far into play now that out-of-position recovery options are generally limited to a punch-out shot. The oppressive nature of the Tulsa summer humidity also makes it tough to keep the grass firm and keen, which along with intruding limbs takes ground options further out of the equation, and probably makes the lush holes feel less varied than they really are.

Jupiter Hills Club – Hills Course

COURSE OPENED 1970

DESIGNER George Fazio

GOLF DIGEST NR

GOLF MAGAZINE 93

The demanding par three 9th, played
uphill and across this yawning bunker

OPPOSITE A pre-restoration picture
of the short 11th, which drops off the
site's principal dune ridge and features
an attractive, angled green site

The Jupiter Hills Club was established in 1969
following a complicated three-way deal that involved
its founding members purchasing land for the State
of Florida in exchange for a section of scrubland at
the southern end of the Jonathan Dickinson State
Park. One of those founding members was George
Fazio, who had identified these dunes as suitable for
golf and then assembled the financiers required to
make the necessary purchases. He also designed the
club's Hills Course, which opened in 1970 but was
altered a few years later when three of its holes were
used to complete the club's second layout.

What attracted Fazio to this property, half
an hour north of Palm Beach, was a natural 60-foot
dune ridge that cuts across the site, the highest in
southern Florida. As well as the size and purity of the
sand, there was also an abundance of pine, oak and
palmetto, which helped create the ideal setting for
the style of golf desired by the membership.
Not surprisingly, the large dunes dominate the
course, particularly around its central regions, where
holes are routed into, along or beside the sandhills.
The opening hole actually dives off the ridge and
heads out toward the less impressive newer holes,
which are located down on the flatter areas. An
elevated approach into the 6th green reintroduces
golfers to the main sand structure, with the next two
holes also boasting exciting cross-valley approach
shots and raised green sites benched into the dunes.
For most, however, the outward nine highlight is the
notorious 9th, a severe uphill par three that is usually
played with a long-iron or fairway wood and heads
across a sprawling scrub bunker toward a target

perched more than 30 feet above the tee.

Aside from a couple of fairly nondescript longer
holes away from the main ridge, the back nine is
more consistently undulating and exciting. The
sweeping, sidehill 10th is a solid starting point, and
neighboring holes at the 11th and 14th are both
respectable pond par threes. The best and most
demanding golf, however, comes closer to the
finish. Both the 16th and 18th are strong par fours
with extremely steep approach shots, each rising
almost vertically across bunkered slopes and into
small greens near the top of the dunes. Sandwiched
between is a long two-shotter that tumbles down and
around this higher ground. Any golfers able to end
their day with pars on these three closing holes are
generally ecstatic.

Although George Fazio's design has remained
largely unaltered over the years, major hurricanes
at the turn of the century destroyed hundreds of
sand pines and altered the look, feel and challenge
of his holes. During 2006 his nephew Tom Fazio
was employed to restore and modernize the Hills
Course. Aside from adding 400 yards to the layout,
he tightened several target areas and exposed more
of the native wastelands. The club also reduced the
par by two shots for those playing from the back tee
markers, making it again one of the most difficult
tests in the region.

Jupiter Hills may not have the subtlety of a
Seminole, or ask the same sort of strategic questions,
but the terrain here is naturally suited to golf and
the number of exciting dune shots helps to keep it
among Florida's most popular courses.

Valhalla Golf Club

COURSE OPENED 1986

DESIGNER Jack Nicklaus

GOLF DIGEST 68

GOLF MAGAZINE NR

Located 20 miles east of downtown Louisville, Valhalla was designed by Jack Nicklaus and conceived by local business luminary Dwight Gahm, whose aim was to create a private golf club that he could develop into Kentucky's premier tournament venue. Opening in 1986, the project was surely one of Nicklaus's most challenging assignments, as not only did his client have lofty expectations but also a site hamstrung by a wide variance in terrain and large flood-prone areas. Further hampering the designers were restrictions on bringing materials onto the property, which forced them to build large lakes and use this fill to create tees, fairways and greens on the low-lying areas.

Despite being relatively young, the desire to test great players under major championship conditions has forced Valhalla to go under the knife on several occasions. First there were minor adjustments and tee extensions made prior to the 1996 and 2000 PGA tournaments. Then, as Ryder Cup 2008 approached, Nicklaus and the club made more substantial alterations, including moving the 6th, 11th and 16th greens, lowering the 8th green and adding back tees and more than a dozen bunkers. Although these recent changes have unquestionably strengthened the course for the better player, they have done little to make it more enjoyable for the average member. Many of the longer holes are now more penal, while few on the course offer genuine strategic playing options. The split fairway par five 7th, for instance, is dissected by water and its main lake was enlarged to make the challenge more exciting. The hole has never really managed to find a balance between strategy and strength, however, as unless you are very accomplished, the tees you play will dictate which side of the fairway you take.

Typical of many expensive modern layouts, Valhalla is best noted for its eye-catching architecture and pristine playing conditions, with members generally hitting from perfect fairways and putting on slick, blemish-free greens often built with tiers and swales to complicate play. Devoid of natural contour and mostly set within the open floodplains, the front nine is dominated by gratuitous mounding and huge powerlines while, by contrast, the back nine is more undulating and heavily treed. Relying less on artificial shapes, it features both a well used creekside area and some steeper higher ground.

A few of the early holes are a little disappointing visually, but things pick up from the narrow par four 5th, which attractively plays through bunkers and then turns up into a tricky plateau target. The par three 8th is another decent hole, though a green with three levels and six target zones does seem a little excessive. On the inward half, better moments include an exciting second shot over a valley into the 12th, the creekside 15th green and the uphill 17th, its target surrounded by rare but effective chipping areas. The pitch into the island 13th green is also fun to play, despite the drive having zero risk-taking possibilities as anything beyond a fairway metal will leave an impossible half-punch into a green built up on rocks and surrounded by a moat.

Purchased by the PGA of America following the successful staging of its 1996 and 2000 Championships, there is no doubt that Valhalla will appeal to those who enjoy playing where the pros play. The course is a long way from Nicklaus's best, however, and is further proof that with length, green grass, space and money you can successfully turn any golf course into a championship venue.

OPPOSITE **Looking back down the 18th fairway**

The Bear's Club

COURSE OPENED 2000
DESIGNER JACK NICKLAUS
GOLF DIGEST NR, GOLF MAGAZINE NR

A gated golf community designed and partly developed by Jack Nicklaus, The Bear's Club is situated on a swampy 400-acre tract of land in the Palm Beach County town of Jupiter. Although the course opened in 2000, Nicklaus began planning this club when he first moved from Ohio to Florida during the 1970s. His aim was to build a quality golf facility, like Muirfield Village, that could be set up precisely the way he desired and shared with a small, exclusive membership.

Not surprisingly, the Nicklaus footprint is all over this property, particularly the golf course, which is carved entirely from the native terrain and nicely distanced from the surrounding housing development. The two-loop routing integrates smoothly with the natural cypress swamps, lakes and wetland areas, its fairways lined by indigenous pines and palmettos. The holes themselves are beautifully built and enhanced by flashed Sandbelt-style bunkering and tricky green complexes that generally play smaller than they appear.

Better areas on the course include the difficult starting holes, the first two with shallow targets falling away toward the rear or side wings and the 3rd bending left around a lake and into a small green hard against the water. The closing run is also very good, the 16th just one of four gorgeous short holes and the 18th a typically dramatic lakeside par five finisher that ends beneath the grand Tuscan-style clubhouse. For the gambling golfer, the aggressive line here is out over water to a peninsula green jutting into the lake. The other standout par five is the 10th, a strategic three-shot test that also runs alongside a lake, a large tier and deep bunkers defending the green for those hitting their second shots too safely away from the water.

Nicklaus set The Bear's Club up as a very private affair, and he doesn't covet publicity or attention for his club. This is a terrific golf experience, however, and he does deserve great credit and recognition for having created one of the finest golf communities anywhere in Florida.

Calusa Pines Golf Club

COURSE OPENED 2001
DESIGNERS Dana Fry, Dr. Michael Hurdzan
GOLF DIGEST 71, GOLF MAGAZINE 58

Located a few miles from Naples, Calusa Pines is a golf-only development that was named after the Calusa Indians who once lived in this part of southwest Florida. The course was designed by Dana Fry and Dr. Michael Hurdzan, who were given the task of transforming a flat and barren 550-acre property into a memorable golf experience. Pivotal to their design plan was a large central mound, almost 60 feet high, which would dominate vistas from the clubhouse and be an integral feature on several key holes.

In order to create the hill, as well as the crucial ground undulations, the team built a series of lakes, using more than a million cubic yards of fill to shape the landscape and push up their green and fairway areas. The entire site was also heavily planted with native ground vegetation as well as hundreds of mature oaks, pines and sabal palms. The design itself is pretty solid. Fairways are nicely rolling and generous, the bunkering deep and well positioned and greens are often raised and generally tie in well with all the earth moving.

Holes of note include the short 3rd, its small green protected on one side by deep bunkers and by a steep fall-off on the other, and the peninsula par three 16th, which drops off the central hill. Of the longer holes, the most interesting are those around the hill as well as the cross-lake par four 9th and the strong and open 5th, which features an elevated target guarded by sand and slopes. The shaping of the par three 11th and the approach into the left-leaning 10th also work particularly well, as does the short par four 8th, a fun gambling hole with a shallow green built into the base of a dune and protected by sand running down its entire left side. What makes the hole so effective is a small pot bunker standing short and right of the green, which aggressive drives need to flirt with in order to set up an eagle putt.

Quiet, private and with an impressive degree of maturity for a course so young, Calusa Pines is an expensive club to join but its membership is treated to some fine golf and excellent conditions year-round.

OPPOSITE **Fry and Hurdzan's bold, believable shaping at Calusa Pines, as seen from the tee at the par three 16th hole**

Holston Hills Country Club

COURSE OPENED 1927
DESIGNER Donald Ross
GOLF DIGEST NR, GOLF MAGAZINE 100

The Holston Hills Country Club was formed in 1927, and its course, one of the best-preserved Donald Ross layouts in America, was built on a rolling property east of Knoxville, Tennessee. Renowned for its deep grass-faced bunkers and steep greens, the course is mostly set beneath the site's major ridge and beautifully routed by Ross across the bumpy lower ground. Although technology has reduced the effectiveness of some driving challenges, the distinctive traps remain fraught with danger while the putting contours, which tend to follow the shape of the land, have become even more treacherous as green speeds have increased.

Each of the nines starts by falling off the main ridge, with the 9th and 18th greens then benched back into the hillside. The par threes, in particular, are outstanding, and varied as they feature a diverse collection of target areas and test a range of shots. These include a short-iron into a pimple green surrounded by sand, a cross-dam mid-iron into a hillock, a rising long-iron and finally a fairway wood at the falling 14th, its putting surface set attractively at the base of a hill. Other notable areas include the Cape-style 2nd, the valley approach into the 3rd green, the skyline pitch shot into the 6th and the split high road/low road par five 7th. The 5th is another excellent three-shotter, played across relatively flat ground but with a series of superbly positioned bunkers to negotiate. Perhaps even more interesting is the 15th, which is cut by mounds from the tee but features a stunning second shot into an elevated green complex protected by humps, traps and a substantial back-to-front tilt.

Although the closing stretch may seem a little soft, it completes a wonderful examination of your game and manages to offer incentives to shoot for birdies with the appropriate risks of ending in deep trouble. As with many well-kept classics of this vintage, scratch golfers may find Holston Hills simple from the tee, but it remains a terrific second shot course with players needing to balance the desire for uphill putts with the need to continually hit beyond the cruel false fronts.

Colonial Country Club – Fort Worth

COURSE OPENED 1936
DESIGNERS John Bredemus, Perry Maxwell
GOLF DIGEST 80, GOLF MAGAZINE 67

Made famous by the exploits of member Ben Hogan, the Colonial Country Club in Fort Worth was founded by Marvin Leonard, who built the club primarily because he wanted to experiment with bentgrass greens in Texas. Frustrated by the coarse Bermuda greens at his home club, Leonard purchased a flat tract of land beside the Trinity River and asked both John Bredemus and Perry Maxwell to advise him on the layout. Each was apparently asked to submit a number of alternate plans, with Leonard using his favorite elements from the various proposals to create his course.

The collated layout is classically understated and remains challenging despite being cramped and of only modest length. Driving is demanding, as the fairways are tightly lined by trees, while the greens are compact, quick and tend to lean sharply forward and feature side areas that reject balls and make the targets feel even smaller. The bunkering is also formidable, the traps generally deep and pressed hard up against the greens.

Interestingly, technology has actually made some of the dogleg holes here more difficult, as they tend to bend quickly and you really need to shape the ball to keep it in play. Hogan once remarked that "a straight ball will get you in more trouble at Colonial than any course I know," and modern professionals used to smashing their drivers dead straight are likely to hit more layback shots from the tee and therefore longer irons into the greens. A classic example is the brutal par four 5th. The final in a trio of holes labeled the Horrible Horseshoe, it bends around the river through tall timber, and unless you can hit a precise power fade you run the risk of either slicing into the hazard or running through the fairway and into a ditch. Strategic doglegs such as the 3rd and 9th are a little more playable, while the closing holes and back nine cross-pond par threes are also very good.

The modern golfer probably expects more than the Colonial Country Club delivers, but Hogan loved this course and it continues to favor the good strikers who can shape the golf ball both ways and consistently hit the small target areas in regulation.

OPPOSITE **Approaching the par four 2nd at the Colonial Country Club in Fort Worth**

The Homestead – Cascades Course

COURSE OPENED 1924
DESIGNER William S. Flynn
GOLF DIGEST 97, GOLF MAGAZINE 61

Surrounded by the Allegheny Mountains of western Virginia, The Homestead is a historic luxury resort located in the delightful spa town of Hot Springs, the birthplace of golfing immortal Sam Snead. The town's first course dates to the 1890s, but its best was designed for the resort by William Flynn in 1924.

Known as Cascades, the layout is wedged in a narrow, sloping valley between large mountains and, despite substantial earthworks being required to make the playing areas level, appears cut directly from its natural surroundings. Flynn's use of the undulating terrain is very impressive, as are his softly contoured green sites, which often break the opposite way to how they appear to lean.

To squeeze 18 holes onto this slender property, Flynn had to build three of his opening holes higher into the hills, on the other side of a busy entrance road. Though this steeper ground is reasonably well used, the best golf is found down on the main property and mostly through the middle of the round. Front nine standouts include the huge par five 5th, which crosses the shoulder of a large hill and has three distinct landing areas, and the rising, sidehill 7th. The best on the back are the cross-pond par three 18th and the unique par four 10th, which falls twice along a staggered fairway shelf. The two-shot 12th is another terrific hole, this time set in an attractive vale alongside the creek. As with many holes here, internal tree growth and the addition of cart paths have somewhat damaged Flynn's design intent, his fairway initially set hard against the creek but now unfortunately separated from the water.

Although a distance behind his finest creations, Flynn's course at Cascades has long been a popular summer stop for holidaying golfers, and the layout will hold particular appeal for those who enjoy playing in such picturesque surrounds.

Ocean Forest Golf Club

COURSE OPENED 1995
DESIGNER Rees Jones with Greg Muirhead
GOLF DIGEST 75, GOLF MAGAZINE 68

A private members club built along an isolated stretch of the south Georgia shoreline, Ocean Forest was designed by Rees Jones in 1995 and is part of a prestige housing development. As its name suggests, the course is both heavily wooded and close by the Atlantic coast, but there is a distinct Low Country feel as the holes wind primarily through flat swamp ponds and saltwater marshes. Generally kept in mint condition, the course is really popular with good players, as fairways are tight, the hazards well used and the small greens tend to be firm and quick.

Each of the nines heads out toward the Hampton River, the front looping back inland and the back winding its way toward, and briefly along, the ocean. Better holes include the short par four opener, pinched by a small lake, the narrow but strategic 2nd hole and the par three 5th, with its attractive river backdrop. Strong fours at the 7th, 8th, 12th and 16th are also good, as are a series of dangerous par fives and cross-marsh par threes at the 15th and 17th, the latter played toward the ocean and a massive green complex surrounded by sand. Concluding a fairly stern examination is the lone beachside hole, the 18th, a rather unforgiving par four played straight along the coast.

In 2007, Rees Jones returned to Ocean Forest to give the track a major facelift, returfing his fairways with zoysia grass, clearing undergrowth to improve vistas, reshaping all his bunkers and adding a couple of hundred yards to the overall length of the course. This is now one of his more enjoyable layouts, with most of your clubs tested and the unusual mix of pines, palms, magnolia trees and live oaks creating a very pleasant environment for the game.

OPPOSITE **Despite its name, the strong par four 18th is the only real ocean hole at Ocean Forest**

East Lake Golf Club

COURSE OPENED 1913
DESIGNERS Donald Ross, Rees Jones
GOLF DIGEST 84, GOLF MAGAZINE 52

The golfing birthplace of legendary amateur Bobby Jones, East Lake was originally created as the country club branch of the Atlanta Athletic Club. It's first course, designed by Tom Bendelow, opened in 1908 but was overhauled by Donald Ross around 1913. Ross arranged his nines on either side of a large central lake and replaced Bendelow's square greens with large, elevated putting surfaces surrounded by tricky gully areas. George Cobb then made changes to the course in preparation for the 1963 Ryder Cup, but soon after the Athletic Club sold the property to developers and the course slowly began to fall into disrepair.

In 1993, with the club bankrupt and the surrounding neighborhood notorious for its high crime rate, a local business philanthropist purchased the course and employed Rees Jones to modernize the holes and rebuild the lost Ross features. It's hard to know precisely how close the current design resembles Ross's intentions, because successive clubhouse fires destroyed most of his plans. The routing appears faithful and Jones has successfully restored the green sites after Cobb had lowered them and flattened some of the more severe contours.

Visually the course is quite bland, however, and the general shaping lacks the sort of creativity one would expect from a quality Ross design. The standout hole is undoubtedly the par three 6th, with its cross-lake tee shot and famous peninsula green. This green complex actually featured on the Bendelow layout, although it was the conclusion of a par five played from a different direction. Other holes lean gently toward the water, but few boast interesting ground movement or use the hazard as an integral part of design. The par five 9th does drop across part of the lake and is likeable for its staggered bunkers and tricky green. The approach across the trenchlike bunker into the 8th is also good, as is the front-to-back green on the downhill 12th hole and the run of strong long holes from the 14th to the 17th.

The turnaround at East Lake and the surrounding area over the past decade or more has been extraordinary. The course itself doesn't really reach great heights, but given the achievements of Bobby Jones, it will forever remain a venue of historical significance.

OPPOSITE **The par three 6th hole**

Grandfather Golf & Country Club

COURSE OPENED 1968
DESIGNER Ellis Maples
GOLF DIGEST 65, GOLF MAGAZINE NR

Situated in the shadows of Grandfather Mountain, one of the highest peaks in North Carolina's Blue Ridge Mountain Range, the Grandfather Golf & Country Club was formed during the 1960s as a private establishment where members could enjoy a range of recreational activities in a scenic and family-friendly environment. From the outset this included golf, and Ellis Maples, who had once worked with Donald Ross, was employed to design the club a championship-quality layout.

Attractively set in a valley between two large mountain ridges, the Maples course is carved through dense forest with its holes generally isolated from one another. This special feeling of seclusion is further enhanced by a series of natural creeks trickling through the site and across several fairways. Although a number of the earlier crossings are not integral to the strategy of the hole, the water is a particularly well-used hazard on the back nine, most notably on the impressive par four 15th. Here a creek pinches the landing area for those hitting a driver from the tee, while the approach is played across a diagonal stream and into a plateau target that falls away on three sides. Other holes of note include the par five 11th, with its large valley fairway and plateau green, the elevated par three 12th and the strong two-shot 18th, which ends with a green cut into the club's 35-acre lake. Hitting toward a distant summit, the par five 6th also features a nicely raised target, while the Ross-like 17th green is notable for its width, angle and the manner in which bunkers are cut into the sides.

With a number of appealing holes pointing toward the impressive peaks and ridges, this is a lovely setting for golf, although the layout itself is clearly a step down in class from the other highly rated courses in the Carolinas.

Sea Island Golf Club – Seaside Course

COURSE OPENED 1999
DESIGNERS Tom Fazio, Harry S. Colt, Charles H. Alison
GOLF DIGEST NR, GOLF MAGAZINE 83

Sea Island is a luxury resort destination located on the Georgia coast, at the southern end of St. Simons Island. Golf at the resort dates back to the 1927 opening of a nine-hole Walter Travis course, which was followed in 1928 by an additional nine holes by English architects Harry Colt and Charles Alison. The resort later added two further nines, but it was not until the 1990s that any attempt was made to tie the four separate courses together into two full-length and cohesive layouts.

Rees Jones was hired to rework the inland holes into the Plantation Course and Tom Fazio was given the plum job of upgrading the coastal Colt/Alison holes and rearranging another nine into a "new" 18-hole Seaside layout. Fazio and his team worked first on the nature of the test, removing hundreds of trees to create a windswept feel and building small dunes and exposed sandy wastes to give the course a more rugged appearance. They also rebuilt tees, fairways, bunkers and greens. While the site is essentially flat, the holes cut attractively through tidal marsh areas and, on the back nine, briefly skirt the Intracoastal Waterway that flows from Boston to Key West.

Although the back nine retains much of the original Colt/Alison routing, particularly from the 10th to the 13th, the front nine was radically changed. Fazio built a number of strong holes like the 4th and 5th, which bend almost 90 degrees around wetlands, but generally struggled to find a strategic balance between testing long hitters and keeping angles relevant for the average golfer. Bigger hitters on the 8th and 15th, for instance, have an easy carry over sand into wide areas, but shorter players are offered little inducement to flirt with danger. The design on several other holes encourages play away from fairway hazards. This is definitely not the case on the 13th, an original Colt/Alison gem that plays obliquely across and then along a marshland and rewards an aggressive drive close to trouble with a superior angle of approach.

This is a beautiful setting for a golf course and the resort itself is rather special, but the flat terrain and lack of interesting architecture is likely to leave connoisseurs a little unimpressed.

OPPOSITE **View from the 10th tee on the Seaside Course at Sea Island**

Sage Valley Golf Club

COURSE OPENED 2001
DESIGNER Tom Fazio
GOLF DIGEST 91, GOLF MAGAZINE NR

Located less than 20 miles northeast of Augusta, the Tom Fazio–designed Sage Valley Golf Club was founded by real estate developer Weldon Wyatt and unashamedly built in the mold of Augusta National. The club is set within an undulating forest of longleaf pines, the 500-acre site originally owned by a timber company which also sold Wyatt an additional 1,000 acres to act as a buffer zone and ensure the facility remains totally secluded.

Despite having a large lake and enough elevation change for interesting golf, this was an expensive course to build, as Fazio transplanted hundreds of fully grown trees, planted azaleas and other flowering shrubs and installed the latest air-circulation system beneath each green to ensure perfect year-round conditioning. As consultant architect at Augusta National, Fazio has a great feel for the aesthetic characteristics that make that particular property so beautiful, and his landscaping work at Sage Valley is of the highest order.

Flowing naturally through the tall pines, the course features generous fairways, quick, sloping greens and attractive bunker shapes that are often used more to frame the hole than to present strategic issues. Although none of the holes could be accurately described as poor or uninteresting, only a few really get the golfing juices flowing. The opening stretch is where most can be found. The 1st is an exciting starter that falls substantially to the fairway below, while the 2nd is a gorgeous par three dropping across part of the main lake to a stunning peninsula green framed by some of Fazio's transplanted pines. The 3rd is then a fine driving hole that doglegs left around the lake. The second shot down to the 5th green, the tempting short par four 6th and gently rising closing hole are among the other noteworthy moments.

Despite lacking the really distinctive and exciting golf holes that you find at the truly great venues, Sage Valley is a solid layout and superior to most of the other modern Augusta clones in the South.

Hawks Ridge Golf Club

COURSE OPENED 1999
DESIGNER Bob Cupp
GOLF DIGEST 100, GOLF MAGAZINE NR

Developed by a couple of business associates, Hawks Ridge is a luxurious golf and residential community built within a 550-acre forest of pine and hardwood in the northern outskirts of Atlanta. Inspired by Augusta National, the course was designed by Bob Cupp, who was only selected as the architect after submitting more than 20 alternate ways to route the layout across the heavily undulating site.

His final routing headed into some of the site's steeper areas and incorporated a small existing lake as well as a larger man-made body of water. Despite similarities with the vegetation, the course is worlds away from Augusta as the terrain in parts is either too steep for sensible golf or has been totally overshaped to remove much of the inherent golfing interest. The 18th is the worst example of excessive shaping. From a massive mound, the hole horseshoes along the main lake with a long carry needed to reach the fairway but few subsequent options for those unable to blast their second straight into the waterside green.

On the positive side, there are a number of attractive holes, including the 2nd, which doglegs along a stream, and the beautiful par three 3rd, which heads across part of a lake. The driveable 6th is also appealing, the hole plunging 75 feet over a creek to a shallow target that will excite and entice the bombers but offer little interest for the rest. The par five 7th will also frustrate the average hitter, as a creek cuts the fairway and forces most to lay back from the tee. The last half of the hole rises up through tall pines and is quite good, as is the strong sidehill par four 9th.

Hawks Ridge has managed to squeeze into *Golf Digest*'s Top 100 and is maintained to an immaculate degree, which helps explain its attraction to certain course raters. For those who believe great grass doesn't necessarily equal great golf, however, it probably stands out as further validation of their viewpoint.

OPPOSITE Looking across the 2nd green at the impossibly immaculate Hawks Ridge golf course

Kiawah Island Club – Cassique Course

COURSE OPENED 2000
DESIGNER Tom Watson with Charlie Arrington
GOLF DIGEST 98, GOLF MAGAZINE NR

The Kiawah Island Club was established as a private facility for property owners on the increasingly popular South Carolina resort island. The club's first golf course opened in 1995 and its second, which is actually located just off Kiawah Island, was completed in 2000. Named Cassique after an Indian chief who once hunted the region, the course occupies agricultural ground alongside the coastal marshes and was designed by Tom Watson, with help from Charlie Arrington.

Built to resemble the links of Great Britain, the course features small pot bunkers and large flowing green sites, but the designers chose to overwhelm Cassique's relatively soft landscape by adding abundant mounding in an effort to create a more dramatic experience. Unfortunately, the shaping is totally unnatural and overdone, but worse most of the holes lack genuine strategic value. The opening stretch is quite decent, but problems start at the split-route 4th, where golfers either take the upper fairway followed by a downhill Dell par three or head down the lower road and then play an uphill par three into the alternate 4th green. The next, a Klondyke-style par five with its green hidden beyond a bunkered ridge, is slightly better but things quickly deteriorate from here. Aside from a decent approach into the 14th green, the back nine has little to recommend it and is punctuated by some awkward architecture on decent coastal land. Holes such as the 15th and 17th touch the tidal marshlands, but each is pinched so tightly that tactical options are extinguished for most players.

With a decent piece of land and an apparently generous budget, the focus on mounding at Cassique seems misguided. The gentle fairway contours also strongly contrast with the heavier peripheral shapes, which only makes the actual holes even more disappointing. Aside from the magnificent manor-style clubhouse, there really is little to recommend here.

The Golf Club at Briar's Creek

COURSE OPENED 2001
DESIGNER Rees Jones
GOLF DIGEST NR, GOLF MAGAZINE 90

Twenty miles southwest of Charleston, South Carolina, the Golf Club at Briar's Creek is an upmarket development built across a 900-acre Low Country landscape covered in enchanting live oaks and an array of unspoilt wetland areas. The golf course was designed by Rees Jones, who was handed the prime terrain and able to make use of pristine saltwater marshes, meandering estuaries and a series of lagoons for his layout.

Largely routed between Briar's Creek and a lake that separates most of the home sites from the golf, the course lacks interesting golf topography, but Jones gave his holes character by sculpting large greens and sprawling bunker shapes. He also built mounding down the sides of fairways, which unfortunately does tend to get a little repetitive. The opening tee shot is a nice introduction to the site, but sets the strategic tone for the round to follow as rightside traps are made redundant by a wide fairway and a green angled to be approached from the left. Interestingly, the next three greens also slope from back right to front left, with other greens angled in a similar way and generally protected by frontal traps cut into their higher side.

The most memorable holes here are those that incorporate a vast tidal marshland. The mid-length 9th, for instance, horseshoes right around the marsh, while the 18th is an all-or-nothing par five that dramatically bends the other way as it nears the green. Most daunting, however, is the 17th, a long, all-carry par three across the quagmire to a small green cruelly falling at the back. Also noteworthy are holes like the 3rd and 14th, which cross swamps and then bend along the hazards.

The entire Briar's Creek facility is extremely impressive, the developer taking a sympathetic approach to the subdivision and preserving as much of the site's great natural beauty as possible. Although it unfortunately doesn't quite boast the quality or originality of the region's best, the layout itself is beautifully maintained and full of solid golf holes.

OPPOSITE The green site on the
par three 2nd hole at Briar's Creek

Shoal Creek

COURSE OPENED 1977
DESIGNER Jack Nicklaus
GOLF DIGEST 50, GOLF MAGAZINE NR

A private invitation-only club located in the picturesque Dunnavant Valley, south of Birmingham, Shoal Creek was opened in 1977 and found infamy when it hosted a controversial PGA Championship in 1990. Beautifully set within view of the Double Oak Mountain, the layout was designed by Jack Nicklaus and has a pleasant sense of seclusion as it is well removed from outside disturbances and the holes are cut through established oak, birch and pine trees that stretch high into the Alabama skies.

Blending attractive foliage with a meandering creek and several ponds, the holes are well routed across the site and the design is noted for its modern length, fast, sloping greens and narrow fairways. Although none of the holes are genuine world-beaters, most are soundly conceived and fun to play. The strategic 15th is a particular favorite, the approach crossing a deep gully and the green angled to leave those driving safely down the right with a very difficult shot. Other notable holes include the par five 6th, which is twice cut by a diagonal creek, and falling cross-water par threes at the 5th and 8th. The severely contoured green on the 4th is also very good, as is the approach into the raised 2nd green, the pitch into the 17th and the strong hillside par three 13th.

Home to one of Nicklaus's most understated layouts, Shoal Creek is a fine club that provides its membership with terrific facilities and a well-cared-for golf course in a peaceful setting. While some of its driving zones have become a little dated by technology, the layout remains a strict test of your game and can easily be tournament readied by speeding greens and growing roughs. Once ranked among the Top 50 courses in the world by *GOLF Magazine*, Shoal Creek doesn't really belong in such exalted company, but it does stand out in quality-starved Alabama.

Trump International Golf Club

COURSE OPENED 1999
DESIGNER Jim Fazio
GOLF DIGEST NR, GOLF MAGAZINE 71

Situated atop an old garbage dump, the Trump International Golf Club was developed by real estate tycoon Donald Trump and its course designed by architect Jim Fazio, apparently in association with his famous client. The club cost a fortune to build, as the amenities are lavish and Fazio moved 3 million cubic yards of earth to transform the flat site into a golfing oasis. Much of the work involved digging deep lakes and using the fill to create mounds; one pile rises almost 60 feet and was once the highest point in the West Palm Beach area.

Squeezed along an arterial road, the layout does get a little cramped in places, though the use of vegetation and heavy shaping has made it feel more spacious. Most of the visuals are dominated by either lakes or mounding, but unfortunately the shaping is fairly unnatural, while few of the water holes offer any real strategic merit. The huge multimillion dollar waterfall behind the par three 17th also seems a big waste of Trump's money, although the hole itself is well built and the modestly contoured peninsula green relatively effective. Other worthwhile holes include the par five 3rd, its green, wetland area and second shot options from back in the fairway all very good. As is the par five 15th, probably the best hole on the course and certainly the most interesting if long enough from the tee to have to choose between tackling the narrow chase-in green entrance or bailing right and then pitching to the target.

As one would expect from such an extravagant facility, water is in play on most holes, turf conditions are generally first-rate and the clubhouse is opulent and eye-catching. The experience itself is likely to satisfy many golfers, but it is hard to see seasoned players being overly impressed, and difficult to justify the decision of the good judges at *GOLF Magazine* to include the course within their Top 100.

OPPOSITE Looking across the 18th green at Trump International, the mega-expensive 17th hole in the background

The Northeast

Regarded by many as the birthplace of American golf, the Northeast is not only full of historical golfing institutions but is also blessed with a number of world-class modern creations. Pictured is the 18th hole at the Sebonack Golf Club on Long Island, one of those recently opened layouts that rests comfortably alongside esteemed neighbors such as Shinnecock Hills and the National Golf Links

The Northeast

Pine Valley

Shinnecock Hills

National Golf Links

Merion

Oakmont

Old Sandwich

Fishers Island

Sebonack

Winged Foot

Eastward Ho!

Friar's Head

Essex County

Somerset Hills

The Country Club

Boston GC

Myopia Hunt Club

Bethpage Black

Garden City

Plainfield

Galloway National

Quaker Ridge

Maidstone

Oak Hill

Baltusrol

Kittansett

Baltimore CC

Yale University

Hudson National

Ridgewood

Piping Rock

The Creek

Lehigh

Laurel Valley

Bayonne

Salem

Congressional

Newport CC

Trump National

While the precise origins of golf in America have been muddied over time, what remains absolutely apparent is that the most historic, interesting and consistently outstanding part of the nation's golf is in the Northeast. It was here that America's oldest clubs were established and most of its 19th century courses created. The USGA was also founded in the area, its National Open and Amateur championships inaugurated during a two-day meeting in Rhode Island in 1895.

Other watershed moments of early American golf, including Francis Ouimet's upset win at Brookline in the 1913 US Open and Bobby Jones's 1930 Grand Slam victory at Merion, took place in the region. Equally significant, for lovers of fine golf, was the arrival of Donald Ross in Boston in 1899 and the opening of the National Golf Links of America in 1909 and Pine Valley a decade later. Both courses helped raise the design bar across the country, and fueled a genuine belief that local tracks could rival the famous British links. Pine Valley's influence cannot be overstated, as it inspired prominent Philadelphia golfers such as A.W. Tillinghast, William Flynn and George Thomas to engage in the practice of golf design. Many of America's best courses were built by these Golden Age prophets who, along with Ross, Macdonald and Raynor, worked heavily in New England and across the mid-Atlantic states.

Continuing the tradition are talented modern designers like Tom Doak, Tom Fazio, Gil Hanse and the team of Bill Coore and Ben Crenshaw, each of whom is responsible for highly regarded courses reviewed within the following pages. Those who were unlucky enough to have been left out include Doak's first private course at Stonewall near Philadelphia and Coore & Crenshaw's charming efforts at Easthampton and New Jersey's Hidden Creek. Of the Golden Agers omitted, the most worthwhile include a little-known but well-preserved Donald Ross layout in upstate New York called Teugega, and his more prestigious Wannamoisett course in Rhode Island. The delightful William Flynn courses of Pennsylvania also have plenty to recommend them; each of Lancaster, Philadelphia Country Club, Huntingdon Valley, Rolling Green and Manufacturers could make a strong case for inclusion among America's Top 100. Another fascinating high-quality relic is the Ekwanok Country Club in Vermont, which has a number of terrific holes and the majority of its Walter Travis design intact.

Whether it's the ruggedness of New England, the seaside splendor of Long Island or the mighty championship tests of Westchester County, New Jersey and Philadelphia, there is more world-class golf in this small corner of the nation than virtually anywhere on earth.

OPPOSITE **Looking down the 12th fairway at Shinnecock Hills, one of the world's truly elite championship layouts**

Pine Valley Golf Club

COURSE OPENED 1919
DESIGNER George Crump
with Harry S. Colt and
others

GOLF DIGEST 1
GOLF MAGAZINE 1

The green site on Crump's
incredible 13th hole

OPPOSITE Despite only measuring
160 yards, the 10th at Pine Valley is
able to instill fear in all who play here

Recognized almost universally as the best golf course on the planet, Pine Valley is built among the sandy pinelands of southern New Jersey, about 20 miles southeast of Philadelphia. The course was founded, financed and primarily designed by hotelier George Crump, who first spotted this remarkable stretch of sand dunes while traveling by train with his golfing pals to Atlantic City. Crump purchased the land in 1912 and spent the next six years living at Pine Valley, searching for holes and scouring the site for the fairway and green locations necessary to build what he hoped would become the ultimate test of golf.

Throughout the design process, Crump consulted extensively with leading golf course architects—including Harry Colt, who had a large input into the final routing. Others, like A.W. Tillinghast, George Thomas, Charles Blair Macdonald and Walter Travis also offered their suggestions. Although he was willing to listen to other peoples' ideas, Crump had strong views on how his masterpiece should be arranged, insisting on keeping each hole isolated and ensuring the routing regularly changed direction. He also strongly believed that bad shots should be punished, and it was this philosophy that dictated much of the Pine Valley design. Sadly, Crump passed away suddenly in early 1918, with only 14 of his holes opened for play. The remaining holes, 12 through 15, were built the following year by Hugh Wilson and William Flynn, who followed his intended plans.

The most penal and visually intimidating test imaginable, Pine Valley is carved through a forest of tall pines with its playing surfaces separated from each other by vast natural expanses of sand and scrub. Though the penalties for a missed shot are severe and absolute, the landing areas from the tee are actually more generous than its fearsome reputation would suggest. There is also a great deal more variety than one might imagine, with the stronger holes offset by a diverse set of par threes and six par fours under 400 yards. With almost perfect balance, the course provides an equal test of your short, mid and long-iron ability, with half the greens demanding an aerial all-carry approach and the others open to a ball bouncing in from the front. The putting contours throughout the layout are quite breathtaking, and despite the sheer peril of missing island targets like the 7th, 8th or 10th, your recovery prospects around any of the open greens are just as dire.

Pine Valley opens with a four-hole loop on the clubhouse side of a river that cuts across the property. Following a wonderful dogleg opener comes the incredible mid-length 2nd, notorious for its daunting approach played over a huge sand hazard cut into the side of a steep ledge. Waiting atop the ledge is an enormous green full of bulging contours, the target sloping sharply to the front and with vertical ridges running through its putting surface. The next jaw-dropper is the 235-yard par three 5th, played directly across the river and into a beautiful green complex benched into a hill. This was Harry Colt's most significant contribution to the layout, as he was the one who suggested the green be pushed back into the hillside, enabling the lower loop of holes to link with those on an elevated ridge.

The remainder of the course is equally dramatic, with tee balls regularly careering across barren wastelands and approach shots played into some of the most frightening targets on earth. The most terrifying include the pushed-up par three 10th, fronted by the infamous Devil's Asshole

bunker, and the tiny pimple green on the par four 8th, which is protected by deep traps and usually approached with either a wedge or three-quarter pitch from an awkward downhill lie. It's not just the short holes that terrorize, the par fives are both genuine three-shotters and dangerous, particularly the deadly 7th, which is cut by a 100-yard long wilderness area known as Hell's Half-Acre. Perhaps the greatest hole of all is Crump's beloved 13th, one of the finest two-shot tests in golf and a hole that he discovered midway through the construction process. Following a drive played across a crested ridge, the fairway turns left around a scrubby ravine, leaving golfers with the option of either hitting directly over the hazard toward the immense target or playing more cautiously out to the open right side and trying to chip and putt for their par.

Despite its heroic qualities, the 13th is a genuine strategic test with multiple routes to the green. The same cannot be said of other holes, and for many the only lingering concerns they have with Pine Valley are the number of forced carries and the severe punishments dealt out to even the slightest mishit. What's cool about the course, however, is just how good the individual holes are and the fact that, generally, the easier the shot the bigger the penalty for a mistake. About the only unremarkable hole is the short par four 12th, which houses a fine front-to-back green site but has unfortunately lost much of its tactical appeal due to tree growth along its left side. Trees have also changed the short 17th from a split fairway par four into a hole

ABOVE View of the final two-thirds of the 7th hole; heaven help those who haven't struck their tee ball long and straight

OPPOSITE The No. 1 ranked course in America ends with one of the great finishers in golf, its green guarded by a bunkered ridge that was once an untidy wasteland

played through a single chute of pines. The other significant difference from the earliest version of the course is the reduction and tidying of some of the exposed waste areas, done primarily to aid with maintenance.

Despite these evolutionary adjustments, and a succession of high-priced, high-profile challengers, Pine Valley remains the benchmark for golf in America. The story behind its creation is one of both incredible vision and great tragedy, Crump's passion and drive to build the perfect golf course inspiring a generation of architects and changing the game in this country forever. The tragedy, of course, was that the genius behind this astonishing club never got to finish the masterpiece himself, nor experience the acclaim that its success has rightfully generated.

Shinnecock Hills Golf Club

COURSE OPENED 1931
DESIGNER William S. Flynn

GOLF DIGEST 2
GOLF MAGAZINE 5

OPPOSITE **Rising high toward Shinnecock's famous clubhouse, the par four 9th concludes an absorbing outward half of golf**

The oldest incorporated golf club in America, Shinnecock Hills was founded in 1891 by wealthy New York businessmen who were introduced to the game during a visit to France the previous year. William Vanderbilt and a group of his Long Island associates had discovered golf while staying in the resort town of Biarritz, and returned to America determined to establish a club upon the shimmering dunes of Southampton.

Laid out to the south of its elevated clubhouse, Shinnecock's first 12 holes were created by Royal Montreal professional Willie Davis but extended to 18 holes in 1895 by Biarritz designer Willie Dunn. Between the Dunn course and William Flynn's 1931 masterpiece, the Shinnecock holes were continually shifted and revised, most significantly around 1917, when Charles Blair Macdonald and Seth Raynor altered the layout to eliminate dangerous railroad crossings. Shortly afterwards, however, a decision to extend the Long Island highway through Southampton forced the club to move again. This time, Philadelphia-based architect William Flynn was hired to assist with the redesign.

Pushed entirely into the northern sandhills, the Flynn course is comprised of 12 new holes and six that were reshaped from the Macdonald/Raynor layout, most notably the controversial Redan 7th. Flynn did a marvelous job tying the existing green sites and his new design features into such an exciting and coherent creation. Flowing naturally across the rolling terrain and changing direction continually to take advantage of both the constant trade winds and the dramatic pitch and fall of the property, the routing is highly sophisticated and alwys engaging. The design is also first class, the lumpy fairways attractively lined by tall bluestem and waving fescue grasses and par defended by rugged, punishing bunker shapes and complicated green sites that are often crowned or built with a pronounced tilt.

The sense that Shinnecock is special hits the very moment you arrive here. Soaking up the historic ambience from the club's iconic Shingle clubhouse, expectant golfers look down upon a course draped beautifully across the windswept undulations of Suffolk County. The opening holes do little to dampen enthusiasm. Turning gently around deep bunkers toward a green angled cleverly to reward those who take a tight line from the tee, the 1st is a wonderfully strategic par four and just about the ideal opener for a course of such quality. The next is an awesome long par three, the tee shot played across a bunkered ridge and into a target built atop a distant plateau. Of the remaining outward holes, standouts include the multiroute par five 5th, where the harder you strive for birdie the more sand you must attack, and the steeply rising 9th, which crosses a series of ridges and leads players onto an inward nine that, hole for hole, is one of the finest in existence.

The back nine begins with a wildly undulating par four, its putting surface perched atop a precipitous ridge and either approached with a long-iron from a level lie or with a blind wedge from down in the sunken valley. Next is a short uphill par three with a small target resting cruelly on an exposed ledge and falling away sharply on all sides. Lined by tall roughs and deep traps, the 12th is a long and direct par four

that may seem relatively uncomplicated yet is proficient at exposing any weakness in your game. Another seemingly straightforward gem is the 14th, an uphill par four heading through a narrow valley toward a saddle green that is much easier to hit and hold for those able to hug the dangerous hillside on the right. Concluding the round is another perfectly balanced stretch of holes; a world-class par five at the 16th is followed by an expertly bunkered short hole and a terrific par four closer that rolls across a series of lovely ridges.

Renowned for being tough but fair, ultimately what makes Shinnecock Hills such an outstanding golf course is the absence of any pedestrian moments and the fact that so many distinguished holes dot its glorious landscape. Strangely, about the only time the layout disappoints is when set up for modern championship events, the narrowing of its fairways tending to render the strategic lines invalid and offering little chance to attack or hit fun recovery shots when out of position. For regular play, however, Shinnecock is simply superb. If it isn't the best course in America, it is certainly one of the leading contenders.

ABOVE The uphill and unforgiving 14th hole, its distant green a much more accessible target from the right side of the fairway

OPPOSITE The magnificently bunkered par five 16th hole

National Golf Links of America

COURSE OPENED 1909

DESIGNER Charles Blair Macdonald

GOLF DIGEST 13

GOLF MAGAZINE 10

View from behind the hidden Alps green, the 3rd, on C.B. Macdonald's groundbreaking National Golf Links of America layout

OPPOSITE Following a diagonal drive across the bay, comes this thrilling approach shot into the 14th green

A giant of early American golf, Charles Blair Macdonald was a pioneering player, administrator and part-time course designer who was raised in Chicago but sent to St. Andrews as a young adult to study at the local university. Mixing with legends like Tom Morris senior and junior, Macdonald quickly fell for the ancient Scottish game and soon found himself on a crusade to increase its popularity in his homeland. He designed the country's first 18-hole course in 1893 and the following year helped institute the USGA. His greatest legacy was to come years later, however, when he retired to Long Island and built the National Golf Links of America.

Macdonald starting planning the National when he moved from Chicago to New York in 1900, the idea being to create what he referred to as the ideal golf course: a seaside layout that would capture the very essence of links golf and faithfully replicate the best holes and features from abroad. After a comprehensive search for suitable ground, he purchased a 205-acre tract of swampy land close to Shinnecock Hills that skirted both Peconic and Bullhead bays and included naturally undulating areas to place his all-star holes.

Armed with sketches and maps of the notable British links, Macdonald started work on the National in 1907, routing and designing the holes himself but hiring a local surveyor named Seth Raynor to assist with their construction. Understanding the need to build a course that not only stretched the better players but also allowed the weaker hitters to get around without great distress, Macdonald devised a strategic out-and-back arrangement with generously proportioned fairways and huge putting surfaces. The playing areas are dotted with punishing bunkers yet continually offer golfers an alternate route into the immense targets. Often crowned to play much smaller than they appear, the greens are shaped with severe internal contours and, when fast, are as challenging as any on the East Coast.

The holes themselves are a mix of direct replicas and hybrids that Macdonald built by merging traditional links elements with the ground movement presented on site. Most of the really faithful replicas occur early in the round. The 2nd, for instance, is a version of the old Sahara hole from Royal St. George's and features a blind tee shot over a small hill and a green that falls away from the fairway and is hidden for those hitting too safely away from left-hand bunkers. The 3rd is a world-famous Alps hole, its drive played across a long diagonal fairway bunker and the approach over a steep hill and into a huge and heavily contoured hidden green. The other really famous copy is the par three 4th, a brilliant Redan hole with its long, angled target built atop a crest that falls naturally away to the rear.

The Short and Eden par threes are also very good, as is the Road hole green complex at the 7th and the Principal's Nose bunkers and double plateau putting surface on the par four 11th. The best of the rest, however, are Macdonald's strategic composite holes, such as the lumpy hog's-back 5th and the classic Cape-style 14th, heading diagonally across water and sand and offering players the option of shortening their approach by biting off more of the hazard from the tee. Set beneath the club's iconic windmill, the

clever punchbowl green on the 16th is
equally memorable, as are steeply pitched
targets on the 10th and 12th and the mid-
length, multiroute 17th, which falls toward the
sea and is deliciously bunkered to reward those
able to hit aggressively up the tighter left-hand
side. The round ends with a tremendous par
five that runs along the bayside bluffs, the hole
presenting golfers with loads of options and
the possibility to both gain and give strokes
back to par.

When Macdonald built the National Golf
Links of America, his ambitious aim was to
produce a layout that would rival the best
links in Britain and, by virtue of its quality,
help to elevate the game in this country to a
higher level. By any measure he succeeded
spectacularly. After running the club for
25 years, during which time he continually
lengthened and refined his holes, Macdonald
passed away in 1939, having left an indelible
mark on the industry at large and a true golfing
monument for a small group of his fortunate
members.

OPPOSITE The true scale and splendor of
the National is apparent in this image of the
15th green and 16th fairway

Merion Golf Club – East Course

COURSE OPENED 1912

DESIGNER Hugh Wilson

GOLF DIGEST 7

GOLF MAGAZINE 7

Approaching the 7th, one of Merion's marvelous short par fours

OPPOSITE **Deep bunkers and water further protect the already demanding par three 9th green**

The origins of Philadelphia's treasured Merion Golf Club date back to the 1865 formation of the Merion Cricket Club, one of America's earliest sporting organizations. Members of the cricket club, who also dabbled in tennis and bowling, built themselves a simple nine-hole golf course on leased land in 1896. The sport's popularity quickly increased and they soon decided to seek a more permanent home, establishing a committee to investigate various options and eventually purchasing a compact tract of land near Ardmore, northwest of the city. Engulfed by suburbia and split by what has become a busy avenue, the land was deemed ideal for quality golf, as one section was dominated by a dramatic old quarry while the other was cut by a series of ridges and a small winding brook.

The committee in charge of building the club's new course was headed by Hugh Wilson, a Scottish immigrant and accomplished amateur golfer. Wilson had never designed a golf course, so during construction he was sent on a half-year trip overseas to study the great British links. Although some of his design concepts were inspired by the holes he saw in Scotland and England, Wilson didn't revert to building replicas, instead creating some delightful hybrids and a number of truly outstanding originals. His course first opened for play in 1912, but he altered it considerably during the early years, adding bunkers, pushing back green sites and rerouting the 10th to 13th holes to eliminate dangerous road crossings.

What makes Merion such a magnificent golf experience is the manner in which every natural feature on the site was incorporated into the design. There is also a superb flow to the routing, with a fierce opening stretch followed by a middle section full of cunning mid-length par fours and an action-packed closing run as tough as any in the game. The greens and bunkers throughout the layout are also exceptional. The intricately contoured targets vary greatly in terms of size, slope and the nature of their settings, while the distinctive jagged-edged bunkers are steeply faced, difficult to escape and so frequently employed that they appear to catch every single errant stroke.

Despite some fantastic holes closer to the clubhouse, the heart of this course lies on the other side of Ardmore Avenue and the 11 gems arranged across the subtle slopes and ridges of the main property. The shortish par fours through the middle of the round are especially good, few offering a genuine incentive for golfers to attack from the tee but all featuring beautiful green sites and testing approach shot challenges. The pitch into the 7th green, set on a natural plateau and guarded by a huge front bunker, is a particular standout, as is the approach into the 11th, its small target pressed hard against the creek. Other world-class holes include the ridgetop par three 3rd and the mighty par four 5th, which pushes 500 yards and bends left along the brook with both its fairway and green leaning strategically toward the water. The putting contours and nasty frontal trap here are incredible, and cleverly punish those who leak their drive too far away from the hazard. The two par fives are also fantastic tests, the 2nd being a narrow uphill teaser that runs along

the road, while the 4th heads in the opposite direction and drops over the creek toward a deceptive green that appears to slant forward yet actually falls away at the rear.

The nature of the terrain changes considerably when back on the clubhouse side of the road, particularly from the par four 16th, which is the first hole to incorporate the quarry. Here the fairway is relatively flat, but the approach is a stunning shot up over the hazard and into a large green site that tumbles boldly into a front right basin. The next is a long and tightly bunkered one-shotter that plunges from the rim of the pit down into a slender green with a false front and superb internal contours. Ending the proceedings is Merion's fabulous finishing par four, made famous by Ben Hogan's 1-iron during the 1950 US Open. After driving over the quarry wall, the approach is played from an undulating fairway up into an imposing target set atop a large crowned plateau.

Hugh Wilson also designed Merion's West Course, but it's the East Course that has always been the club's crowning jewel. The layout hasn't really changed much in the years since his passing, although the fairways have narrowed and the rough has become a more prominent hazard. The holes have also continued to be stretched in an effort to thwart today's power-hitting professionals. Despite this added length, the great thing about Merion is that it still doesn't feel super-long, yet continues to provide a stern examination of all golfers and all playing abilities.

ABOVE **The dangerously bunkered green site on the par five 4th**

OPPOSITE **The awesome cross-quarry approach shot into the 16th hole at Merion**

Oakmont Country Club

COURSE OPENED 1903
DESIGNERS Henry Fownes,
William Fownes

GOLF DIGEST 5
GOLF MAGAZINE 6

William Fownes repeated his
Church Pews idea at the strong,
sidehill 15th hole

OPPOSITE One of the shortest fours at
Oakmont, the 14th is still a demanding
hole with its green site surrounded by
fescue grasses and its narrowing fairway
lined by a dozen bunkers

One of the most demanding layouts in world golf, the Oakmont Country Club was founded in 1903 by Pittsburgh industrialist Henry C. Fownes. An accomplished amateur golfer, Fownes designed the course himself on rolling pastureland he had purchased northeast of the city. Together with son William, he then spent the next 30 years refining and strengthening his holes, polishing the layout into the internationally respected jewel we see today.

Initially inspired by the open linksland of Britain, Oakmont was built to be a strong but uncomplicated course that would reward accurate hitting but punish severely those who stray. Both father and son believed that golf needed to be difficult in order to remain interesting, and were equally convinced that bunkers were the game's most appropriate hazard. Much of their work, therefore, involved adding bunkers—including the notorious Church Pews, which the younger Fownes created during the 1930s. They also built some of the finest and most treacherous green sites anywhere in golf. The quality and variety of their greens work is truly extraordinary, with the targets leaning in every direction and shaped to demand golfers attempt all manner of approach shots and from a range of different lies and angles.

Divided in two by the Pennsylvania Turnpike, Oakmont features a two-loop routing that flows beautifully across the sloping terrain in much the same manner as it did when first arranged. The holes are now longer, narrower and more heavily bunkered, but structurally it hasn't change in over a century. The difficulties here are apparent from the very outset, the opening fairway pinched uncomfortably tight by sand and noted for a semiblind approach that heads over a crest toward a fast green angled sharply away from play. Following a short uphill par four with a steep green and a stack of penal bunkers comes the world-famous 3rd, a magnificent two-shotter that climbs steadily up a small hill toward an attractive away-sloping target resting atop a plateau. The hole is, of course, best known for the Church Pews, a unique wasteland bunker divided by a series of grassy ridges that guards both the left side of this fairway and the adjacent par five 4th. These ridges were created to ensure players hitting into the enlarged trap were duly punished, and although a series of bunkers would serve the same purpose, there is no denying the aesthetic appeal of this distinctive feature.

Other great areas on the front nine include the crested par four 7th, with its strategically leaning green site forcing brave golfers to chase their ball through sand in order to get near certain hole locations. The 8th is then a classic half-par hole that pushes 300 yards from an elevated back tee, its inviting target protected by a long Sahara bunker that can either be attacked or avoided according to one's ambition. Standouts on the back nine include the horrendously tough approach into the 10th, which must be flighted perfectly as both the fairway and green fall away to the left, forcing you either to flirt with right-side bunkers or to try hitting a controlled fade from a draw lie. The front-to-back putting surface on the long par five 12th is also exceptional, while the par four 15th is rightly

celebrated for an awesome sidehill approach heading into an immense target that is angled toward an elongated bunker and full of cunning breaks. The closing stretch is also very strong, particularly the picturesque 18th with its deep fairway bunkers, softly rising approach and boldly contoured green complex.

The key difference between a course like Oakmont and other penal layouts is the variety of the Fownes' design and the number of outstanding individual holes they managed to create. Unusually for its vintage, this course was always intended to be brutal and one has to admire the club for adhering so stringently to the early design philosophies as it continues to pinch fairways, add back tees and reposition bunkers. They did famously lose their way during the 1960s, when thousands of trees were planted through the interior of the course, but thankfully these have since been removed and the vistas and open characteristics of the site restored. Although it's probably too demanding for many who aspire to play here, for skillful golfers Oakmont provides the ultimate examination of their ability to think clearly, hit accurately and putt truly.

OPPOSITE The mighty 3rd hole is dominated by the original Church Pews bunker

Old Sandwich Golf Club

COURSE OPENED 2005
DESIGNERS Bill Coore,
Ben Crenshaw

GOLF DIGEST NR
GOLF MAGAZINE 45

Pushing 240 yards, the 4th is a lovely one-shotter with a huge green full of internal movement

OPPOSITE The 15th is another of Old Sandwich's beautifully bunkered short holes

Set amongst the glorious pinehills and spacious sand dunes of eastern Massachusetts, the Old Sandwich golf course was designed by Bill Coore and Ben Crenshaw and first opened for play in 2005. Located a short drive south of Plymouth and within three miles of Cape Cod, this private members club was founded on a property seemingly destined for golf, its landscape blessed with plenty of heavy elevation change, abundant sand deposits and an attractive mix of pine, fescue and blueberry undergrowth.

Typically kept in firm condition and with genuine links characteristics, the playing corridors here are quite generous, but the designers continually force good players to flirt with danger in order to set up decent angles and approaches. Despite the ideal golfing ground, the architects deserve great credit for creating such a gripping layout and for building some of their most impressive greens and bunkers. Set on natural ledges, plateaus, within hollows or benched into the hills, the targets are generally open and often built with shaved fronts and sophisticated internal contouring. The clever chipping areas around the greens provide a comprehensive test of your ability to visualize and execute appropriate recovery shots, while the rugged bunker shapes also form a crucial part of the strategic examination and are particularly striking when cut into the scrubby dunes.

The round begins with a stroll from the rustic Shingle Style clubhouse across a lake toward the opening tee, the water sensibly omitted from the routing so as not to scar this otherwise pristine golfing environment. The holes themselves are beautifully built, and were constructed using only materials from the site. The only substantial earthworks were to a large sand hill that blocked the 1st fairway, the structure simply sliced away and its fill used to build the greens and tees. Hitting across this apparently natural sandy blowout is an early highlight, as is the hole itself, a multioption par five with a terrific green set on a subtle spur. The next gem is the 4th, the first in a set of nicely varied and attractive par threes. Measuring well over 200 yards from the back tee, the hole falls dramatically across a shallow vale and into a huge flowing green with lots of internal movement.

Other outstanding areas on the front nine include the uphill, sidehill 8th and the gently bending 7th, its green an islandlike target with rounded edges that is almost entirely surrounded by sand. The short par three 9th is another stunner, the hole completely manufactured by Coore and Crenshaw, who made the exquisitely contoured green site appear cut from the virgin terrain. The back nine is dominated by some rather bold fairway shapes and a number of spectacular targets, most notably on the twisting, tumbling par five 13th, whose green is built on a small shelf and framed by magnificent bunkers cut into the dune behind. The closing stretch is also very strong, particularly the modern par four finishing hole and par threes at the 15th and 17th, the latter rising up into a tiered ledge that

is angled toward the tee and offers little chance of recovery for those unable to hit in regulation.

While Old Sandwich has some obvious showstoppers, there is strategic interest across the layout and few areas likely to cause golfers any major concerns. The quality of its holes, as well as the club's special sense of privacy and seclusion, make the course a wonderful addition to this strong golfing region and, more significantly, help push it up among the leading few layouts anywhere by this talented design duo. It would be hard to argue that, hole for hole, Old Sandwich is in quite the same class as Sand Hills, but the greens, bunkers, routing balance and design variety are all outstanding. By any accurate measure, this fine course must be regarded as one of the best modern tracks in America.

ABOVE Approaching the islandlike putting complex on the mid-length 7th hole

OPPOSITE The 17th is the last of the glorious par threes at Old Sandwich, its green built on a ledge and leaning steeply toward the tee

Fishers Island Club

COURSE OPENED 1926

DESIGNER Seth Raynor

GOLF DIGEST 16

GOLF MAGAZINE 20

There are few par threes in the Northeast more dramatic than the 5th at Fishers Island

OPPOSITE The unconventional 9th green, with front and back tiers and a flatter central channel

A small, skinny landmass on the eastern edge of the Long Island Sound, Fishers Island is a popular summer retreat for well-to-do New Yorkers and home to one of America's most exclusive Golden Age golf courses. The origins of the course date back to 1925, when a corporation was formed to develop the eastern two-thirds of the island into a recreation and housing precinct. The Fishers Island Club was part of this development, and Seth Raynor was hired to plan its golf course. Construction began in the spring of 1925 with the official opening the following summer, only a few months after the designer's sudden passing.

Occupying a rugged and undulating headland, the Raynor layout is superbly routed in a loop along both the north and south coastlines, as well as a narrow entrance isthmus. As was his modus operandi, Raynor built replica versions of the favored holes of his mentor Charles Blair Macdonald, most blessed with uninterrupted views out toward the Connecticut shoreline. The greens in particular are exceptional, the large targets often set high on plateaus and exposed to the winds, making this a course that can play much longer and much harder than the scorecard suggests. Compounding your troubles are massive sand traps and tight, bouncy fairways lined by nasty roughs and a series of tidal ponds and marshes.

Although Fishers Island is dotted with fine golf holes, there are two stretches that provide most of the excitement. The first great run starts at the 3rd, a short uphill par four with a narrowing fairway and a steeply raised skyline green. The 4th is then a spectacular two-shotter along the sea, best remembered for a falling approach shot played into a hidden punchbowl target set against the craggy coastline.

Concluding an extraordinary seaside stretch is the 5th, a Biarritz-style par three with its tee and big, square green elevated on either side of a yawning chasm.

The next memorable run starts with a series of cruel green sites, the 8th featuring a particularly nasty Road hole–type target angled across play and the 9th a double-plateau green pushed back against the water. Continuing the theme is the short 11th, a brilliant copy of the famous Eden hole at St. Andrews. Built with a huge green set atop a knoll, par here is protected by the slope of the putting surface and some of the deepest greenside traps imaginable. The 18th is another great hole, first heading across part of the harbor and then deceptively uphill into a multitiered target protected by deep bunkers and a sharp false front. About the only slightly disappointing part of this course is the area immediately preceding this magnificent closer. Both the 15th and 17th are strangely bland holes built without driving hazards or any great interest on the green, while in between is a replica of the St. Andrews Short hole which, like the Redan 2nd, lacks the natural attributes of Raynor's best par threes.

Although these holes fail to take the shine off the experience of playing here, they do highlight the shortcomings of using a nongolf designer who never saw the original versions of the holes he copied nor any alternatives that may have been better suited to the land. That said, Raynor did a remarkable job routing this course and the quality of his work, as much as the memorable setting, make it well worthy of its lofty ranking. Despite having several courses under construction when he passed away, Fishers Island was undoubtedly Raynor's best and it remains his crowning achievement.

Sebonack Golf Club

COURSE OPENED 2006
DESIGNERS Tom Doak,
Jack Nicklaus

GOLF DIGEST NR
GOLF MAGAZINE 76

The long, downhill par three 4th

OPPOSITE Rising toward the Sebonack clubhouse, the 3rd is a strong four with plenty of sand and a steep green site

The 2006 opening of Southampton's Sebonack Golf Club was one of the most eagerly anticipated in many a decade. For a start, the course was built immediately beside the hallowed golfing ground of the National Golf Links of America, and second it was the result of a rather unlikely design collaboration between Tom Doak and Jack Nicklaus. Despite fundamental differences in their approach to golf course architecture, the pair was brought together by the club's developer, Michael Pascucci, who initially offered Nicklaus the design job but later saw Doak's effort at Pacific Dunes and decided to persuade them to work together.

Built partially atop the bluffs that overlook the Great Peconic Bay, the Sebonack site was first considered for golf back in 1906, when it was part of a larger estate that Charles Blair Macdonald was inspecting for his golfing monument. Macdonald eventually bypassed the land in favor of neighboring links ground that ran alongside Bullhead Bay. Interestingly, his club again passed on the property several years later, when it was offered as a gift from one of its founding members. When Pascucci purchased the site in 2001 it was much as Macdonald had left it, heavily treed but with an ideal sandy base and an abundance of raw golf undulation hidden beneath the brush.

Given the nature of the land and its proximity to some of the world's greatest golf, both designers poured a great deal of time and energy into this course, working hard to ensure it would stand comfortably alongside its esteemed neighbors. The routing of the layout was crucial to its success, and

it was Doak who came up with the final plan, setting the holes partly within a sloping inland forest and partly atop an elevated bayside ledge. He also had a major influence on the look and feel of the course, particularly the manner in which the undulating fairways, free-flowing tees, lumpy greens and shaggy bunkers blend with the native terrain. This was a genuine collaboration, however, and thanks to the Nicklaus team the holes are longer and the wild green complexes smaller than on other Doak courses, making the test a little more challenging for accomplished players.

Throughout the round there are a number of world-class moments, including the short par four opening hole and the majestic three-shot closer, which occupy the open dune ground and rather unconventionally head toward the same area. Enhanced by classically handsome bunker shapes, the 2nd is another fantastic hole, its tee shot played through a pair of stately elm trees and its approach uphill into a nasty pimple green that features a large frontal hump to torment golfers taking the aerial route. The 3rd green is again elevated and equally severe on those unable to throw their ball beyond its steep false front. Most of the remaining holes are among the forested section, with outward half highlights including the downhill par three 4th and the driveable 5th and par five 9th, both of which are cleverly bunkered to entice bigger hitters to attack.

The final nine is even more impressive and starts with a couple of exciting par fours, the 10th rising into a tightly contoured green atop a ridge and the 11th falling across a crest and then staring straight

down toward the bay. Also enjoying a superb water backdrop, the par three 12th is another great hole, with its small putting surface set attractively on a natural spur. Other highpoints include the finishing work on the 14th and the greenside shaping on the par five 15th, its cascading target cut into a shallow dune and framed by sprawling sand traps. Hopping along the shoreline, the 18th completes a terrific collection of long holes and provides a fitting end to a magnificent day's golf. Aside from uninterrupted views across the bay, the hole is noted for beautiful bunkers that pinch its landing zones and a fascinating green site built with a sunken front section, an upper tier and a cool central ridge.

Although there are a couple of uncomfortable areas here and a few fairway traps that seem out of sync with the general design principles, the compromises made by Doak and Nicklaus on this course fail to take the shine off the overall quality of its holes. Sebonack may not have turned out precisely how either would have wanted, but this is a wonderful layout that is sure to improve as it matures over the years. Whether it was an astute decision to bring such divergent design ideas together on this project will ultimately depend on how many golfers pay the club's astronomical initiation fees.

ABOVE The final nine at Sebonack begins with this well-bunkered par four, which leads golfers back toward the forested area

OPPOSITE The 18th is a fine three-shot test played right along the Southampton shoreline

Winged Foot Golf Club – East & West Courses

COURSES OPENED 1923

DESIGNER Albert W. Tillinghast

GOLF DIGEST West 8, East 43
GOLF MAGAZINE West 13, East 38

Tillinghast's expertly bunkered par three 10th hole on the West Course

OPPOSITE The 9th West which, like the 18th hole, heads back toward Winged Foot's grand clubhouse

The origins of the Winged Foot Golf Club date to 1920, when a group of keen golfers from the New York Athletic Club decided to build a golf course among the green, fertile pastures of Westchester County. Their search for suitable land brought them to the town of Mamaroneck and an elevated 280-acre property close to the established Quaker Ridge course. Following its acquisition A.W. Tillinghast, who was already prolific in the region, was appointed as golf architect and instructed to design 36 championship standard holes. Work started in 1922, with both the East and West courses opening for play the following year.

Despite occupying one of the highest points in the area, the topography at Winged Foot is actually quite flat. Tillinghast did well to incorporate some subtle ground movement into his design, but what makes these holes special is the creativity he displayed around the green sites. The core challenge across both layouts is provided by vividly bunkered targets that are generally pitched steeply from back-to-front and complicated by side wings, ridges and false fronts. As modern putting speeds have increased, these contours have become even more severe, and perhaps more fiendish than Tillinghast could have envisaged.

Longer, tighter, harder and more dramatic, the West Course is the club's centerpiece and provides a comprehensive test of every facet of your game. Built on either side of the final eight holes on the East Course, its two nines are littered with long, skinny par fours, exacting par threes and tempting par fives that are really only scoring holes

for long hitters who are able to keep their ball in play. Rather than easing gently into the round, the West Course opens with a rigorous stretch of holes that are as dangerous as any on the course. Aside from a number of cleverly canted green complexes, highlights of the opening nine include the gorgeously bunkered par five 9th and the short two-shot 6th, with its tiny green tucked beyond a deep bunker and easier to hit the farther and more aggressively you can drive.

On the back nine, holes within the undulating western section, such as the 14th and 15th, are outstanding, as is the par three 10th, its broad green leaning toward the tee but with heavy sand on either side and some torturous putting contours. The closing holes are also superb and particularly brutal in tournament play, when the narrow 16th is converted into a par four and the final two greens are rock hard and fast. Favoring a different shape of shot from the tee, both the 17th and 18th have slender fairways and incredibly unforgiving greens, the home hole noted for an astoundingly difficult target built into a rise and with a big false front, deep swale and steep slopes off its back and sides.

By contrast, the golf on the East Course is slightly less intense, primarily because it is shorter, more open and some of the original green slopes have been softened over the years. There are still a number of flowing and intricately shaped target areas, such as the 9th, 10th and 14th, as well as several that are abruptly angled and built atop small plateaus or steep knolls. The finishing stretch is particularly impressive, as are the early holes east

of the clubhouse, which are routed across the most diverse territory on the site.

Despite superficial changes in presentation and general appearance, a look at an aerial image of Winged Foot from 1925 shows that, aside from back tees and the odd shifted bunker, structurally both layouts have been remarkably well preserved. The biggest concern is how trees have started to cramp the West Course, limbs occasionally obstructing an interesting design feature or even a direct route to the green. The putting surface on the 2nd, for example, features a marvelous back right shelf, which was clearly designed to be difficult to access after right-sided drives but is now completely blocked by trees and inaccessible for anyone not bombing long down the left.

The other concern with the modern setup of the West Course is the proliferation of back tees, which were considered essential to combat technology but jut so far into preceding fairways that they compromise any sense of intimacy or flow within the routing. These problems aside, Winged Foot remains one of the foremost championship venues in America, and for most golfers a round on either of its courses will be the experience of a lifetime.

OPPOSITE One of the most dangerous greens in golf, the putting surface on 18 West features a sizeable false front and severe internal breaks

Eastward Ho! Country Club

COURSE OPENED 1924

DESIGNER Herbert Fowler

GOLF DIGEST NR

GOLF MAGAZINE NR

"I am quite certain that this course will compare favorably with the leading courses in the United Kingdom and will be second to none of them."

HERBERT FOWLER

OPPOSITE **Perfect view of the 6th green at Eastward Ho! and the club's picturesque Cape Cod setting**

Originally founded as the Chatham Country Club, Eastward Ho! is a unique Golden Age golf course situated on a narrow and bumpy Cape Cod peninsula known as Nickerson's Neck, which eats into the waters of Pleasant Bay. The club was established in 1922 by a group of Bostonians who hired Herbert Fowler to build them a traditional links-style layout they could enjoy during their summer vacations. Fowler, who had previously revised England's oldest links at Westward Ho!, arranged his holes in a large figure eight on either side of a central clubhouse, the opening nine stretching east toward the ocean and the back nine looping west along the shores of the bay.

Fowler's course was completed in 1924 and is a true minimalist masterpiece, with the heaving ground undulations left untouched and the layout uncluttered by excessive bunkering or unnecessarily extravagant putting shapes. There are few level lies anywhere on the property and even fewer commonplace golf holes, starting with a par four opener that rises across twisted ridges toward a green built into a distant hill. The view from atop this green out over much of the outward half is quite spectacular. As are the two short par fours that follow and the stunning one-shot 4th, with its green resting atop a small, bunkerless knoll.

Even more memorable is the 420-yard journey along the par four 6th, this adventurous hole heading across the brow of one hill toward a seaside target carved into the top of another. Here, strong and straight drives are pushed toward the steeply banked green site, while those leaking to the right are kicked into a sunken valley, leaving an approach shot that is both longer and blind across another large mound. The short, rising 7th and mid-length 8th are also terrific, but the remaining front nine highlight is unquestionably the par four 9th, which tiptoes precariously along a narrowing ridge. Again the advantage for an accurate drive is enormous, as the putting surface falls sharply on both sides and approaching from a sidehill lie in the rough is fraught with danger.

On the back nine, the ridges are generally less irregular and the contours slightly smaller than on the front side. The exception is the 18th, a magnificent two-shot test that crashes wildly into a distant valley before climbing straight uphill into a crowned target falling cruelly at the front and rear. Equally unforgettable are bold roller coaster fairways at the 11th and 12th, both with small plateau greens that are blind for those unable to hit their earlier shots beyond the farthest ridge. The par threes are also outstanding, the long 10th with a green tucked beside a small hill and the shorter 15th with its triple-tiered green virtually pressed against the shoreline.

Despite great satisfaction with the current setup, Eastward Ho! did suffer a long period of neglect when the club allowed trees to propagate heavily across its windswept

slopes. Thankfully, since the start of the century, thousands have been removed, the transformation back to its raw, virgin state even more drastic than what occurred at Oakmont. Not only are the fairways and greens once again exposed to the region's shifting winds, but the sweeping vistas and turf conditions have also improved tremendously.

Aside from its general lack of recognition, what's most remarkable about this course is the dizzying scale of the property and the sheer number of fantastic holes it has. Unfortunately for golfers worldwide, developers don't build courses like this anymore, and more's the pity, for Eastward Ho! is one of the most enjoyable layouts to play anywhere in America and its uncomplicated quality should remind us all of the pleasures of golfing on naturally suitable ground. Unlike many modern courses, where you walk off the 18th and seek immediate refuge from the torture, here you are likely to start longing for another game the moment the round has ended.

ABOVE **Your round at Eastward Ho! starts with this steeply climbing mid-length opener**

OPPOSITE **It ends here – at the strong and undulating par four 18th**

Friar's Head

COURSE OPENED 2002
DESIGNERS Bill Coore,
Ben Crenshaw

GOLF DIGEST NR
GOLF MAGAZINE 22

Surrounded by sand, the par three 10th features one of the largest greens in the US

OPPOSITE Looking across the 9th green and back up the fairway toward the main dune ridge at Friar's Head

Situated among the pristine parabolic dunes of Baiting Hollow, on the North Shore of Long Island, Friar's Head is an exclusive golf-only establishment that was designed by the acclaimed architectural team of Bill Coore and Ben Crenshaw. Fresh from the astonishing success of Sand Hills, Coore and Crenshaw were first introduced to this 300-acre plus property in 1997 and immediately recognized the opportunity it afforded them to create another modern golfing masterpiece. After many months spent considering various routings, and a two-year construction period, the course opened for play in 2002.

Unlike those endless rolling sand hills in Nebraska, this particular site featured both heaving dunes and a flatter tract of farming ground. Finding a way to link these contrasting landforms together was crucial to the course's success. With great skill, the design team was able to devise a routing scheme that switches effortlessly between the sand and softer ground, with minimal earthworks required to build the holes and, importantly, short walks between greens and tees. What gives the layout such an appealing, coherent feel is the strategic nature of the design and the bold jagged-edged bunkers, which are especially impressive when collapsing into the native sand. The green sites are also a key design feature, the greens varying greatly in the nature of their contours and the size of the putting area, from tiny postage stamps at the 16th and 17th to the half-acre target at the 10th.

For a visiting golfer, your first look at this

course is almost overwhelming. The sight of glorious white sand, giant dune ridges and distant sea views all greet you from the clubhouse and whet the appetite for the day's golf ahead. Although much of the course is then arranged across the flatter lowlands, Coore and Crenshaw's construction team was able to shape these areas so well that they almost match the golf available on the more dramatic terrain. The fairway bunkering on the longer transitional holes is particularly effective. As are the creative green complexes through the early stages of the back nine, such as the split-level target at the flat par five 11th, with its sunken back bowl.

Golf at Friar's Head is all about the sand, however, and it's the holes routed around the property's most dominant ridge that steal most of the headlines. The opening hole is quite an introduction, the mid-length par four cut by sandy scrub and rising sharply into a blind putting surface that rests atop a 40-foot hill. The adjacent 9th is equally eye-catching as it tumbles down the bank and bends around a waste area toward a beautiful green site fashioned from a stretch of exposed sand. The back nine then starts with one of the most remarkable par threes in golf. Set amongst the dunes, the hole measures anything from 130 to 230 yards, depending on tee location and where the flag is located on the enormous, partly hidden green.

Unquestionably the most outstanding section of the course, however, is the run home, starting with the brilliant par five 14th. Rising slowly

through immense forested dunes, the hole is technically reachable in two shots but the putting surface is raised, heavily contoured and tucked dangerously beneath giant converging sand ridges. The next is equally spectacular. From an elevated tee, this long par four turns through a natural valley before rising into a cool plateau green. Perched precariously above a deep hollow, the smaller tabletop green on the undulating 16th is another great target, as is the thumbnail-size green on the treacherous par three 17th, which is benched into a ridge and totally exposed to the elements. Like at Sand Hills, the round ends with a gorgeous short hole followed by a strong two-shotter, here the 18th fairway bends around the shoulder of a large hill before rolling up into a steeply pitched target positioned beneath the imposing clubhouse.

Although the entire layout here is first class, the wild dune holes are simply breathtaking and the final five are as dramatic as any on the American East Coast. Coore and Crenshaw have built an awesome reputation over the past decade and Friar's Head is further proof of both their talent for working with great golf land, but more importantly of their ability to shape disparate landforms into an exciting and cohesive golfing experience.

ABOVE Native grasses and jagged bunkers enhance lowland holes like the par three 12th

OPPOSITE The finishing stretch at Friar's Head is world-class, and includes the dramatic par four 15th

Essex County Club

COURSE OPENED 1917

DESIGNER Donald Ross

GOLF DIGEST NR

GOLF MAGAZINE NR

Crashing down from atop one hill
and around a couple of others, the
18th is a splendid closing par four

OPPOSITE The 9th green at Essex
is protected by deep bunkers and
natural ground contours

Established principally as a horse and leisure club, the Essex County Club was born in 1893 in the small Massachusetts town of Manchester by the Sea. The club's first course was a basic nine-holer, which was expanded to 18 in 1917 by the great Donald Ross. Ross had arrived in Boston in 1899, and although he left for Pinehurst the following year, he continued to return to New England during the summers, living at Essex for several years while he oversaw the construction of its new holes.

What makes Essex such an outstanding course is its spectacular golf topography and Ross's willingness to let the bumpy landscape dictate his design. Routing holes to make best use of the terrain, he created a unique links-style layout that mixes some dizzying undulation with an attractive mix of pine and fescue. The greens are generously proportioned but cleverly shaped to play tighter and more complicated than they appear, while the rugged bunkering complements the nature of the property and asks the appropriate range of strategic questions.

Although the inward nine boasts the most exciting land, there are blind drives, hidden greens and wild fairway contours throughout the layout. There are also a large number of clever mid-length par fours. The best two are the 2nd and the 6th, both almost driveable under favorable conditions yet built with nasty crowned greens that demand birdie seekers take an aggressive line off the tee. The other really interesting outward holes are the 8th, with its

blind split-level fairway, and the long par five 3rd, which features a unique bathtub-shaped depression in its green. This target apparently dates back to the original 1893 course and is said to be the oldest green in the country.

The fun on the back nine starts at the 10th, which plays partly across the shoulder of a hill and has plenty of fairway width but a green so steeply angled that it encourages drives out to the narrow left side. Other fine holes include the blind, tumbling 12th and the gorgeous tree-lined 13th, with its crowned target set on a ledge beneath a rocky embankment. The quartet of quirky finishing par fours are also great fun, especially the short 17th, an Alps hole that climbs more than 100 feet, and the longer 18th, which drops even farther over and then around a couple of large hills toward a small, domed green set immediately beyond a brook. The showstopper, however, is the 11th, a stunning Redan-like par three with its green sitting atop a steep plateau and guarded by a series of enormous bunkers.

Essex is a wonderful old golf club and in its rugged, natural state perhaps best reflects how the architect himself would have preferred his more famous courses remain. With the exception of his work at Pinehurst, Ross probably spent more time personally working on these holes than at any other course he designed. Despite its low profile and absence from major ranking lists, those who can tolerate the bouncy fairways, wild greens and uneven lies will rejoice at having discovered one of golf's true hidden gems.

Somerset Hills Country Club

COURSE OPENED 1918

DESIGNER Albert W. Tillinghast

GOLF DIGEST 57

GOLF MAGAZINE 49

Tillinghast's heavily fortified
18th green at Somerset Hills

OPPOSITE The 2nd is a tighter,
but equally brilliant, version of the
much-copied Redan hole

The prestigious Somerset Hills Country Club was founded in 1899, its early members golfing on a cramped nine-hole course beside the Ravine Lake in north-central New Jersey. Lacking the space required for a full 18 holes, the club soon looked to expand and in 1916 purchased a vast estate in the nearby hills of Bernardsville. A.W. Tillinghast was hired to construct their new course, building his front nine across an open, spacious field and setting the back nine among a heavily wooded area that touched a natural dam and enjoyed great elevation variances.

Somerset Hills was one of Tillinghast's earliest designs, and also one of his most creative. The course tests almost every club in your bag and offers golfers endless variety with some unusual hazard arrangements and a range of approach shot challenges. The use of droplet mounds, whether grassed over or part of a bunker complex, is particularly intriguing, as are some of the experimental putting contours, which are often difficult to decipher. A number of targets, for example, are cleverly angled one way but look as if they lean the other, while some that appear flat are actually quite steep.

Less obviously dramatic than the back nine, the front is built across a softly moving meadow that once housed a racetrack. After a strong, bending par four opening hole, the 2nd is a fearsome Redan-style par three that features a narrow putting surface set atop an exposed knob, the target sloping steeply to its back left corner. The 3rd is then an innocuous looking mid-length hole with a wide-open fairway but a treacherous green site built on a steep hill and best approached from the more dangerous left-hand side. The lovely, sweeping

approach into the crested 7th green is also very good, as is the long, one-shot 8th, played through chocolate-drop bunker mounds and into a green complete with small, random humps.

Enjoying the pick of the golf terrain, the homeward nine starts with the only hole modified significantly from the Tillinghast design, its green pushed onto a plateau and the par extended from four to five. The hole is of only moderate interest, but the rest is first-rate, starting with the fantastic par four 11th, which falls toward the lower basin area, turns around a hill and then rises into a brilliant green that tumbles sharply to the left. The next is a delicious par three with a peninsula green that extends into the dam, its putting surface leaning toward the water to ensure that golfers bailing toward dry land face a precarious recovery shot. Set atop a higher ledge, the next three holes are quality mid-length par fours with outstanding green sites. The target on the steadily rising 13th, for instance, is cut by a broad valley and features heartbreaking hole locations both within the valley and atop an upper tier.

Aside from changes to the 10th, the Somerset Hills Country Club has diligently preserved this great track and they deserve credit for resisting the urge to modify holes or soften their marvelous green shapes. At various times they have had issues with tree growth and the loss of playing areas, but in recent years a carefully supervised restoration program has successfully returned much of the layout to the original Tillinghast plan. What's cool about this course are not the things that Tillinghast experimented with here and then took onto later projects, but the unique design features that he rarely tried anywhere else.

The Country Club – Clyde/Squirrel Course

COURSE OPENED 1893

DESIGNERS Various

GOLF DIGEST 20

GOLF MAGAZINE 23

Originally established as an equestrian club by a group of blue-blooded Bostonians, The Country Club was formed in 1882 near the town of Brookline, southwest of the city. Golf was introduced to the property in 1893, with the opening of a rudimentary six-hole course built by members around the club's polo field and racetrack. With help from Scottish professional Willie Campbell, the layout grew to nine holes the following year, and by the end of the century had expanded to a full 18.

By the early 1900s, golf had become the members' principal pastime and an additional tract of land was purchased to allow the club to lengthen its layout in preparation for the rubber-cored ball. This version of the course remains in place today and is best remembered as the host venue for the historic 1913 US Open, won by a young local amateur named Francis Ouimet. In 1927, the club added a third nine by William Flynn, and in subsequent championships a composite layout was created with three and a half Flynn holes replacing three of the shorter originals. Although both Geoffrey Cornish and Rees Jones have since made alterations to these composite holes, the routing and general design style remains largely unaltered.

Nestled on about 240 acres of beautifully undulating golfing ground, the landscape in places here is reminiscent of the London heathland but with a distinct New England flavor. Across the three nines, the greens are outstanding and are so small and cleverly tilted that when playing firm, they become its primary defense. The rugged bunkering and naturally occurring fescue areas provide a brilliant contrast to the playing corridors and help further to define these wonderful targets.

What makes Brookline such great fun is the constant undulation and the fact that the routing continually alters your direction of play. The better holes tend to reside on the best bits of terrain, with the first such gem being the 3rd, a world-class par four that heads through a narrow valley and then twists around a steep, rocky ledge. For those unable to smash their drive beyond the ledge, the approach will be a long-iron or wood shot that needs to skirt past some nasty frontal traps and onto a small green that backs against a road. The next standout is the subtly bending 5th, its drive heading blind across a small hill and the approach played into a sharply angled right-to-left target. The downhill pitch into the minuscule 4th green is also fantastic, as is the par three 7th, its unique double-plateau putting surface apparently a remnant from the original 1893 course. The par five 11th (Composite 9th) is another quality hole on quality ground. Again, a large rocky ledge can be carried by the brave golfer who wants to get home in two, but this time the green sits atop a well-bunkered ridge and is much less intimidating to approach with a wedge in your hand.

The Country Club was America's first organized recreational club, and it's hard to visit Brookline and not feel nostalgic or sentimental. With its classical style of design and wonderfully unpredictable golf terrain, the course itself is truly superb, particularly when conditions are firm and fast. The fact that it doesn't bear the hallmark of a single golf architect, but is instead the product of many varied minds, makes it even more remarkable.

OPPOSITE **Posing all kinds of dilemmas both from the tee and into the green, the 3rd is unquestionably Brookline's standout hole**

Boston Golf Club

COURSE OPENED 2005
DESIGNER Gil Hanse

GOLF DIGEST NR
GOLF MAGAZINE NR

A true 300-yard teaser, the 5th hole ends with this anorexic putting target

OPPOSITE The 14th hole at Boston is a healthy par four that bends slightly right toward this well-protected green

One of the more dramatic modern courses in American golf, the private Boston Golf Club is situated south of Boston and built upon an abandoned rock quarry near the small township of Hingham, Massachusetts. Opening in 2005, the course was designed by architect Gil Hanse, who skilfully incorporated abrupt elevation changes, dense woodland and sheer rocky ledges into an attractive, traditional-style layout.

The overwhelming highlight of Hanse's work here is the believability of his shaping. The sand and gravel base made it easier for the design team to create contours that match the existing natural terrain, but the work done was first class. Fairways crash and rise with great irregularity, the holes enhanced by beautifully constructed bunkers that are often fringed by bracken or shaggy tufts of native grass. The varied and heavily contoured greens are another standout feature; the targets are generally open at the front, yet consistently more difficult to approach the safer you drive from the tee.

Arranged in two nines on either side of an arterial road, the course begins with a grueling opening stretch that includes a tough three-shotter and a couple of crafty par fours. The 3rd is especially tricky, as its ideal landing area is partly obscured and its shallow half-pipe green is angled across the fairway and placed immediately beyond a nasty gully. The next glamour holes are the 5th and 6th, the latter a superbly bunkered par three set within a shallow clearing, and the 5th a remarkable short par four housing one of the narrowest greens in the world. Protected by a gnarly waste bunker, the putting surface here is only a few paces wide and perched atop a vertical spur that falls sharply on all sides. Unless driving right up close to the sand, it is only accessible with a precisely judged bump along the ground.

From the tightest green imaginable to one of the most expansive, the next outstanding hole is the par four 12th, its impressive target straddled atop a gentle ridge and falling steeply both front and back. The par fives later in the round are also special, particularly the 15th, which rises and falls and is cleverly bunkered to make players flirt with sand along its left side or face a blind third shot across a pronounced fairway hump. Unusually, the round ends with a par three finishing hole, its attractive green resting on a ledge beneath a forested ridge.

About the only areas that don't work are long par threes over hazards, the small and awkward 13th green and the Principal's Nose bunkers on the solid 16th, the traps well built but failing to encourage aggressive play. The biggest single issue, however, is the long distance between nines and the fact that the course is unwalkable for many. Some will also be concerned with the manner in which Hanse has kept his foot on the gas from the opening hole through to the finishing green. You don't really get a breather anywhere on this layout, as disaster waits around every corner. If struggling with your game, therefore, this is not really a course that you can ever get comfortable playing.

That said, the membership here is mostly made up of accomplished golfers and the best parts of the course are truly world-class. Given its modern length and difficulty, it wouldn't surprise to see the Boston Golf Club start appearing prominently on Top 100 ranking tables in the very near future.

Myopia Hunt Club

COURSE OPENED 1896

DESIGNER Herbert Leeds

GOLF DIGEST NR

GOLF MAGAZINE 86

The short but frighteningly
difficult cross-pond 9th hole

OPPOSITE Approaching the 18th green

Supposedly founded by a group of bespectacled men from Boston, the charming Myopia Hunt Club was established as a golf, horse and hunting club in the village of South Hamilton in 1894. Designed by member Herbert Leeds, the first nine holes were opened in 1896, with the full 18 completed by 1901.

Built across a series of unspoilt hills, in the most peaceful and secluded setting imaginable, the course is dominated by a broad central ridge, with a number of holes routed up, down and across its rugged fescue-strewn slopes. This is classic turn-of-the-century New England–style golf, but although there are blind shots, hidden greens and punishing central bunkers, the shapes here are generally softer than at Brookline and Essex, meaning you are less likely to get harsh kicks and uneven lies.

Leeds spent the best part of 30 years refining Myopia, and the quality and variety of his design work is very impressive. Like Henry Fownes at Oakmont, he believed in protecting par by aggressively bunkering holes and famously used to watch good players closely and then build bunkers wherever he felt their poor shots had not been sufficiently punished. He also dug his existing traps deeper if escape became too simple and mixed irregularly shaped trenchlike bunkers with smaller, narrow pits where it is difficult to even take a proper swing at the ball. The greens are also severe, a number so steeply pitched that they only have a handful of pin locations.

The starting holes here are particularly intriguing. The opener measures less than 280 yards but is played along a shoulder of the main hill toward a small, angled skyline green site. Those who drive strong and straight off this tee are likely to make birdie, while anyone who hits too safely to the right is left battling for their par. Plunging off the hill and onto the linksy lower ground, the short par five 2nd is another birdie hole for those able to avoid bunkers and safely find its hidden punchbowl green. The next few holes will take plenty of shots back, however, starting with a monster one-shotter at the 3rd, which features deep bunkers and a small target that you attack at your peril. The 4th then bends left around a marsh area and its green leans so sharply forward that driving away from the hazard leaves a frightening approach. Even if you hit this green in regulation, it is quite possible to putt your ball back into the frontal traps.

Other notable holes include the beautifully undulating 7th and the impossibly narrow par three 9th, its target only a few yards wide and surrounded almost entirely by sand. Perhaps the hardest par on the course, the 12th is also outstanding as it meanders up through a shallow, twisting valley toward another tiny green site. The finishing stretch is memorable for a falling par three at the 16th, a clever mid-length sleeper at the 17th and a brilliant closer that features a tight, leaning fairway and a daunting approach that heads across deep bunkers and into a menacing target.

Incredibly, Myopia Hunt Club has barely changed since it last hosted the US Open in 1908. There was a period when the site had become overplanted, but the removal of hundreds of trees has helped the fescues thrive and returned the layout's spacious links characteristics. This really is a wonderful place to golf; the terrain is ideal, the holes are constantly engaging and the only distraction as you play is from the occasional horse trotting by.

Bethpage State Park – Black Course

COURSE OPENED 1936

DESIGNER Albert W. Tillinghast

GOLF DIGEST 26

GOLF MAGAZINE 21

Built during the heart of the Great Depression, the Bethpage State Park was a remarkably ambitious municipal golf development spread across almost 1,500 acres of woodland in central Long Island. The vision behind the park was Robert Moses, the influential president of the Long Island Parks Commission, who spent much of his tenure acquiring land on the island for recreational pursuits. During the early 1930s, his commission purchased the vast Bethpage estate in the village of Farmingdale and set about transforming it into a first-class golf facility for New York residents. Architect A.W. Tillinghast was hired to design three new courses for the property and to modify an existing Devereaux Emmet layout.

Tillinghast's courses were constructed by park superintendent Joseph Burbeck, and each was named after a color according to the skill level it best suited. Opening in 1936, the Black Course was designed from the outset to be the fiercest test at Bethpage and was given its share of the best land on site. Built on a sandy base, the holes are routed across a combination of broad, open slopes and more dramatic forested hills. The design focuses heavily on difficulty, particularly from the tee, where you are either hitting through thick roughs to narrow slices of fairway, or flirting with spectacular sand hazards that protrude strategically into the holes. The putting shapes are less terrifying than at other Tillinghast courses, but getting onto the greens here is more complicated, as many are steeply elevated or

protected by deep greenside bunkers that are difficult to escape.

Given its length, forced carries and grueling hazards, Bethpage Black is the sort of course that can easily overwhelm a golfer not quite on his form. Thankfully, the opening few holes aren't overly taxing, the 1st green is in fact one of the few here that will accept a well-judged bouncing approach from those good enough to hit its slender fairway. The rest of the front nine is not so forgiving, although there are still rewards for strong and sensible play. The 4th, for instance, is a world-class three-shotter that first bends around a cavernous sand trap before rising across a pair of bunkered ledges. Fours can be made on this hole, but taking an aggressive driving line close to the first bunker is the only way to get on or near the green in two. The next is an intimidating par four played through a twisted valley, the hole favoring a sliced drive partly across a sprawling diagonal bunker, followed by a precise uphill approach shot into a small green that rests atop a plateau. The strategic use of an oblique waste hazard on the par five 7th is also very impressive, as is the short cross-pond 8th, with its green pushed into a natural amphitheater.

Less consistently dramatic than the front side, the back starts with some relatively subtle golf laid out across an open meadow. Set beyond a deep hollow, the pushed-up 10th green is a fantastic target, as is the slender, angled putting surface on the par three 14th, which is played across an attractive gorge. The 15th is then

OPPOSITE Expansive bunker complexes dominate the long but engaging par five 4th

one of the hardest par fours imaginable, the hole pushing 480 yards and featuring a tight, turning fairway and a skinny hilltop green. Pars are like birdies here, but shots are easily lost on the closing holes as well. Both the 16th and 17th greens are tightly bunkered and dangerous, while the 18th is a frighteningly narrow par four that climbs noticeably into its small, slick putting target.

Not surprisingly, the Black Course has enjoyed somewhat of a rankings renaissance in recent years, with exposure from hosting the 2002 US Open and improvements made by Rees Jones prior to the event helping push the course well into America's Top 30. Aside from lengthening the layout beyond 7,300 yards, Jones successfully restored the scale and nature of Tillinghast's magnificent bunkering scheme and also made alterations that have improved the condition of the course considerably.

There are five courses in total at Bethpage State Park, and as much as one may admire the modern Black layout, it still isn't really recommended for general consumption, because the holes are too hard for high handicappers and often there are no places for struggling golfers to miss their shots. A sign beside the first tee, warning that the course is only recommended for highly skilled players, basically says it all.

ABOVE The only way to secure a par on the 18th is to split this narrow fairway with your drive

OPPOSITE Water, sand and rough grasses surround the par three 8th

The Garden City Golf Club

COURSE OPENED 1899

DESIGNERS Devereux Emmet,
Walter Travis

GOLF DIGEST 56
GOLF MAGAZINE 32

Deep bunkers guard the
16th green

OPPOSITE A sweeping view of
Garden City's softly rolling 4th hole

Surrounded by the bustling suburbs of Nassau County, the Garden City Golf Club is a low-key private men's club that was founded in 1899 on the site of a nine-hole course built the previous year by Devereux Emmet. Emmet's course was extended to 18 holes and later revised and lengthened by legendary golfer Walter Travis during his ten-year reign as Chairman of the club's Green Committee. Admiring the Emmet routing, Travis lamented the shallowness of his traps and the lack of interesting green contours. He transformed the course by adding some 50 bunkers, deepening others and reshaping all 18 green sites.

Built upon the expansive Hempstead Plains, the topography at Garden City isn't overly dramatic, but the course is beautifully routed and the designers did a superb job squeezing quality holes out of fairly unremarkable landforms. Appearing quite straightforward, the layout isn't long nor overly complicated, as the fairways are rather generous and the greens come with only subtle breaks and open fronts. The yawning traps and tall native grasses are brutal on stray golfers, however, and the greens are often canted in such a way as to encourage the player to take undue risks from the tee.

With plenty of half-par holes and hazards arranged to create genuine risk/reward dilemmas, Garden City is particularly well suited to matchplay. It is also quite unconventional, the course opening with a reachable par four and closing with a cross-lake par three. Aside from deciding whether to attack the 1st green by biting off more of the rough, the first real highlight comes at the 2nd, a

stunning par three heading over an old quarry pit toward a slender green sloping away from the tee. Other exceptional front nine features include the strategic cross-bunker and highly contoured plateau green on the par five 4th and the rising hog's-back fairway and wasteland bunker at the cunning mid-length 9th.

More consistently outstanding, the back nine starts with a wonderfully simple par four that is noted for its fallaway green and a vast fairway that is bunkered to encourage players to hit closer to sand than may be prudent. The run of clever par fours from the 14th is equally memorable, particularly the 450-yard 15th, which is split by a deep bunker that separates a lower landing zone from a deceptively angled green set atop an upper fairway shelf. The ending is also very impressive, the 17th a short par five with a tricky front-to-back target and the 18th a brilliant par three inspired by the Eden hole at St. Andrews and boasting the steepest putting green on the course.

Seemingly trapped within a time capsule, the Travis/Emmet design here has been remarkably well preserved over the years, with the only significant alteration being the flattening of mounds that originally ran through either side of the 12th green. Steeped in the traditions of early American golf, Garden City is an unpretentious treasure that continues to excite and delight the well-connected New Yorkers who play here. It isn't the best layout on Long Island, but it does have obvious appeal and, not surprisingly, has developed itself a considerable global following.

Plainfield Country Club

COURSE OPENED 1921

DESIGNER Donald Ross

GOLF DIGEST 85

GOLF MAGAZINE 70

The small, saddled green
on the par three 11th

OPPOSITE Ending one of the
most underrated nines in American
golf is the mid-length 9th hole

One of the surprise packages of northern New Jersey, the Plainfield County Club was established in 1890, but today golfs on a restored Donald Ross masterpiece that dates back to 1921. Built atop the lush, rolling slopes of Edison, the Ross layout is noted for its ferociously contoured greens and a brilliant routing that makes perfect use of both the natural pitch and fall of the land as well as a large principal ridge that cuts across the site.

Despite its obvious quality, the present course has endured much change over the years, starting with a club decision in the 1930s to abandon its 17th and 18th holes in favor of a driving range. Ross helped accommodate the range by reshuffling his holes, converting two into the terrific par five 12th and then designing three new holes on additional land the club had acquired. These new holes were reshaped by Geoffrey Cornish during the 1960s and also changed when a natural stream was replaced by a couple of ponds. Built on the flattest part of the property, and without the direct supervision of Donald Ross, they were unlikely ever to have been highlights here, but are now quite disappointing when compared with the rest of the layout.

The main site, by contrast, has lots of interesting undulation, the fairways traversing great sweeping ridges and the greens attractively set among natural depressions or atop bold crests. Aside from the three flat holes, the strength of the course is the absence of dreary ground or moderate design. The opening stretch is quite outstanding, starting with a couple of strong par fours routed across left-leaning fairways. The 1st features a remarkably severe target whose back right portion is several feet higher than the front left, while the 2nd boasts a thrilling approach shot across a bunkered valley and into crested green cut into the side of a mound. The strong, dipping par four 7th is another tremendous hole, this time its approach played from a falling fairway over a deep cross-bunker and into a semisunken green.

The golf around the turn is equally outstanding. The heavily tilted 9th green and skinny half-pipe 10th are both terrific conclusions to quality mid-length par fours, while the 11th is a beautiful short par three played across a valley and into a small, steep green saddled atop a ridge. Also wonderful is the par five 12th, which is complicated by a tight driving zone and a drainage ditch that splits the final third of its fairway and then wraps around the left side of its target. The 16th is another intriguing par five, its fairway cut by an enormous bunker complex and its vast putting surface flowing beautifully back-to-front from beneath the 17th tee. Ending the round are a couple of fine doglegging two-shotters, the 17th turning sharply to the right and heading uphill and the final hole bending the other way but also rising into a lovely crowned green site.

Like many courses of this vintage, Plainfield suffered badly as a result of overplanting, but the layout has been transformed by a major restoration program undertaken by architect Gil Hanse. Starting in 2000, Hanse worked on returning greens and fairways to their original specifications and removed hundreds of trees to open up vistas and improve turf conditions. Now more successfully preserved, the course is still relatively unheralded, but it comes highly recommended for all fans of classic golf design.

Galloway National Golf Club

COURSE OPENED 1995
DESIGNER Tom Fazio

GOLF DIGEST 74
GOLF MAGAZINE NR

"Galloway National has unique personality, character, strength and variety."

TOM FAZIO

Opening in 1995, Galloway National was developed by banker Vernon Hill, a regular golfer in the Atlantic City region who became so frustrated by slow play on the local courses that he decided to build his own private golf club. With an associate, he purchased a magnificent 200-acre tract of pinehills about ten miles north of the city, and employed Tom Fazio to shape the property into a world-class golfing retreat.

Partly sited on the marshy banks of Reeds Bay, the course falls beautifully across the rolling terrain, enjoying stunning views of Atlantic City and out toward the New Jersey shoreline. The routing is a little complicated owing to the fact that the layout had to incorporate three separate parcels of land, and because parts of the coastline were protected. Pushing long, flowing holes against the bay was impossible, so Fazio instead arranged for two early par threes to play directly along the reeds, and for another at the end of the round to head straight out toward the shoreline. The rest of the course is carved through a dense pine forest, the holes enjoying a sense of isolation and blessed with vast expanses of sand and dramatic natural contours.

About the only thing Galloway National lacks is a really strategic short par four. The other two-shot holes are terrific, as are the par fives and the group of distinctive par threes, which get progressively longer throughout the round. The 2nd only requires a short iron, but it crosses the bay and houses a small, crowned green that is pressed against the reeds on one side and collapses violently to a sunken chipping zone on the other. Heading back the opposite way, the mid-iron 5th also features a carry over the marsh, this time to a larger target protected by a steep false front. The downhill 17th, by contrast, is usually played with a rescue club or fairway wood and its big, sloping green is open and shaped to feed well-struck balls toward seemingly inaccessible pin locations.

The longer holes are also very interesting, particularly those on the front nine set amongst the sand and scrub. The opening hole, for instance, bends around a waste area and into a superb green perched atop a small, dangerous plateau. The drive and pitch 3rd hole and longer, left-bending 4th both have really demanding approach shots into shallow greens, as does the 6th, a tremendous short par five dominated by a huge bunkered gully off the tee and a minuscule-looking target. Even more impressive, the 7th is a gently rolling par four that turns left across a sprawling waste area toward a slightly raised green resting beautifully within its sandy surrounds. The outward half ends with another great, gambling par five. Strong players who can drive accurately beyond a dune crest here are given the opportunity to attack a large and intricately shaped target that rewards really good shots with eagle opportunities but nudges the slight mishit into three-putt territory.

From the 10th the course changes character a little, as the back nine is longer, harder and a little more unforgiving on golfers striving too hard

OPPOSITE **The 2nd at Galloway National is a delightful short hole noted for its sharply perched green**

for pars and birdies. Water comes into play on several holes, while the yawning bunkers and sloping putting surfaces seem to be even more punishing. The two standout holes are the 17th, which stares straight out across the Atlantic City skyline, and the uphill par four 15th, which features a spectacular second shot over an expansive bunker complex. This craterlike hazard was actually added by Fazio as an afterthought, and helps to complicate an already difficult approach by obscuring a large green site that was built with both a sharp front and a hump through its right side.

With a distinct Pine Valley feel to some of its holes, Galloway National has almost all of the elements required for great golf, the views, sandy carries, sloping lies and bold undulations all helping to give it a genuine sense of real quality. The turf conditioning is also first-rate. Although the internal ponds and occasional long walk between green and tee aren't ideal, this is a very strong golf course and clearly among Fazio's leading few designs.

ABOVE **Brooding skies overlook the par four 1st hole**

OPPOSITE **The 5th is another fine par three that heads across the reeds and toward the Atlantic City skyline**

Quaker Ridge Golf Club

COURSE OPENED 1918

DESIGNER Albert W. Tillinghast

GOLF DIGEST 33

GOLF MAGAZINE 37

Located directly across the road from Winged Foot, the Quaker Ridge Golf Club is an equally prestigious, though quietly unassuming, club that was established in 1916 on the site of a short nine-hole course built the previous year. A.W. Tillinghast was hired by the founding membership to redesign these existing holes and add a further nine, his full course ready for play by 1918. During the mid-1920s the club acquired an additional tract of land and Tillinghast returned to rearrange their holes and extend the layout to its current configuration.

In between, Tillinghast had designed the Winged Foot courses, and comparisons between the two clubs are almost unavoidable. Like most old courses in the heart of Westchester County, both properties are now heavily treed and nicely undulating, with plenty of natural ground movement integrated into the design. If anything, the topography at Quaker Ridge is more uniformly interesting and the tight fairways less dependant upon choking roughs to provide a comprehensive driving examination. Although the bunkers aren't as punishing as those at Winged Foot, nor the greens as severely contoured, the shaping is superb throughout the course, with the targets nestled snugly into the terrain and built with more than enough slope to test the better players.

Essentially laid out in two loops, the opening eight holes are arranged in a counter-clockwise ring around the club's perimeter, with the final ten mostly heading the other way across the interior. The 1st hole provides a marvelous introduction to the challenge that lies ahead here, the tree-lined par five rising beyond a large cross-bunker and into the steepest green site on the property. The other par five is also very good, as are the set of distinguished par threes, but it's the long two-shotters that really stand out as exceptional. Ten measure in excess of 400 yards, and each has a unique green complex and fascinating strategic characteristics. The 4th, for instance, tiptoes along a skinny ridge with a high road/low road fairway and angled green. Both the 6th and 7th bend gently from right-to-left, the 6th featuring a tricky sidehill approach into a subtle target and the 7th heading toward a gloriously bunkered plateau green that leans ominously forward toward the approaching golfer.

Other high points include the narrow, rising 12th hole and uphill approach shots into the 15th and 16th greens. The 18th is also superb, its fairway climbing slowly into a target positioned beautifully beyond a soft ridge and beneath the classical Tudor-style clubhouse. On the negative side, fully grown trees have altered the nature of design on several of the key holes by intruding too far into the line of play. Robert Trent Jones, and later his son Rees, also altered some supposedly dated features. The loss of sprawling cross traps on the par five 14th and a crucial driving bunker built into the right hill on the 6th are the most glaring omissions.

Despite these minor concerns, this Golden Age gem remains mostly in its original condition, the greens and bunkering as innovative and visually appealing as first conceived. Tillinghast's distinctive design style and clever routing, together with the club's low-key elegance, have made Quaker Ridge stand out as one of the genuine golfing treasures of metropolitan New York.

OPPOSITE The approach into the 11th green at Quaker Ridge is played across a creek and into a green leaning toward the water

Maidstone Club

COURSE OPENED 1924
DESIGNER Willie Park Jr.

GOLF DIGEST 72
GOLF MAGAZINE 39

Aerial view of the 11th,
12th and 13th holes

OPPOSITE Willie Park routed
his 9th hole right along the East
Hampton sand dunes

A prestigious East Hampton institution, the Maidstone Club was established in 1891, but its members didn't start golfing until the introduction of a modest three-hole course a few years later. As the game's popularity increased, so too did its golf course, from three to seven to nine and finally to a full 18 holes by 1898. This first full course was inland of the sea, and it wasn't until the club's 1922 decision to expand to 36 holes that it evolved into the gem that is so widely admired today.

Champion Scottish golfer Willie Park Jr. was hired to plan the new courses and was given permission to push his holes closer to the Atlantic shoreline. Although the second course was subsequently reduced to nine holes, the championship layout has survived virtually intact from Park's original proposal. Its opening and closing holes are partly routed on the inland side of a large tidal pond, with the central 12 squeezed onto a tight 80-acre peninsula wedged between the water and the spotless beachside dunes. To many, this section is as close to genuine linksland as exists in America, and Park's uncomplicated design complements the soft, bumpy terrain perfectly. Conscious of the fact that wind can drastically alter the nature of the course, he was careful not to overdesign his holes and instead kept green and bunker shapes relatively simple and in tune with their surrounds.

While the holes away from the beach are solid and well designed, the best golf at Maidstone is found around the pond and on the sandy peninsula. The first really outstanding hole is the 6th, its fairway bending around a wetland area and its green built with a higher left side to complicate the approach for those unable to hug the water with their drive. The short 8th is another fine hole, this time with its putting surface angled away from the tee and partly obscured by a sand dune. The most celebrated holes, however, are back-to-back par fours at the 9th and 10th. Running alongside the Atlantic, the fairway on the 9th is sheltered by tall dunes and its approach is played uphill into a plateau green set beyond a deep hollow. This looks like one of the most naturally attractive links holes in the country, but the fairway was actually created by Park's team, who cut away part of a dune and then pushed the sand to the side to create the ridge that separates it from the 10th. The final, obvious glamour hole is the short par three 14th, which heads straight toward the ocean and an isolated green site surrounded by sandy scrub.

Willie Park passed away shortly after Maidstone opened, and sadly he never saw the finished product. His brother John was responsible for building the course and little has changed since he first had it ready for play in 1924. Modern issues include cart damage on the unirrigated fairways and its general lack of length, many golfers unimpressed by things like having three par fives under 500 yards in a four-hole stretch. The beauty of these holes, however, is that they rarely play the same way on consecutive days and one of the great challenges here is hanging onto the shots gained on downwind holes when the wind is into your face.

While Park gets great credit for his design at Maidstone, the club deserves equal praise for the firm and bouncy manner in which the fairways and greens are maintained. Although there is no doubt the course wouldn't rate quite so highly were it surrounded by the big guns on the British coastline, this traditional old layout is terrific fun to play and will particularly delight passionate enthusiasts of Golden Age design.

Oak Hill Country Club – East Course

COURSE OPENED 1926
DESIGNERS Donald Ross,
Robert Trent Jones,
George Fazio, Tom Fazio

GOLF DIGEST 25
GOLF MAGAZINE 31

Looking across the 12th
green at Oak Hill East

OPPOSITE The 2nd hole is a
beautiful par four with an elevated
approach into an undersized target

Established by a group of affluent Rochester businessmen, the Oak Hill Country Club began life in 1901 on a small nine-hole pasture course beside the Genesee River. The course was soon expanded to 18 holes, but in 1921 the University of Rochester proposed a land swap, offering the club 355 acres of farming land in the nearby town of Pittsford in exchange for its riverside property. The university would also pay for a new clubhouse and the construction of two 18-hole courses. Donald Ross was then asked to consider the land's suitability for golf, his enthusiastic report convincing members to accept the deal.

What impressed Ross so much about this site was its mix of high ridges and rolling hills, as well as a meandering creek that wandered across some of the flatter areas of the property. His original plans made careful use of the natural elevation, with the West Course set mostly among the steep ridges and the East holes dropping between the lowland areas and a large central hill. Both courses opened in 1926, and were soon accompanied by thousands of trees, mainly oaks, that were planted by a prominent member and now dominate the landscape.

Interestingly, Ross considered the West Course to be best suited for hosting championship play, but it was the more spacious East layout that tournament organizers were drawn to, primarily because it could be lengthened, narrowed and made more difficult. As a result, the East Course has become the club's centerpiece, but it has also been changed the most significantly. Aside from the growth of trees and the softening of green slopes to accommodate greater putting speeds, back tees and bunkers were added by Robert Trent Jones in the 1950s and the par three 6th and 15th holes were redesigned by George and Tom Fazio in 1976. The Fazios also made major alterations to the 5th and 18th greens, the latter

moved forward by 30 yards to accommodate grandstands.

Despite the fact that trees have altered the nature of the challenge and hurt some of the better holes, Ross's outstanding use of existing ground contours ensures plenty of exciting golf. Better moments include an uphill approach into a small, concealed green at the 2nd, the wonderfully bunkered plateau par three 3rd and the wildly undulating 9th, which turns around the entrance road and rises steadily into a cool target. The ride up the massive 13th fairway, and the pitch into the elevated and sharply angled 14th green, are also thrilling. Of greatest disappointment is the general loss of Ross's distinctive green shapes and the fact that the first three Fazio targets seem unduly complicated and are out of character with the rest of the course. Equally concerning is how the profusion of trees along the 7th fairway have turned a magnificent, strategic two-shot hole, with multiple angles of approach, into a one-dimensional uphill slog.

Shorter, wider, quirky and less punishing than the East Course, the West has a more authentic set of Ross greens and bunkers and an equal number of top-shelf holes. These include the gorgeous par three 4th, with a nasty frontal depression in its putting surface, and the long, rolling par five 6th. The downhill par three 8th and mid-length 9th are also worthy of mention, while on the back nine the star attraction is the fabulous par four 13th, played across one sizeable ridge and up into a green atop the next one.

With its historic ambience, superb amenities and spectacular Tudor-style clubhouse, Oak Hill has become a landmark American country club and is the most celebrated championship venue in upstate New York. Although neither of its courses is quite in the Pinehurst No. 2 or Seminole league, both do compare very favorably to Ross's other famous layouts.

Baltusrol Golf Club – Lower & Upper Courses

COURSES OPENED 1922
DESIGNER Albert W. Tillinghast

GOLF DIGEST
Lower 44, Upper NR
GOLF MAGAZINE
Lower 29, Upper 66

Established by a New York socialite in the mid-1890s, the Baltusrol Golf Club is located a short drive west of Manhattan and set in the foothills of a northern New Jersey mountain. Although the club's original course was a primitive nine-holer, it quickly expanded to 18 holes and was soon of sufficient standard to host numerous national championships. By 1918, however, growing demand for tee times had forced the club to look at building a second layout, with prominent architect A.W. Tillinghast hired to do the design work.

Unimpressed by the existing course, Tillinghast rather boldly suggested the club would be better off abandoning it entirely and instead building 36 brand new holes. Surprisingly, they agreed, and the designer set about routing his two layouts across the site, setting the Upper Course partly into the base of the mountain and arranging the Lower holes down on the flatter valley floor. While both courses were essentially new, Tillinghast did incorporate several existing green sites into his design.

Despite lacking the dramatic terrain of the Upper holes and being a little too heavily treed, the more uniformly demanding Lower Course has plenty of tournament pedigree and is the course that visitors most want to play. Not surprisingly, its best holes are those built across the subtle undulations, the first significant hole being the 2nd, a mid-length par four whose narrow, rising fairway is cut by an expanse of sand and whose steeply leaning green is protected by eight nasty traps. The 3rd is another undulating beauty, this time sweeping down and left through tall trees and featuring a demanding approach played across a creek toward a large, angled green guarded by deep bunkers.

Elsewhere, attractive elevated green sites at the 5th and 15th are quite impressive as are approach shots into adjacent targets at the 6th and 14th and the tricky par four 13th, which bends along a rerouted creek. Across the rest of the course, holes are mainly noted for relentlessly narrow landing areas, creative bunker arrangements and tight green complexes.

The Upper Course, by contrast, is shorter and more open, and starts by heading along the base of the hills before settling onto the flatter ground beside the Lower holes. The layout is best recommended for early sidehill holes like the par three 3rd, said to be an original from the 1895 design, and the steeply benched right-to-left green on the split-fairway 4th. On the lower areas, raised targets at the 10th, 12th and 13th stand out, as does the par four finishing hole, rolling uphill toward a green site placed beyond a small saddle and pinched between sand.

Baltusrol has tried as hard as any club to combat modern technology, and since Tillinghast's passing both courses have been changed substantially, if not structurally. During the 1940s, Robert Trent Jones added 400 yards and countless fairway bunkers to the Lower Course in an effort to attract major championship play back to the club. During the ensuing years, they have continued to toughen their holes by adding more back tees, encouraging even denser roughs and allowing trees to grow and intrude even farther into the line of play.

Although neither layout here is world-class, Baltusrol is an outstanding golf club and the opportunity to play at such a revered venue, and on such demanding holes, will be a tremendous attraction to many golfers.

OPPOSITE **Hidden from the tee, the green at the 2nd hole on the Lower Course is surrounded by bunkers**

The Course at Yale University

COURSE OPENED 1926
DESIGNERS Seth Raynor,
Charles Blair Macdonald

GOLF DIGEST NR
GOLF MAGAZINE 75

Looking across Yale's remarkable 9th green

OPPOSITE **The tumbling fairway and daunting green on the par four 8th**

Golf at Connecticut's prestigious Yale University dates to the 1890s, when a professor of law organized for a course to be built in New Haven for interested students and local residents. As the game's popularity increased, students started to find it difficult to access tee times, so when a 700-acre woodland was bequeathed to the school in 1924, the University decided to build its own course.

Heavily forested, hilly and full of rock and swamp, the property itself was far from ideal for golf, but the founders had a generous budget and managed to convince retired designer Charles Blair Macdonald to act as a consultant on their project. His associate Seth Raynor was responsible for the routing and prepared design plans for each hole, with Charles Banks supervising their construction after Raynor's death. The process involved in building the course was so arduous and expensive that original plans to build 36 holes on the site were shelved when the first layout was completed.

When it opened, in 1926, Yale was widely hailed as the first great University course in the country. What impressed so much about the early layout was the adventurous nature of the design and the scale and drama of its topography. Incorporating ponds, lakes, rocky ledges and dramatic hills and valleys into the course, the Raynor holes are noted for their wildly undulating fairways, cavernous bunkers and greens that, even by Raynor's standards, are enormous and aggressively contoured.

Interestingly, the par threes here are the same foursome found at the nearby Fishers Island Club, and again they show the limits of imitation versus creation. Although the Short, Redan and Eden holes are quite good, they are not among Raynor's best, and these replicas do get less interesting the more of them you see. The infamous Biarritz 9th, on the other hand, is simply magnificent and more than lives up to its billing as one of America's great par threes. Crossing a natural pond in much the same way that the original French hole crossed the ocean, the tee shot is played slightly downhill to a massive green that is 60 yards long, set at the base of a hill and sliced in two by a five-foot gully.

The par fours and fives also feature elements of the leading holes from Europe, with some interesting variations. The 17th, for instance, combines a double plateau green with a Principals Nose–style bunker complex short of the putting surface. The 8th is another Yale gem, the Cape-style par four tumbling left and featuring a sunken green tilted severely toward a 20-foot bunker on the left-hand side. Other holes of note include the quirky, blind 3rd and the strategic two-shot 4th, which favors a brave drive close to water followed by a precise iron into an elevated green protected by a deep Road hole–type bunker. The 18th is also very cool, the hole a long par five that will be thrice blind unless you are able to smash two big balls to the top of a large hill that runs through the center of the fairway.

Sadly, the Course at Yale has changed considerably in the years since it opened. Cart paths now scar its rugged landscape, while a handful of greens and bunkers have been moved and unnecessarily recontoured. Although the layout is now a distance behind Macdonald and Raynor's best efforts elsewhere, it does still come highly recommended, if only for the experience of playing what is clearly the world's most dramatic version of the now-extinct Biarritz hole.

Hudson National Golf Club

COURSE OPENED 1996

DESIGNER Tom Fazio

GOLF DIGEST 90

GOLF MAGAZINE NR

"From my first day of walking the land, I felt a dramatic and spectacular golf course would evolve."

TOM FAZIO

OPPOSITE The appeal of Hudson National is apparent from the par three 16th

OVERLEAF Heading for home, the view from the 18th tee

Located high within the rocky hills of northern Westchester County, the Hudson National Golf Club occupies a historic tract of land in Croton-on-Hudson, approximately 45 minutes from Manhattan. Designed by Tom Fazio, the course opened in 1996, but construction started two years earlier with much of that period spent blasting more than 100,000 cubic yards of rock from the site and leveling the hillside to enable holes to be routed across its steep terrain.

Set more than 400 feet above the Hudson River, with spectacular views from many of its holes, this remarkable property had actually housed a nine-hole course during the 1920s. The remains of its old stone clubhouse, apparently torched by arsonists during the Depression, was integrated into the design by Fazio, who also used an established forest and some unique rock outcroppings cleverly within his layout.

Although Fazio's approach to the design here is undoubtedly contemporary, his gently rolling fairways and use of off-color native vegetation and golden fescues has successfully given the course a classical appearance. The elevation changes are generally used to create scenic rather than strategic holes, but the bunkering is attractively sculpted and the greens feature plenty of sideways movement, in places even being built with tightly mowed chipping areas that make up-and-downs less repetitive.

While the opening and closing holes are routed along an elevated ridge close to the clubhouse, the majority of the course is set down within a broad valley where most of the earthworks were carried out. The crucial hole in this process was the 5th, a transitional par four that drops steeply from the upper area down into the valley below. Better holes within this lower section include the mid-length 7th, with its rolling fairway and perched green, and the long par three 8th, which demands an all-carry tee shot across a wetland. The twisting 10th fairway, a double dogleg for those unwilling to take on the driving hazards, and the strong par four 15th, which bends around and then heads into a rocky ledge, are also very good. As is the short, uphill par four 17th, which narrows and gets progressively easier to birdie the farther and more dangerous you can drive from the tee. The holes most likely to live longest in the memory, however, are the gently bending 4th, framed by the ruins of an old stone chimney, and the 250-yard par three 16th, with its picture postcard views of the Hudson River.

Despite its obvious golfing qualities, the overriding appeal of Hudson National has less to do with great golf and is more about its beautiful setting and long-range outlook across the river and stone ruins. The quality of the hand-cut bentgrass fairways will also keep many players coming back for more. Thankfully, the best holes here, though a distance behind Fazio's finest creations, are mostly fun, challenging and very pleasant to play, and there are more than enough of them to please the majority of discerning golfers.

Piping Rock Club

COURSE OPENED 1913
DESIGNERS Charles Blair Macdonald, Seth Raynor
GOLF DIGEST NR, GOLF MAGAZINE 92

Significant for its role in helping Seth Raynor establish himself as a genuine golf course architect, the Piping Rock Club was founded in 1911 within the exclusive Long Island village of Locust Valley. Mixing polo and hunting with the emerging sport of golf, the club purchased a 340-acre meadow and hired Charles Blair Macdonald to oversee the creation of its golfing facilities. The tempestuous designer prepared routing plans for the course but became so frustrated at having to sacrifice prime land for horses that he instead sent Raynor to construct his holes.

Fresh from building the nearby National Golf Links, the pair again chose to include copies of Macdonald's favorite European holes. Interestingly, the first ten had to be arranged in a large loop around a polo field and racetrack that were both later abandoned when golf's popularity exploded. Remnants of the track remain visible in a sweeping ridge that cuts across the 7th fairway and directly in front of the par three 3rd, a tremendous Redan hole with its large rear-leaning green guarded by a ten-foot bunker. Another outstanding replica is the 9th, the first Biarritz hole that either designer attempted and a wonderful par three with a pronounced apron swale and massive putting surface. Also impressive is the sharply tiered target on the par five 6th and the Road hole–style green at the 8th, which has a more forgiving entrance than the original at St. Andrews but a fearsome pot bunker in its front side and longer, trenchlike traps along its rear.

By contrast with the spacious front nine, the back is tighter and heads partly into an elevated woodland. Better holes include the Alps-style 12th and the 300-yard 13th, which features a large, tiered green built atop an abrupt knoll and set almost 20 feet above the level of the fairway. The uphill approach into the away-sloping 16th green is also very good.

Piping Rock was the first course Macdonald and Raynor built after the National, and it was also the first time they attempted to transpose the ideal hole concept onto an inland site. Many believe it was the success of these replica holes that emboldened Raynor to use them again on his later design projects.

The Creek Club

COURSE OPENED 1923
DESIGNERS Charles Blair Macdonald, Seth Raynor, William S. Flynn
GOLF DIGEST NR, GOLF MAGAZINE 99

Founded as an exclusive club for the super-rich residents of Locust Valley, The Creek Club opened in 1923 and was initially designed by Charles Blair Macdonald, one of its founding members. Built by his understudy Seth Raynor, much of the course was set down on lower ground beside the Long Island Sound, and during the formative years these lower areas flooded badly during heavy rains. With Raynor deceased and Macdonald at odds with the board on how to rectify the situation, William Flynn was hired to look at possible solutions. Working mostly on the 9th to the 13th, Flynn fixed the problem by creating a dike and using the fill to raise fairways and some greens. He also added bunkers on a handful of holes.

Opening with a series of parkland par fours, the layout tumbles from a forested ridge down toward a tidal creek that separates the property from the sea. Linking the two areas is the 6th hole, a wonderful two-shotter that features a unique bowl-shaped green surrounded by mounds and wrapped around an immense front bunker. Uphill shots into the 9th and 14th greens are also very good, as is the tremendous twin-plateau target on the 15th, which is set beyond a deep hollow and usually approached from a hanging lie. The most memorable holes, however, are those around the creek, particularly the 10th, which is a driveable Cape-style par four that crosses the inlet toward a fairway pressed against the beach. The 11th is then a superb Biarritz par three, with an enormous island target that is at least 75 yards long and cut into two large tiers by a shallow swale.

Slow deterioration of this course between the 1940s and '80s was mercifully reversed during a recent restoration project headed by Tom Doak, who successfully replaced bunkers and returned lost green shapes to their original proportions. Although the opening and closing holes are still a little underwhelming, The Creek Club is again a delightful test of golf and its best holes are more than worthy of acclaim.

OPPOSITE **The Creek Club's highly original 6th green**

Lehigh Country Club

COURSE OPENED 1928
DESIGNER William S. Flynn
GOLF DIGEST NR, GOLF MAGAZINE NR

Founded in 1908, Pennsylvania's Lehigh Country Club moved to its present location a few miles southwest of Allentown in 1928, when a new course designed by William Flynn first opened for play. Set beside the Little Lehigh Creek, much of the layout is routed across a lush, rolling ledge, but the property also features a sunken creekside valley that Flynn skillfully incorporated into both nines.

Flynn did a great job building this golf course, creating some interesting sidehill holes and instilling tremendous variety into his putting surfaces. Complicating play is the fact that the targets are often tilted more severely than they appear. The highlight of the course, however, is the routing, and the manner in which the holes are arranged across what is a steep and fairly difficult site. A number of holes plunge into or across the attractive basin area, such as the par three 7th, which drops almost 100 feet over the creek to a green pressed hard against the hazard, or the mid-length 4th, which falls from the upper ledge over the water but then rises into a beautiful green site benched into an opposing ridge. Both the 12th and 13th head along the flat ground beside the creek, while the preceding hole is a riotous par five that slings right to left from the tee and then crashes dramatically down into the valley. Away from the water, better features include the big shoulder on the left side of the 3rd green, the narrow fronted 5th green and a fine front-to-back target on the downhill 10th.

Lehigh doesn't really have any world-class golf holes, but 1 through 18 are about as strong and consistent as anything in the Flynn portfolio. Pleasingly, the club has resisted the trend toward narrowing its fairways and strengthening its holes, leaving admirers of classic golf architecture to enjoy what remains a strategic and relevant test of golf.

Laurel Valley Golf Club

COURSE OPENED 1959
DESIGNERS Dick Wilson, Arnold Palmer, Ed Seay
GOLF DIGEST 82, GOLF MAGAZINE NR

Set within an attractive valley between the Laurel and Chestnut Ridge Mountains, the Laurel Valley golf course was originally designed by Dick Wilson in 1959 but later modified by one the club's founding fathers, western Pennsylvania native Arnold Palmer.

Built on a swampy hunting estate, the areas in close proximity to the elevated clubhouse occupy nicely undulating ground, but much of the course is routed across a small public road on land that is quite flat. Palmer, and his design associate Ed Seay, started adjusting the Wilson holes during the 1980s, the pair's most significant alterations being to the 10th green and the rerouting of the par three 17th and the long par five 11th, which once bent right but now follows an elevated plateau and dives to the left. They also stretched the 18th to a par five and pushed its green closer to a pond. Throughout the rest of the course, greens and fairways were subtly reshaped, with the flatter holes generally more heavily bunkered.

Despite these changes working reasonably well, the course suffers a little from the contrasting design styles and is still hurt by the lack of interesting terrain. Aside from the holes heading back toward the clubhouse, and a brief stretch through the inward nine that runs alongside a heavily treed ridge, the best moments include the cross-pond approach into the 7th and the right-bending par four 10th, which follows a stream toward a green pressed against the water.

Laurel Valley is a very pleasant golf club that has fine amenities and fairways that are generally kept in super condition. Although the abundant plantings of the early members have helped to delineate holes and enhance the parkland nature of the experience, the course itself is fairly unremarkable.

OPPOSITE **The tightly bunkered 11th green at Laurel Valley**

Bayonne Golf Club

COURSE OPENED 2006
DESIGNER Eric Bergstol
GOLF DIGEST NR, GOLF MAGAZINE NR

One of the more remarkable golf developments of modern times, New Jersey's Bayonne Golf Club was financed and designed by amateur architect Eric Bergstol and built upon an industrial waterfront that looks across the Hudson River toward lower Manhattan.

Bergstol's design was inspired by the heaving links of Ireland and Great Britain, but to transform this reclaimed landfill into a believable golfscape he had to import more than 7 million cubic yards of fill, mostly muck from the dredging of New York Harbor. This material was used to construct a series of towering fescue-covered dunes and create lumpy golf corridors protected by heavily sloped greens and nasty links bunkers. Although a few of the greens are unnecessarily extreme, they do feature plenty of exciting hole locations that members will delight in discovering how best to attack.

Despite so much earth being pushed around on this project, the front nine lacks playing space and several of the early holes are actually designed to force players to back off from using their driver. The inward nine is much better. Moving closer to the harbor, the golf here is more spacious and varied, attacking the wind from all directions. The best holes are the most authentically British, the 12th and 13th tumbling to and from the water and complicated by cunningly positioned bunkers and bewildering greens. The multilevel putting surface on the par five 13th is a real treat and set attractively in the shadows of the resplendent naval clubhouse and its 150-foot flagpole. Falling toward the shoreline, the views on the 14th and 16th are also quite special, while the Cape-style 17th is a bruising par four that crosses part of the river and ends with a rolling green squeezed between dunes.

Bayonne was a monumental engineering achievement and, at upwards of $100 million, it is one of the most expensive clubs ever built in America. Despite the fact that it does give you the opportunity to hit some really cool golf shots, the layout will really only work for those prepared to suspend rationality and embrace the fun of playing this type of golf in the heart of an industrial wasteland.

OPPOSITE **The man-made dunes and views on the 8th hole at Bayonne**

Salem Country Club

COURSE OPENED 1926
DESIGNER Donald Ross
GOLF DIGEST NR, GOLF MAGAZINE 96

The origins of the Salem Country Club date back to 1895 and a short nine-hole course built in the seaside city of Salem, north of Boston. The membership quickly grew, and in 1925 the club moved to a heavily treed farm in nearby Peabody, where prolific architect Donald Ross was able to build them a new full-length 18-holer.

Despite thousands of trees being felled during construction, in terms of terrain Ross left the rolling landscape virtually untouched and produced a quality layout full of interesting holes and creative green complexes. Controlling your approach shots here is the key to good scoring, as the green contouring varies greatly and keeping your ball under the hole throughout the round is essential.

Among the highlights are stirring approach shots into the uphill opening green and the trio of finishing fours, each with putting contours that are more complicated than first apparent. The long, downhill par three 6th and the shorter 12th, with its tiered green banked into a rise, are also very good. As is the strong par four 9th, which follows a bumpy fairway shelf and then falls across water into a green pitched steeply to the front. Best of all, however, is the mid-length par four 13th, played first into a fairway hollow and then up into a lumpy, triple-tiered target set on a slight elevation. Ross apparently once described this green as the finest he had ever designed.

What differentiates Salem from other New England courses of this vintage is its manicured, parkland appearance and the absence of rugged native grasses. The modern layout remains very true to the original Ross design and although a number of drive bunkers have become dated by technology, the addition of some sensible back tees has ensured the course remains a relevant test of your golfing smarts.

Congressional Country Club – Blue Course

COURSE OPENED 1962
DESIGNERS Robert Trent Jones, Rees Jones
GOLF DIGEST 86, GOLF MAGAZINE 51

Founded by a group of influential politicians and wealthy businessmen, the Congressional Country Club is located in Bethesda, Maryland, about half an hour northwest of the nation's capital. The club's original 18-hole course was designed by Devereux Emmett and opened for play in 1924. It was radically overhauled in 1962, however, when Robert Trent Jones extended the facility to 36 holes, splitting the existing course in two and using half the holes for his Blue and Gold courses.

With greater length and difficulty, the Blue Course is the club's preferred championship test, and as a result it has been altered more regularly to keep pace with the modern game. Rees Jones renovated the course in 1990 and again in 2007, when he switched the par three 18th to head the other way across a lake and play as the 10th hole. The terrific par four 17th, with its peninsula green angled toward the water, now acts as the finisher. This change helped create a better conclusion for tournaments, but it destroyed any flow that the back nine might have enjoyed. Already cursed with long walks to the 12th and 18th tee boxes, you now have to walk backwards to get to the 11th tee and then trek behind the 10th green and back up the incline toward the clubhouse after putting out on the 18th.

These issues would be more worrying if they spoilt something truly outstanding, for Congressional, despite its history and status, is a rather uninspiring place to golf. Aside from the new 18th hole, there is little to recommend on a Blue Course dominated by thick rough, symmetrical mounding and some rather unsightly green and bunker shapes. The Gold Course is shorter and less difficult, but also unremarkable save for a clever hog's-back par four at the 17th, with its green said to have been designed by Donald Ross shortly after the first course opened.

Although both layouts at Congressional will appeal to certain golfers when set up in tournament mode, the truth is there are hundreds of superior courses across the United States.

OPPOSITE The new par three 10th hole on Congressional's Blue Course

Newport Country Club

COURSE OPENED 1894
DESIGNERS Albert W. Tillinghast, Donald Ross, William Davis
GOLF DIGEST NR, GOLF MAGAZINE 64

Among the five founding members of the USGA, the Newport Country Club is one of the nation's most historic golfing institutions, having hosted both the inaugural US Amateur and US Open Championships in 1895. The club's first nine holes were designed by head professional William Davis the previous year, and extended to 18 holes by Donald Ross in 1915. A.W. Tillinghast then significantly remodeled the course during the 1920s.

Set partly beside the Rhode Island coastline, this is a classically rugged links-style layout that is exposed to constant sea winds and built with small, sloping greens, tight fairways, thick fescue roughs and deep bunkers. Both the long and short holes can be tricky and totally change character according to whether the winds are helping or hindering. Key front nine holes include the crosswind par three 8th and the long, rising 9th, which features a deep cross-bunker on the right and an elevated approach into a green leaning hard to the left.

The back nine starts with a loop of holes inland of the clubhouse, followed by the famous 14th, the second of consecutive par threes and supposedly the opening hole in the original 1894 routing. Falling from beneath the lavish clubhouse, the putting surface here is narrow and built on a nasty plateau that is guarded by a huge bunker on one side and a steep fall-off on the other. Running along an out-of-bounds area and with a green ringed by water and sand, the 16th is another dangerous proposition.

A throwback to the golden days of early American golf, the fairways here are irrigated by Mother Nature and when dry and firm provide modern golfers with a strict examination of their ability to control ball flight and bounce into the tight target areas. Newport isn't as consistently outstanding as the best seaside courses in America, but its par of 70 is quite a challenge, and for history buffs the experience alone makes it worthy of recommendation.

Trump National Golf Club – Old Course

COURSE OPENED 2004
DESIGNER Tom Fazio
GOLF DIGEST NR, GOLF MAGAZINE 54

Located a few miles west of the USGA headquarters in Far Hills, New Jersey, the Old Course at the Trump National Golf Club was designed by Tom Fazio and opened for member play in 2004. Set amongst the gentle slopes of Bedminster, the course was initially developed by a company that struggled to finance its construction following the September 11 attacks in 2001. The partly built layout was later purchased by Donald Trump, who established a private club on the property, supervised the completion of the course and then added a second track a few years later.

Well built and attractively finished, the Fazio course is certain to please a key golf demographic, as its conditioning and amenities are first class and there are plenty of water holes and eye-catching architecture. Design-wise, however, there is little new or exceptional, particularly out among the more open areas where the vast playing areas and large, sprawling bunkers offer little strategic interest or any real advantage to golfers hitting into dangerous areas. The best holes are probably the one-shotters. The three that play over ponds are all decent, while the longer 14th, which crosses a rough-covered ditch, features a fun and effective rolling green site. Less effective is the course's signature hole, the downhill par four 6th, which bends a little right and plays toward a peninsula green jutting into a lake. Despite being aesthetically attractive, the putting surface is unduly complicated by a hump through its front half and a split tier through the back, both of which can kick well-struck irons, headed toward the heart of the green, off into the water.

With a few good holes and enough redeeming features to keep most players entertained, Trump National is superior to the other Trump courses but still a long way from the best in this region. For those who have experienced lots of quality golf, its inclusion among *GOLF Magazine's* Top 100 will be a surprise.

OPPOSITE **The picture-perfect 16th hole at Trump National**

Ratings & Rankings

Ratings & Rankings

As outlined in the introduction to this book, most of the courses featured in *Planet Golf USA* appear on the 2007–08 Top 100 ranking lists of *Golf Digest* and *GOLF Magazine*, the most widely read publications in our sport. Thanks to determination, persistence and a supportive network of local golf contacts, I was fortunate during my travels to be able to visit 99 of the courses on the *Golf Digest* list and 98 from *GOLF Magazine*. The intention initially wasn't to review additional courses, but after experiencing the likes of Essex County Club, White Bear Yacht Club, Colorado, Kingsley, Chambers Bay, Boston, Erin Hills and Kapalua Plantation, I decided that I couldn't publish a book on America's great layouts and omit such obvious gems.

Without wishing to enter the "which list is more accurate" debate, it is apparent that both have quite serious flaws and that neither panel is really able to provide golfers with an accurate overview of quality. This is principally because the tastes and preferences of the individual raters vary so greatly, but also because exclusive clubs and tough, lush tournament venues continue to receive an unhealthy edge over their competition. Some of America's best courses regularly host championship events, but so too do some of the most overrated. The same is also true of those ultra-elite clubs that virtually no one can play.

Throughout both *Planet Golf* books, the focus of my analysis has been entirely on the golf course itself, and more specifically how good its individual holes are. While golfing in total privacy and on hand-mown fairways and blemish-free greens is appealing, conditioning and exclusivity alone don't guarantee great golf holes and it is, after all, great golf holes that maketh great golf courses.

The main problem I see with US ranking lists is that, aside from the top 30 or 40 courses here, which are stronger than anywhere else in the world, the next two or three hundred are so difficult to differentiate that getting a panel of people to grade them accurately is next to impossible. Needless to say, after seeing more than 800 of the world's finest courses myself over the past four years, I feel well qualified both to comment on ranking lists and to offer up an alternative view on what are the great courses in golf.

Therefore, aside from listing what I regard as the best, hardest and most spectacular holes in the USA, I have also compiled a *Planet Golf – World 100* list of my own. While I don't expect readers to treat this table as an "official" ranking of the globe's premier layouts, I do hope that, given the breadth of research that went into compiling these two *Planet Golf* volumes, it will be seen as carefully considered and credible. As new clubs are built and existing courses upgraded, so too will the *Planet Golf – World 100* evolve, any shifts or amendments available via www.planetgolf.com.au.

Darius Oliver

OPPOSITE **The world-class par three 11th at Pacific Dunes**

Best Holes – Par Threes

Best Par Threes

Cypress Point 16
Pacific Dunes 11
Cypress Point 15
Augusta National 12
Pine Valley 5
Fishers Island 5
Sand Hills 17
Pebble Beach 7
Essex County 11
Pine Valley 10
San Francisco GC 7
Chicago GC 7
Yale 9
Crystal Downs 9
Merion (East) 3
National Golf Links of America 4
Bel-Air CC 10
Ballyneal 15
Riviera 4
Camargo 15
Shinnecock Hills 11
Plainfield 11
Cypress Point 7
Ballyneal 3

Bandon Trails 17
Sand Hills 3
Prairie Dunes 2
Pine Valley 3
Camargo 5
Kingsley 2
Bandon Trails 5
Friar's Head 10
Dunes Club 2 *MI*
Garden City 2
Chechessee Creek 7 *SC*
Shinnecock Hills 2
Pinehurst (No. 2) 17
Fishers Island 11
Winged Foot (West) 10
The Valley Club of Montecito 8
Seminole 17
Colorado GC 2
Los Angeles CC (North) 15
Old Sandwich 4
Olympic Club (Lake) 3
Pacific Dunes 17
TPC Sawgrass (Stadium) 17
Sand Hills 13
Kittansett 3

Somerset Hills 2
Eastward Ho! 15
The Creek 11
Whistling Straits (Straits) 7
Galloway National 2
Myopia Hunt 9
Los Angeles CC (North) 9
Bandon Dunes 6
Chambers Bay 15
Pinehurst (No. 2) 9
Teugega CC 12 *NY*
Yeamans Hall 3
Old Sandwich 9
National Golf Links of America 6
Bandon Trails 2
Somerset Hills 12
Bandon Dunes 12
Sage Valley 2
Shadow Creek 17
Maidstone 14
Whistling Straits (Straits) 17
Pacific Dunes 5
Chambers Bay 17
Chechessee Creek 13 *SC*
Teugega CC 15 *NY*

Best set of Par Threes

Cypress Point
Pine Valley
Pacific Dunes
Camargo
Sand Hills
Merion (East)
The Valley Club of Montecito
Ballyneal
Chicago GC
Shinnecock Hills
Crystal Downs
Bandon Trails
National Golf Links of America
Los Angeles CC (North)
Chechessee Creek *SC*
Bandon Dunes
Old Sandwich
Prairie Dunes
Augusta National
Chambers Bay
Essex County
Holston Hills
Friar's Head
Riviera

Cypress Point 16th

Bandon Trails 17th

Galloway National 2nd

Camargo Club 5th

Colorado GC
Seminole
San Francisco GC
Harbour Town
Ekwanok *VT*
Pasatiempo
Pebble Beach
Somerset Hills
Pinehurst (No. 2)
Maidstone
Sebonack
Kingsley
Teugega CC *NY*
Monterey Peninsula CC (Shore)
Shadow Creek
Bel-Air CC
Kapalua (Plantation)
Wild Horse *NE*
Galloway National
Yeamans Hall
Links at Cuscowilla *GA*
Cherry Hills
Boston GC

Hardest Par Threes

Wolf Creek 3 *NV*
Pine Valley 5
Cypress Point 16
Castle Pines 16
Briar's Creek 17
Oakland Hills (South) 17
Pebble Beach 17
Shinnecock Hills 7
Fishers Island 5
Yale 9
Kiawah (Ocean) 17
Cherry Hills 8
Oakmont 8
Whistling Straits (Straits) 12
Crystal Downs 11
Victoria National 16
Olympic Club (Lake) 3
Shinnecock Hills 11
Rolling Green 14 *PA*
Merion (East) 3
Myopia Hunt 3
The Concession 4 *FL*
Bel-Air CC 10
Merion (East) 17

Most Spectacular Par Threes

Cypress Point 16
Cypress Point 15
Pacific Dunes 11
Pebble Beach 7
Whistling Straits (Straits) 7
Bandon Dunes 6
Whistling Straits (Straits) 17
Fishers Island 5
Bandon Dunes 12
Sand Hills 17
Whistling Straits (Straits) 12
Yale 9
Friar's Head 10
Pacific Dunes 10
San Francisco GC 7
Monterey Peninsula CC (Dunes) 14
Pine Valley 5
Chambers Bay 15
Bel-Air CC 10
Spyglass Hill 3
Diamond Creek 17 *NC*
Princeville (Prince) 7
Ballyneal 15
Arcadia Bluffs 13

TPC Sawgrass (Stadium) 17
Augusta National 12
The Creek 11
Essex County 11
Black Diamond Ranch (Quarry) 13
Maidstone 14
Kittansett 3
Sanctuary 5
Sage Valley 2
Old Tabby Links 17 *SC*
Galloway National 17
Harbour Town 17
Eastward Ho! 15
Shadow Creek 17
Bayonne 14
Galloway National 2
Ballyneal 3
Hudson National 16
Fishers Island 11
Chambers Bay 9
Bandon Dunes 15
PGA West (Stadium) 17 *CA*
Victoria National 5
Merion (East) 17
Wade Hampton 17

Colorado GC 17th

The Golf Club at Briar's Creek 17th

Whistling Straits (Straits) 7th

Essex County Club 11th

Best Holes – Par Fours

Best Par Fours (under 360 yards)

Cypress Point 9
Riviera 10
Pacific Dunes 6
Crystal Downs 5
Ballyneal 7
Sand Hills 7
Pine Valley 8
Bandon Trails 14
National Golf Links of America 2
Essex County 6
Fishers Island 3
Merion (East) 7
Bandon Trails 8
Salem 13
Boston 5
Crystal Downs 7
Pacific Dunes 16
Myopia Hunt 1
Ekwanok 14 *VT*
Crystal Downs 17
Bandon Dunes 16
Shoreacres 13
Ballyneal 14
Easthampton 12 *NY*

Victoria National 2
The Creek 15
Muirfield Village 14
Pine Valley 17
Interlachen 6
The Golf Club 13
Oak Hill (West) 9
Augusta National 3
Yeamans Hall 10
Sebonack 1
The Creek 10
Shoreacres 2
Forest Highlands (Canyon) 17
Essex County 2
The Valley Club of Montecito 6
Eastward Ho! 8
Lehigh 4
Oakmont 14
Pete Dye 6
Interlachen 10
Calusa Pines 8
Eastward Ho! 12
Olympic Club (Lake) 18
Wannamoisett 7 *RI*
Seminole 12

Best Par Fours (over 360 yards)

Pine Valley 13
Augusta National 11
Pasatiempo 16
Sand Hills 18
Pebble Beach 9
Cypress Point 8
Pacific Dunes 13
Pebble Beach 8
Cypress Point 17
Pasatiempo 11
Merion (East) 5
Seminole 6
Pinehurst (No. 2) 5
Prairie Dunes 8
National Golf Links of America 17
Oakmont 3
The Country Club (Clyde/Squirrel) 3
Cypress Point 13
Shinnecock Hills 14
Pebble Beach 10
Pine Valley 2
Merion (East) 16
Pine Valley 4
Merion (East) 18

Prairie Dunes 18
Ballyneal 1
Bandon Trails 13
White Bear Yacht 5
Bandon Dunes 5
Pacific Dunes 7
Seminole 4
Lost Dunes 11
Bandon Trails 15
Shoreacres 11
Crystal Downs 1
Shinnecock Hills 9
Myopia Hunt 4
Colorado GC 9
Kapalua (Plantation) 17
Fishers Island 4
Sand Hills 12
Sebonack 2
Peachtree 12
National Golf Links of America 10
Pine Valley 18
Shinnecock Hills 1
Sand Hills 4
The Golf Club 6
Olympia Fields (North) 3

Riviera 10th

Victoria National 2nd

Pasatiempo 16th

Lost Dunes 11th